THE TRANS-SIBERIAN RAILWAY

THE TRANS-SIBERIAN RAILWAY

A TRAVELLER'S ANTHOLOGY

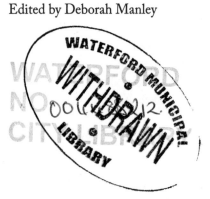

Edited by Deborah Manley

Signal Books
Oxford

First published in the UK in 2009 by
Signal Books Limited
36 Minster Road
Oxford
OX4 1LY
www.signalbooks.co.uk

A catalogue record for this book is available from the British Library

ISBN 978-1-904955-49-8 Paper

Cover Design: Baseline Arts
Cover Images: Kubalibre/dreamstime.com; istockphoto.com
Images: dreamstime.com; istockphoto.com
Production: Devdan Sen
Printed in India

Contents

1
THE DREAM 1

2
THE RAILWAY 27

3
THE TRAIN *49*

4
PREPARATIONS FOR THE JOURNEY *79*

Contents

5
REVOLUTION AND WAR 93

6
SIBERIANS, TRAVELLERS AND WORKERS 115

7
INTO RUSSIA AND ONWARD FROM MOSCOW 137

8
IRKUTSK *193*

9
CROSSING LAKE BAIKAL *207*

Contents

Dedication ~
Valentina, Boris, Olga, Sveta and Barbara with
whom I have travelled.

FOREWORD

> 'Best of all, he would tell me of the great train that ran across
> half the world ... He held me enthralled then, and today, a life-
> time later, the spell still holds.'
>
> Lesley Blanch, *Journey into the Mind's Eye*

The spell that Lesley Blanch's 'Traveller' cast captured me, too, through her
enchanted *Journey into the Mind's Eye*, it was her writing that was the inspiration for my initial journey on this railway as it must have been for
many others.

I first met Deborah Manley in the studios of the BBC almost twenty
years ago. She had just finished compiling the original edition of this anthology for travellers and I'd recently completed my *Trans-Siberian
Handbook*, a practical guidebook. We had both spent long and enjoyable
days in the Reading Room of the British Library, then still under the great
dome in the British Museum, tracking down many of the wonderful books
from which Deborah has selected the colourful pieces reproduced here.
How well they wrote, we agreed, these early rail travellers.

Even before the opening of the railway, adventurers had been drawn to
Siberia. This was the great age of the Victorian traveller, usually monied
and upper-class, who spent the greater part of their lives exploring lesser-
known regions of the world, writing long and often highly readable accounts of their adventures and their encounters with the 'natives'. Siberia
attracted almost as many of this brave breed as did Africa and India. The
remoteness of the region was one draw; the difficulty in getting there and
the perceived dangers were others. To most people in the Western world the
word 'Siberia' meant only one thing: an inhospitable land of exiled murderers and other ruthless criminals who paid for their sins by working in its
infamous salt mines. While some of the first exiles sent over the Urals did
indeed toil in salt mines, most of them mined gold, silver or coal. There
were actually very few salt mines.

Once travelling across the great Siberian plain by the normal forms of
transport of the time, *tarantass* (carriage) or sledge had been tried, these
foreign adventurers resorted to such new-fangled inventions as the bicycle
(RL Jefferson in 1896) and the car (the Italian Prince Borghese in an Itala
in 1907) but it was the new rail service linking Europe with the Far East

established at the turn of the nineteenth century that caused the greatest interest. Readers like Lesley Blanch who had journeyed in their mind's eye with intrepid spirits such as Kate Marsden through her *On Sledge and Horseback to the Outcast Siberian Lepers*, could now contemplate making the journey across Siberia themselves within the safety of a railway carriage.

'This Railway will take its place amongst the most important works of the world ... Russia is awakening at last and moving forward,' wrote one of the first foreign rail travellers, Michael Myers Shoemaker (*The Great Siberian Railway from St Petersburg to Pekin*, 1903). This was true though he was not to know that a setback to the moving forward would come in 1917 and last until almost the end of the century. The Ministry of Ways and Communications was forward-looking not only in the building of the railway but, on its completion, in setting about a publicity exercise as professional as any public relations campaign of the twenty-first century.

In an attempt to lure both passengers and freight onto the line the Ministry took a large stand at the Paris 'Exposition Universelle' of 1900 and also published their own guidebook for travellers, the *Russian Guide to the Great Siberian Railway*. At the Paris Exposition, amongst photographs and maps of Siberia, with Kyrgyz, Buryat and Goldi robes and artefacts, there were several carriages to be operated by the Belgian Wagons-Lits Company on the new railway. They were furnished in the most sumptuous style, with spacious compartments in the sleeping carriages, each with an en suite lavatory. The other carriages contained a smoking-room in Chinese style, a library and music-room complete with piano. In the two restaurant cars, decorated with mahogany panelling and heavy curtains, visitors to the exhibition could dine on the luxurious fare that was promised on the journey itself. To give diners the feeling of crossing Siberia, a length of canvas on which was painted a Siberian panorama of wide steppes, dense *taiga* and little villages of log cabins, could be seen through the windows. To complete the illusion, the panorama was attached to a long belt of canvas mounted on rollers and made to move past the windows. Visitors were intrigued and impressed and more than a few soon set off on the epic trip. The reality, they were to discover, was a little different from what they experienced at the Exposition.

The new railway certainly made Siberia more accessible to foreign visitors but it brought a new set of dangers, all of which provided colourful copy for travel writers. It was shoddily constructed: derailments and accidents were commonplace. 'The engine has smashed up,' said a jolly Russian sailor in broken English. 'She is sixty years old and was made in Glasgow. She is no use any more' ... 'The poor old engine was now towed to her last berth ... I had whipped out my "Kodak" and taken her photograph, thinking of Turner's 'Fighting Temeraire".' (Annette Meakin, *A Ribbon of Iron*, 1901).

Reading the anecdotes in this anthology one is, of course, struck by how much has changed. When the first Trans-Siberian travellers set out, large swathes of the world map were coloured pink as part of the British Empire, British steam engines pulled Russian trains and communication was by means of telegraph rather than the internet. Yet it's also apparent to the modern Trans-Siberian traveller how much the overall experience of the journey has remained the same. To quote Annette Meakin again: 'The Siberian express is a kind of "Liberty Hall", where you can shut your door and sleep all day if you prefer it, or eat and drink, smoke and play cards if you like that better. ... Time passes very pleasantly on such a train'. Smokers may now have been relegated to the chilly area between the carriages but all the rest remains true.

Another interesting point which the reader and traveller today may discern from excerpts in this book is that some things that were part of the pre-Revolutionary Trans-Siberian experience have now returned with the demise of communism. Travelling in 1901, John Foster Fraser reports, in *The Real Siberia*, that locals did good business on the platforms selling 'dumplings with hashed meat and seasoning inside ... huge loaves of new made bread, bottles of beer, pails of milk, apples, grapes, and fifty other things.' During the communist years this was not the case but nowadays many platforms are lined with *babushkas* hawking everything from pramfuls of fresh raspberries to piles of smoked *omul*, the fish found only in Lake Baikal.

In this jet age most of us have lost touch with the travel experience that is slow enough to give us a real concept of the geographical distance we've covered. Quite apart from being environmentally unfriendly, to the twenty-first-century traveller air travel has become mind-numbingly routine and unexciting. To embark on a long-distance rail journey, spending days on a train and crossing thousands of miles of the surface of the earth, is just as thrilling now as it was a century ago and in this anthology what comes across is that excitement, the pure joy of doing this on the

Trans-Siberian Railway despite the setbacks and hardships. As Eric Newby says, 'The Trans-Siberian is the big train ride. All the rest are peanuts.' Nothing can change that.

Bryn Thomas
Hindhead, 2008

INTRODUCTION

Some few years after we had travelled from Liverpool Street to Hong Kong, when what was in effect a second revolution began to change the Soviet Union back into a Russia surrounded by neighbouring states, and to change Russia from a communist to a quasi-capitalist country, I travelled often along the line of the Trans-Siberian – or at least, the first 24 hours of it on my way to and from the great city of Perm on the Khama river. My home city of Oxford had formed a partnership between universities and with the budding voluntary sector of the Perm Region and at least once a year I travelled thither to plan the next link in a long chain of work together. I always went by train – usually from Moscow, once from St Petersburg, and often I travelled in winter – unlike most of the travellers in this book.

One February it was so chillingly cold in Moscow that we wept with pain when we had to remove our gloves in order to show the *provodnik* our train tickets and passports before we could climb up into the warmth. But once aboard the great Russian train it was always the same thrill to face the long journey ahead – to Perm a mere 24 hours, not the long stretch of days of the trans-Siberian journey.

In winter there was a wonderful pleasure in looking out in the morning's first light to see the tracks of the animals which had crossed the snow on the railway overnight. My last journey was slightly longer – from St Petersburg to Perm – and it was in the summer with all the beauty which the warmth brings to the countryside. The train stopped very occasionally for about twenty minutes at large stations and everyone clambered down to stretch their legs, breathe the fresh air and look for anything of interest. There was little, except for the occasional extremely well-bred dogs being exercised along the platform. But quite soon capitalism took hold and local women would meet the train to make a 'market' of the occasion, selling ice cream in summer and small cakes and biscuits and handiwork in winter.

And soon when the train crossed the Khama river and slowed into Perm and the end of the journey we felt as if we were coming home to friends rather than stepping down from the train to strangers. Often we would be accompanied back to Moscow by a companion whose mother would have loaded him or her with enough food for the whole journey lest the dining car did not feed us.

Over several years we saw Russians climb out of the terrible hardships of the changes their government required of them and gradually they regained some of the security of their past. But through that decade of hardship, the train journey always held the magic it had held for me on the first journey across Russia and Siberia.

Deborah Manley
Oxford, 2008

INTRODUCTION TO 1988 EDITION

Perhaps no other journey on earth has captured people's imagination as powerfully as the crossing of Russia by the Trans-Siberian Railway. It is a dream that knows no frontiers. My friends longed to go with me. When I returned, people sought me out to hear about the journey and to see my photographs. A well-travelled Tongan woman told me it was the one journey she still wanted to make. For a Turkish interpreter it was, next to walking the Tigris and Euphrates, his most cherished dream. My travelling companion was an American friend; in our party were two Danes, a Belgian, three other Americans (two of them over seventy), an Australian goldminer and an assortment of Scots and English. We were typical of the groups who make the journey today.

The 5,900 miles of the Trans-Siberian Railway took nearly a quarter of a century to build, but much of it was finished in half that time. The go-ahead for the great enterprise was given in 1891, and construction was inaugurated by the Tsarevitch Nicholas at Vladivostok on 31 May 1891. Work began at both ends and, within twelve years, the line was in place except for two sections: the crossing of the great freshwater Lake Baikal and the 800 mile stretch through Manchuria (the Chinese Eastern Railway) which was in foreign territory. Some people believed that Manchuria would, as a direct result, be absorbed into Russia, but it was not to be. In 1895, about 66,000 men (and their accompanying womenfolk and children) were engaged in construction work. There were 36,629 navvies, 13,080 carters, 5,851 surfacemen, 4,310 carpenters, 4,096 stone-masons and 2,091 riveters.

The first train from Moscow arrived in triumph at Irkutsk, the 'Paris of Siberia', on 16 August 1898. The land to the south of Lake Baikal is mountainous, but before completion of the Circumbaikal loop it was possible to negotiate the lake during the winter by laying rails across the ice, with some consequent tragedies. After 1900 the lake was crossed by an ice-breaking train ferry, the *Baikal*, which had been prefabricated in Britain and reassembled on the lake shore by British technicians. The Japanese threat leading up to the Russo-Japanese War of 1905, and the prospect of having to move troops and supplies to the east, encouraged the hasty completion of the Circumbaikal loop with, at kilometre 5,204, the first tunnel on the route from Moscow. The train is at this point about half way between

Vladivostok and Moscow.

By 1900 it was possible, by using railway and steamer, to travel right across the continent. In 1916 the line north of the Chinese border along the Amur River was opened. The whole line was now within Russian territory and it was no longer necessary for Cossack guards to ride shotgun to protect the train against Manchurian bandits. Now there was an uninterrupted rail link on Russian soil from Moscow to the Pacific, in effect from any city on the European mainland to Vladivostok.

After the 1917 Revolution the Compagnie de Wagon-Lits abandoned their Russian service but, unable to use elsewhere the carriages built for the wider gauge of the Russian railways, sold them to the Soviet railway administration. Work on the railway continued and by 1939 the Trans-Siberian Railway was double track from end to end and in some sections triple track. More recently much of the line has been duplicated along a new course to the north.

The Trans-Siberian line today starts at the extraordinary Yaroslavl Station in Moscow, (strangely reminiscent in style of the post houses along the old road to Siberia), winds across the plains of Russia, crossing the Volga (the longest river in Europe), and passes through the Urals. Shortly before Sverdlovsk, at the 1,777 kilometre post from Moscow, the train passes a simple white obelisk. On one side is carved in Cyrillic letters 'Europe' and on the other 'Asia'; it is less dramatic but as memorable as crossing the Dardanelles from Europe into Asia. From the obelisk the line soon reaches Sverdlovsk (once again Ekaterinburg). The earlier line, and many of the travellers in this book, went south via Ufa and Chelyabinsk. The line continues to Omsk on the Irtysh river, Novosibirsk (where the bridge was completed over the River Ob in 1897), Tomsk, Krasnoyarsk, and on to Irkutsk on the Angara river, not far from where it flows into Lake Baikal.

The line creeps round the southern shore of the lake, with the drama of that first tunnel, and continues to Ulan-Ude. Near here a line turns south to the Mongolian capital of Ulan Bator and onward across the Gobi Desert to the Chinese border and beyond. The main Trans-Siberian line continues through Chita, along the valley of the Amur River and the Chinese border to Khabarovsk, and from there turns south to the fortress town of Vladivostok. But, for a foreigner, in Soviet days, the journey ended at Nakhodka on the Sea of Japan, 9,428 kilometres from Moscow. Now one again travels through to the great port of Vladivostock.

The extent of the journey and the area covered was well described by George Kennan in 1891 (in *Siberia and the Exile System*):

> If it were possible to move entire countries from one part of the world to another, you could take the whole United States of America from Maine to California and from Lake Superior to the Gulf of Mexico, and set it down in the middle of Siberia, without touching anywhere the boundaries of the latter territory. You could then take Alaska and all the States of Europe, with the single exception of Russia, and fit them into the remaining margin like the pieces of a dissected map; and after thus having accommodated all of the United States, including Alaska, and all of Europe, except Russia, you would still have more than 300,000 square miles of Siberian territory to spare.

Once the railway had been built across this great territory, people came from all over the world to travel along it. The Trans-Siberian travellers always had stories to tell, and many of them have written them, from Annette Meakin, who in 1900 with her mother accomplished her ambition to be the first Englishwoman to cover the entire route, to Bob Geldof and, of course, Eric Newby. Early books about the railway sold like hot-cakes and fuelled the dream.

The Trans-Siberian journey has fascinated people for many reasons, of which the foremost is probably the terrain. Yet, even today, little is known of it beyond the 'ribbon of iron'. Equally the 6,000 miles of railway from Moscow to Vladivostok is a human achievement that vies with the construction of the Great Wall of China, which many of the railway's travellers will pass through on their journey. It is twice the distance of the railway line between New York and San Francisco.

Thirdly, there is the magic of distance, time and place. Liverpool Street Station in London to Vladivostok on the Sea of Japan takes more than six days, instead of the dozen or so hours required by air. Even now, as tourists fill the carriages, there is a sense of mystery – of places once long shut off from foreigners, of a history surrounded in secrecy, of names like Omsk, Tomsk, Irkutsk and Ulan Bator.

But most of all the fascination is with the people who have gone before, went even before the railway was there, and the people who went never to return: the convicts and exiles, and Tsar Nicholas and his family who were taken off the train at Ekaterinburg to die in a small room.

For me the journey is unforgettable. It led me to read anything I could find about it, taking me into second-hand bookshops in market towns, to the British Library and the Bodleian, to the Russian Studies Department of Leeds University, to stalls in the Portobello Road, to the Intourist office, to seek others' accounts. This book is the result of that search.

Within the book the date given with the title of each piece is the date of the journey, not the date of subsequent publication. The title of the book is given with the excerpt only when the author wrote more than one book from which I chose excerpts. Otherwise the titles of the books will be found in the author's biographical details or in the bibliography. Sadly I was unable to track down details about all the writers whose experiences appear in this book. Their original spelling has been preserved.

Lastly I would like to thank Barbara Shear who came with me and enjoyed almost every moment from beginning to end and my husband who has listened endlessly to the tales of both the journey and the making of this book.

Deborah Manley
London, 1988

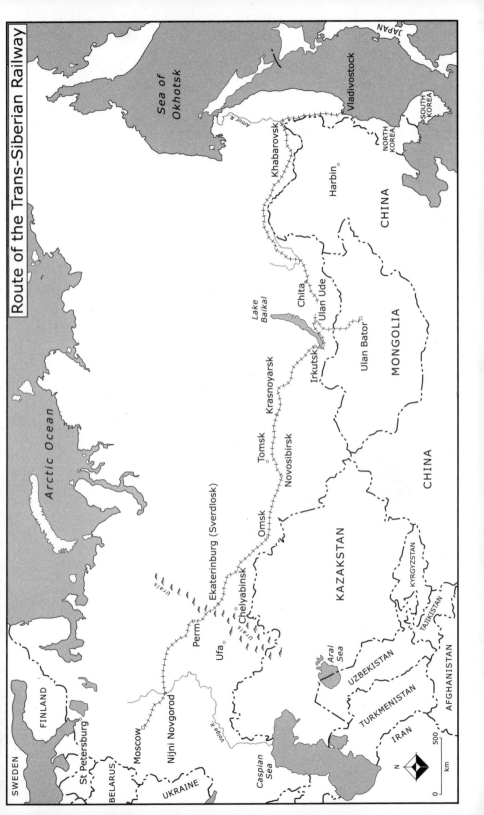

1

THE DREAM

We stood in the hall of the Armoury Museum in Moscow. We had just seen the Great Siberian Railway Easter egg made by Michael Perkin in Fabergé's workshop with its scale-model of the train. In the afternoon we would be on the train itself. We got talking to some Americans, recognized from our massive hotel, and we learned they had been to Leningrad, to Georgia, even to Samarkand.

"And you?" they asked politely.

"This afternoon we board the Trans-Siberian railway to travel to Hong Kong."

"Now that," said one, his eyes lighting up, "is the trip I *really* want to do."

This chapter is devoted to descriptions of this fascination with the great journey. Perhaps the most eloquent was written by Lesley Blanch who was, through her childhood and into adult life, obsessed by the idea of a journey to Siberia. Excerpts from Baedeker (1914) set the scene, and must have been read by many who never actually boarded the train. Bassett Digby, who first travelled the route in 1910 and returned more than once, also describes the size of the country and gives glimpses of what can be seen along the way. Lindon Bates Jr describes a whole day on the train in 1908. Sir Henry Norman, MP, discusses the strategic dream of the railway in 1901. Harry de Windt, who went this way both before and after the railway was built, provides a comparison. Lindon Bates Junior discusses the potential of the line in 1908, A. Rado records the Soviet government's commitment to the railway and finally Paul Theroux, who returned from his great railway journey (told in *The Great Railway Bazaar*) on the Trans-Siberian Railway, tells of the journey westwards and the people encountered along the way.

The Trans-Siberian Railway Thundering Through the House
Lesley Blanch, 1968

Sometimes he told me fairy stories – Russian legends, Ilya Mourametz the heroic, or Konyiok Gorbunok, the little hump-backed horse who brought his master such good fortune; or the magical cat, chained to a tree, who sang verses when he circled to the right, and told fairy tales when he went to the left … Best of all, he would tell of the great train that ran half across the world – the most luxurious and splendid train that ever was – the Trans-Siberian.

He held me enthralled then, and today, a life time later, the spell still holds. He told me the train's history, its beginnings (first mooted, it seemed, by an Englishman, a Mr. Dull by name); how a Tzar had said, 'Let the Railway be built!' And it was. He told me of its mileage, five thousand (to the Canadian Pacific's three thousand); of its splendours: brass bedsteads instead of bunks; libraries, hot baths, and grand pianos to while away the hours. (From Moscow to Irkutsk, barely a half way point to Vladivostok, was nearly a week's travelling.) Of its miseries; of prison wagons, iron barred trucks hitched on at some wayside halt where the shackled lines of wretched creatures could be heard clanking their chains, often five pounds of wooden logs added to the heavy irons – and singing their traditional exiles' begging song, the Miloserdanaya, a sort of funeral chant of doom and despair.

How I loved him! How I loved his Traveller's tales and the way he brought the Trans-Siberian railway thundering through the house. There was a chapel on the train, he said; a candle-lit ikon-filled chapel where the long-haired, long-bearded Orthodox priests ('*Popes* we call them') gathered the pious together before a gilded iconostas, praying and swaying as the great engine snaked across the steppes. Piety ran the length of the train. Piety and patriotism: love of a country. As the train rattled across the bridge over the Volga, every man stood up and doffed his cap to Mother Volga.

I knew it all by heart. Every Wednesday and Saturday, the Trans-Siberian train pulled out of Moscow and for seven days ate up the eastward miles to Irkutsk, and farther, into the heart of Siberia, through the Trans-Baikal provinces, edging the Mongol steppes and the yellow dust-clouds of the Gobi desert. There was a branch line to Outer Mongolia–another, along the Amur, to bandit-infested Manchuria, and at last, ten days later–Vladivostok, Russian outlet of life and death on the Sea of Japan. One extension of the line led to 'The gates were scarlet lacquer, a hundred and fifty feet high, and stuck with the heads of malefactors,' said the Traveller, spreading beef-dripping with a lavish hand.

For me, nothing was ever the same again. I had fallen in love with the Traveller's travels. Gradually, I became possessed by love of a horizon and a train which would take me there; of a fabled engine and an imagined landscape, seen through a pair of narrowed eyes set slant-wise in a yellow Mongol face. These Asiatic wastes were to become, for me, the landscape of my heart, that secret landscape of longing which glides before our eyes between sleeping and waking; a region I could not fathom, into which I was drawn, ever deeper, more voluptuously, till it became both a challenge and a retreat. It was another dimension where I could refuge from the rooms and streets about which I moved, docile but apart. From the first, the Traveller had understood my in-fatuation for Asia, and every time he came to see me, he brought some object which told of those horizons. A chunk of malachite or a Kazakh fox-skin cap (which smelt rather rank) and once, a bunchuk, or stan-dard, decorated with the dangling horse-tails of a Mongol chieftain. I was enraptured.

From Moscow to Vladivostok
Baedeker, 1914

8134 V. (5391 M.). Railway from Moscow to Tchelyabinsk, 2056 V.; Trans-Siberian Railway from Tchelyabinsk to Irkutsk, 3049 V.; Trans-Baikal Railway from Irkutsk to Mandshuriya, 1424 V.; Chinese Eastern Railway from Mandshuriya to Pogranitchnaya, 1388 V.;

Ussuri Railway from Pogranitchnaya to Vladivostok, 217 V.–*Customs Examination*. On the outward journey Chinese officials examine passengers' luggage at Mandshuriya, and Russian officials at Pogranitchnaya (registered luggage at Vladivostok). On the return journey there is a Chinese examination at Pogranitchnaya, and Russian examinations at Mandshuriya, Tankhoi, and Irkutsk. – Two EXPRESS TRAINS weekly in 8⅔ days, one being operated by the International Sleeping Car Co., and the other by the State Railways. Carriages are changed at Irkutsk. Fares 327 rb. 44, 212 rb. 77 cop. (first-class compartment reserved for a single traveller 523 rb. 70 cop.); from Berlin to Vladivostok 673 *M*, 424¾ *M*; from London to Vladivostok 37-38*l.*, 23-25*l.* The first-class compartments or sections are for two persons, the second-class for four. The railway tickets (apply early) are available for 22 days if bought in Russia, or 3 months if bought elsewhere. If the journey is broken, it is necessary to obtain a new seat ticket for the rest of the journey. Thus, *e.g.*, a new seat-ticket from Omsk to Irkutsk costs 18 rb. 40 or 13 rb. 80 cop. The amount of luggage allowed free is 60 Russian lbs. (54 lbs.), but through passengers from foreign countries are entitled to twice as much. Each additional 10 lbs. (9 lbs.) costs 2 rb. 69 cop. The charges in the Dining Car are B. 55 cop., déj. 1¼, D. 1½ rb. –MAIL TRAIN daily in 18 days (fares 158 rb. 93, 96 rb. 76 cop.; carriages changed at Tchelyabinsk, Irkutsk, and Mandshuriya). Also 'PASSENGER TRAIN' daily as far as Mandshuriya (seat ticket, see p. xxiii). – The journey from Moscow to *Tsuruga* (Yokohama) viâ Vladivostok takes 12 days (fares 365 rb. 19, 250 rb. 51 cop.); to *Nagasaki* 12 days (fares 380 rb. 48, 265 rb. 81 cop.); to *Shanghai* 14 days (fares 410 rb. 7, 295 rb. 39 cop.).

FROM ST. PETERSBURG TO VLADIVOSTOK, viâ Perm and Tchelyabinsk. 8269 V. (5481 M.), express train twice weekly in 9 days (fares 329 rb. 35, 214 rb. 25 cop.). Carriages are changed at Irkutsk. Comp. R. 35.

Through passengers from W. Europe to the Far East must have their passports *visé* by a Russian consul (comp. pp. XVIII, XIX); registered luggage is not examined before it reaches the frontier of the country of destination. Tickets (available for 2 years) are obtainable for the journey to the Far East by railway and back by steamer, or vice versâ. The steamer-journey may be begun or ended at Shanghai,

Yokohama, Kobe, or Nagasaki.

Siberia has an area (4,784,034 sq. M.) 1½ times greater than Europe, $2\frac{1}{3}$ times larger than Russia in Europe, and more than 40 times larger than the United Kingdom of Great Britain and Ireland. In 1910 its population was estimated at 8,220,000. It extends from the Ural Mts. (59° E. long.) on the W. to the Sea of Japan and the Okhotsk and Behring Seas on the E. (Cape Deshnev or East Cape, 174° 24' E. long.), and from the Arctic Ocean on the N. to China on the S. It is divided into the two *Governments of Tomsk* and *Tobolsk* (which together formerly constituted the General-Government of West Siberia); the *General-Government of Irkutsk*, which includes the Governments of Yeniseisk and Irkutsk and the Territories of Yakutsk and Transbaikal; and the *General- Government of the Amur Territory*, comprising the Amur and Maritime Provinces, Kamtchatka, and the N. half of the island of Sakhalin. The N.W. part of the *General-Government of the Steppes* (the Akmolinsk and Semipalatinsk Territories) belongs officially to Russian Central Asia.

Western Siberia, from the Urals to the Yeniséi, is for the most part a flat plain, with good arable land and pastures in its central and S. portions. Eastern Siberia, which is three times as large, is mountainous and less fertile, labouring under the disadvantages of a severe climate in its W. part and of periodical inundations in the E. In N. Siberia most of the ground is covered with forest *(Taigá)*, gradually passing over into a waste of barren lands *(Tundras)*, which are frozen for the greater part of the year and marshy in the summer. To the S. and S.E. are the *Altái Mts.* (p. 526), the chief peak of which is the Byelúkha (14,900 ft.); the *Sayán Mts.* (highest peak *Munku-Sarduik*, 11,275 ft.); the *Yáblonovi Hills;* and the *Stanovói Hills*, all of crystalline formation. – Into the Arctic Ocean flow the *Ob* (2240 M. long), with its greatest tributary the *Irtúish* or *Irtýsh* (about 2200 M. in Siberia and 330 M. in China, where it is known as the Black Irtúish); the *Yeniséi* (about 2490 M. long); and the *Lena* (2860 M. long). The *Amúr* (p. 587), which with the *Argún* is over 2720 M. long, flows into the Sea of Okhótsk. The largest lake is *Lake Baikál* (p. 533).

The CLIMATE of Siberia runs to extremes both of heat and of cold; the winter is long and the air dry except on the E. coast. The coldest month is January, the hottest July. At Tomsk the range is from –3.3°

Fahr. to + 65.6°, while the mean annual temperature is + 30.7°. The corresponding figures at Irkutsk are: 5.4°, + 65.1°, and + 31.3°; at Blago-vyeshtchensk, on the Amúr: 13.9°, + 70.5°, and + 33.3°; at Vladivostok: 14.1°, + 87.1°, and + 40.3° F. Siberia is rich in coniferous trees. The deciduous trees of W. Siberia lack variety, consisting mainly of birches, aspens, alders, and poplars; to the E. of the Yáblonovi range the list receives many additions, such as the oak, walnut, and elm. The Territory of the Amúr, on the other hand, abounds in deciduous trees. Siberia is especially rich in minerals. These include gold (output in 1909, 2895 pud or 1,524,762 oz.), silver, lead, copper, iron, coal, and graphite. Exports to the W. include wheat, rye, oats, and butter (in 1911 more than 4,300.000 pud or 69,320 tons, most of it viâ Windau).

The great majority of the INHABITANTS of Siberia, especially those in the towns and along the railway, are Russians, including free immigrants (peasants and Cossacks) and the exiles and their descendants (comp. p. 261). [Between 1896 and 1910 there were 3,970,000 immigrants.] The Turkish (Kirghizes, Tartars, Yakuts), Finnish (Voguls, Ostyaks), and Mongolian (Teleuts, Buriats, Samoyedes, Tunguses) races are also represented. The exiles, most of whom are to be found in E. Siberia, consist of criminals condemned to penal servitude, those compelled to settle in prescribed communities, and those banished by administrative process. As a result of an Imperial Ukase of June 10th, 1900. the banishment to Siberia has been considerably limited.

HISTORY. The Russian conquest of Siberia began in the reign of *Iván the Terrible*, who in 1574 invested the merchants *Jacob* and *Gregory Stróganov* with the right to build forts upon the banks of the rivers Toból, Irtúish, etc. In 1575, for the protection of their extensive domains, the Stróganovs took into their service 800 Cossacks under *Yermák*, the former Volga pirate, who penetrated far into the interior of Sibería, and (on Oct. 26th, 1581) captured *Iskér* or *Sibír* (p. 528), the capital of the Siberian Tartar Empire. Yermák was drowned after a fight in 1584 while attempting to escape by swimming across the Irtúish–Thence forward the Russians pressed steadily eastward and northward, and easíly vanquished the inhabitants who opposed them. Tobolsk was founded in 1587, Tomsk in 1604, Yakutsk in 1632, Irkutsk in 1652. In 1649 the Cossack Hetman *Khabaróv* fitted out an expedition to take possession of the Amúr district, but the peace of

Nertchinsk (1689) gave this territory back to China. The scientific exploration of the land was undertaken during the reign of Peter the Great, when Behring discovered the strait which bears his name. In 1854 *Count Muravyév* (Amúrski), Governor-General of Eastern Siberia, descended the Amúr with a military force, and in 1857 the left bank of that river was ceded to Russia by China. In 1860, by the treaty of Peking, Russia acquired the Ussurí province; and in the same year Vladivostok was founded. During the construction of the Trans-Siberian Railway (1891-1903) the Russians leased the peninsula of Kuan-tung (with Port Arthur) from the Chinese (1898). The Russians occupied Manchuria in 1900, and their refusal to evacuate it at the request of Japan brought on the Russo-Japanese war of 1904, which ended in the defeat of the Russians. By the Peace of Portsmouth (1905) Russia lost Kuan-tung, Manchuria, and the S. half of Sakhalin.

The best TRAVELLING SEASON for Siberia extends from the middle of May (O. S.) to the middle of June. July is a very hot month, but August is pleasant, while September is a favourable season for Manchuria (voyage on the Amúr, see p. 539). Those who make the trip in summer should take light clothing and a warm overcoat, while woollen underwear is the best safeguard against the sudden changes of temperature. Travellers should *on no account* drink *unboiled water*. High goloshes or 'rubber boots' are desirable, as the unpaved streets of the towns are almost impassable in spring and autumn; in winter felt overshoes or 'arctics' are also necessary. A mosquito-veil is desirable in E. Siberia and Manchuria during the summer. It is desirable to carry a revolver in Manchuria and in trips away from the railway. – The HOTELS are almost invariably dear and indifferent. Bed-linen, soap, etc., should always be taken. A disturbing feature is the inevitable concert or 'singsong' in the dining room, which usually lasts far into the night. Travel in Siberia is about one-third more expensive than in Russia in Europe.

The traveller must be on his guard against *Thieves*. Thus, when he quits his compartment at a railway station he should have the door locked by the provodnik (p. xxi).

Travellers in Siberia should avoid carrying large sums of money on them. Instead they should have orders on the *Russo-Asiatic Bank* (comp. p. 96), on the *Commercial Bank of Siberia*, or (for the East) on the firm of *Kunst & Albers* at Vladivostok (branch at Hamburg).

BIBLIOGRAPHY. More or less extensive accounts of Siberia will be found in the following works: *A. Bordeaux*, Sibérie et Californie (Paris, 1903).– *A. J. Dmitriev-Mamonov* and *A. F. Zdziarski*, Guide to the Great Siberian Railway (1900). – J. *F. Fraser*, The Real Siberia (1902). – *W. Gerrare*, Greater Russia (1903).– *Sir A. Hosie*, Manchuria (1901). – G. *Kennan*, Siberia and the Exile System (4th ed., 1897) and Tent Life in Siberia (New York, 1893). –*J. Legras*, En Sibérie (Paris, 1913). – *M. P. Price*, Siberia of Today (1912). – *P. A. Stolypin & A. V. Krivoshein*, Kolonisation Sibiriens (Berlin, 1912).– *M. L. Taft*, Strange Siberia (New York, 1911). – *S. Turner*, Siberia (2nd ed., 1911). – *Chas. Wenyon*, Four Thousand Miles across Siberia (5th ed., 1909).– *R. L. Wright* and *Bassett Digby*, Through Siberia (1913).

I'll Give You Siberia!
Lesley Blanch, 1968

'Siberia! I'll give you Siberia – you with your chilblains,' said my nurse, when I whined to go out in the brown-edged, slushy London snow. I was hardening myself, in preparation for journeys to Omsk and Tomsk (later I named two kittens after these towns) and the mysterious, icy-sounding places along the Trans-Siberian's way. Verkhné-Udinsk, Chita and Chailor Gol were names round which the tempests of Asia howled. Nevertheless Nanny, who had now left us, showed an understanding of my peculiar passion, and next Christmas sent me a purple-bound volume (a come-by chance, off a barrow in the Portobello Road) entitled *On Sledge and Horseback to the Outcast Siberian Lepers* by Kate Marsden – New York (1892.)

'Must have been off her rocker,' said cook, when I read her the more dramatic passages. Moreover she was adamant in her refusal to make *pelmeni*, pieces of stuffed pasta, a celebrated Tartar dish, of which the Traveller had given me the recipe.

'Staple Siberian diet,' he said. 'Filthy, but filling.' He also added it was very hard to make.

'Which is as maybe,' said cook darkly, basting the roast in a crimson glow of professional complacency.

Nor was she any more co-operative when I dwelled on the habits of Jenghis Khan's troops who were required to carry a sheep's stomach full of desiccated dried meat, and another of powdered milk flour under their saddles, thus being ever at the ready to gallop off on some foray.

'But it would only be like getting a haggis,' I pleaded, when she refused to supply a sheep's stomach. I had planned to attach it to my tricycle, and thus provided, pedal furiously off down the path to Asia.

The Sheer Size of It
Bassett Digby, 1928

Pull out the map and have a look at Siberia. The outline of the United States will help you to get an accurate idea of the distances.

Picture yourself starting off from Leningrad, one gloomy Leningrad February afternoon. If it is a typical gloomy February afternoon you'll be glad to be starting off anywhere. Look at the departure board in the ramshackle railway station. Adventure beckons. Trains are leaving for Archangel, up on the White Sea, and the Crimean seashore resorts down on the Black Sea, for Rumania, for Vienna, for Central Asian destinations within a morning's horse-ride of the frontiers of mysterious Afghanistan, and for Manchuria and China. Truly a wonderful range of destinations!

You clamber up into the cars ... A bell is clanged. No one among the jostling throng on the platform pays any attention to it. A few minutes later it clangs again. Now the doors become jammed with crowds of friends answering the "All ashore!" signal, simultaneously with crowds of tardy passengers answering what *they* interpret as the "All aboard!" signal. The latter are laden with those extraordinary assortments of hand baggage peculiar to Russia and Siberia. It is no use asking me how one passenger can board a Russian train through the thick of a descending cataract of "see-ers off," while laden with a large brass *samovar* (tea-urn), a huge wicker-work basket with the lid coming off; a wooden sugar box full of pots and pans and crockery, with no lid at all; a bundle of bedding and an armful of sled-runners. I can only advise you to go and see for yourself. Every one is frantically imploring some one else to do what some one else does not in the least want, or intend, to do, with a view to easing the congestion. Yet, against all probability, and practically all possibility, the comers come and the goers go by the time the station bell is clanged three times. The locomotive gives an answering hoot, a mournful hoot. With a jerk and a clang the couplings come taut – and off you go.

Now what do you see? Nothing at all, unless you are lucky. There are double windows in the cars to keep out the intense cold, and the majority of them frost over, so that you have to go down the corridor to the end platform if you want to get a glimpse of the landscape. And there are only half-a-dozen different glimpses all told. Every additional glimpse is a repetition of one of the others. A vast ocean of deep snow, now with occasional birch trees, now with fir forest breaking its monotony. Occasional snowed-under villages of stockaded log cabins, on distant slopes. Occasional rough sledges drawn by dejected-looking, head-hanging horses. The fence by the track-side; and the telegraph poles, staggering this way and that.

This depressing monotony, broken only by a half-hour stop tomorrow at Vologda station, the junction for Archangel, and a stop on the following day at the town of Perm, lasts all the way to the Ural mountains. How eagerly you await the sight of this famous range, after the tedious journey across the plains! But if you expect anything jagged, towering, picturesque, like the Rockies or the Pyrenees, you will be sadly disappointed. The earth merely heaves itself up in gradually steepening, forested hills, for a couple of hundred miles. Now and again there is a glimpse of a sheer cliff or a deep gorge or a pinnacle of rock, but, for the most part, such of the range as you can see is as tame as the Blue "mountains" of Pennsylvania. There is an hour's stop at the great station of Ekaterineburg, the chief mining town of this range of rich mineral deposits. Then down the train trundles to level ground again, and out on to the plains of Western Siberia ...

If any one told me that the west of Siberia was uninteresting I should immediately deny it and embark upon a priggish dissertation about the vileness of writers of guide-books, whose interest in lovely wild flowers, queer smells (and majestic stinks), home-made chimneys, what peasants are eating for supper at yonder table under the trellised vine, the occasions when stockings should be worn, how cats are treated, what people pin up on the wall, the etiquette of singing at wineshops, butterflies, the things that various sorts of people read, the songs of birds, the way the local fish are caught and which are the brutes among them that the Devil himself stuffed with bones, what the villagers do when they fall ill, the animals in the woods around and their queer ways and so forth, is nil. For why judge the allure of every place by the monuments it contains, The View, or the tradition that some one or other whose name got into books somewhere or other, did or said something there sometime or other (or even passed through, one sultry July afternoon, in a drunken stupor)? I should tell you that if, by some miraculous dispensation of Providence, I were enabled to kick every writer who had dismissed as "not worth a visit" or "without interest" places that I have found extremely interesting though totally destitute of historical parlour tricks, or Views, one pair of boots would not last for the job.

Dreaming with Baedeker
Lesley Blanch, 1968

I sat on the noisy terrace of a brasserie, waiting for the interminable café *filtre* to fill my cup and wishing passionately that it was a *tchai-khana* in Russian Turkestan – the kind the Traveller had so often described to me in his tales. But he had gone, and with him, his tales; and now Kamran was lost too. With a sense of abandonment that verged on panic I turned inward, into that other world of fantasy that always waited for me, that was only a sigh away.

I scuffled in my bag and tugged out the chunky little red volume which alternated with Herzen's Memoirs as my daily reading. My affection for Baedeker's *Russie 1895* (French Edition) which rivalled and often contradicted that other treasure, Murray's Handbook of Russia for 1893, was mystifying to my French and Russian friends. They constantly reminded me that it was out of date. But then I, too, was out of date, keeping company with a ghost who had known Russia at that time. Apart from the fact that the Russia of which Baedeker writes is no more and that present-day guide books suggest enormous itineraries and cover distances which are only realizable by the use of jet planes and fast cars, there is another, striking difference.

These earlier guide books are all obsessed by the same question – *how to pass the time* (when of course, the real problem is how to stop it passing so quickly, especially if one is in the faraway realms on which Baedeker and his kind dwell). But on that particular Mayday of desolation at the Mairie des Lilas time undeniably seemed to drag. So, ordering another *café filtre* I opened my guide book and took flight to Russia, to St. Petersburg, 1895 ...

The magic never failed. Paris faded; the spire of the Admiralty gleamed before me, the old familiar smell of sun-flower seeds, wet leather and salted fish assailed me. I was home, safely home ...

Emploi du temps, says Baedeker, listing his suggestions – all of them, to me, mouth-watering prospects, but it is clear Baedeker doubts his reader's abilities to pass the time in Russia without his aid. Murray goes further and devotes a long passage to eating, counselling and explaining the typical Russian cuisine for adventurous British stomachs. Is there, perhaps, a faint trace of cynicism to be detected? Of patronage, perhaps? In listing *Botvinia* merely as 'a soup of a green colour,' or describing *Porosionok pod khrenum,* cold boiled sucking pig with horseradish, as 'not a pretty dish but very eatable', and dismissing various local cheeses warily, 'should the digestion or habit require them', we can also detect a dyspeptic note. Murray follows up this gastronomic section with one headed SANITARY PECULIARITIES, and I imagine the editors sitting back, a good day's work done. That will keep the tourists busy! After the red pottage (or the green soup?), the exceeding bitter cry. Just let them try out those dishes. They have been warned, and then, if they feel poorly, we have listed reliable pharmacies and doctors too, say Murray's editors complacently, going off for a mutton chop at their club.

But Baedeker knows his French readers are not to be fobbed off with any suggestions about eating as an *emploi du temps.* They have been brought up in the noble traditions of the French cuisine and for them eating is not an *emploi du temps;* it is a whole way of life, a whole civilization. They are not to be distracted by picturesque *plats.* They must be given other suggestions for passing their time abroad. But so insistent are the editors on this *emploi du temps,* this pressing question of how to pass the hours, that I begin to envisage numberless tourists, all raging with boredom, all pacing up and down the confines of the variously graded hotels, throughout the world. In cities and remote provinces alike, the same ennui, the same gnawing preoccupation – *how to pass the time?* At the Hotel de France, the Imperial, de la Poste, du Commerce, the Schweizerhof, the Victoria, or, for bold travellers in southern Russia, *Cafés Tartares en face de la Gare. Malpropres.* The *emploi du temps* here will probably be how to obtain insecticides but the preoccupation of the editors is always the same: how to pass the time. In Russia? They wouldn't have to tell *me*.

A Day in 1908
Lindon Bates Jr

You rise with the rest, draw on your fur cap and gloves, work into the heavy fur-lined overcoat, and clamber down to the platform. A little wooden station-house painted white is opposite the carriage door. It has projecting eaves and quaint many-paned windows. In front of it is a post with a large brazen bell. On the big signboard you can spell out from the Russian letters "Zlatoust." This is the summit station of the pass that crosses the Urals. Around are standing stolid sheep-skinned figures, bearded peasants just in from their sledges, which are ranked outside the fence. Fur-capped mechanics, carrying wrenches and hammers, move from car to car to tighten bolts and test wheels for the long eastward pull. Uniformed station attendants are here and there, some with files of bills of lading. As you walk down the platform among the crowd, you come upon a soldier, duffle-coated and muffled in his capote, standing stoically with fixed bayonet. Forty paces further there is another, and beyond still another, all the length of the platform, and far up the line. What a symbol of Russian rule are these silent sentries! And what a mute tale is told in the necessity for a guard at every railroad halting-place in the Empire!

You stroll along toward the engine. Huge and box-like are the big steel cars, five of which compose the train. Two second-class wagons painted in mustard yellow are rearmost, then come the first-class, painted black, next the "wagon restoran" and the luggage-van, where the much advertised and little used bath-room and gymnasium are located. The engine is a big machine, but of low power, unable to make much speed; and the high grades and the road-bed, poor in many places, additionally limit progress. It is apparent why the train rarely moves at a rate greater than twenty miles an hour.

At first you do not notice the cold. But now that you have walked for a few minutes along the platform, it seems to gather itself for an attack, as if it had a personality. You draw erect with tense muscles, for the system sets itself instinctively on guard. The light breeze that stirs begins to smart and sting like lashes across the face.

The hand drawn for a moment from the fleece-lined glove, stiffens into numbed uselessness. As you march rapidly up and down the platform, an involuntary shiver shakes you from head to foot. A fellow passenger, remarking it, observes:– "It is not cold today, in fact, quite warm. *Ochen jarko.*"

You walk together to the big thermometer that hangs by the station-door. It is marked with the Réaumur Scale, and your brain is too torpid for multiplications. But the slightly built official, known as a government engineer by green-bordered uniform and crossed hammers on his cap, is inspecting the mercury also. "Eight degrees below zero Fahrenheit," he says. "Quite warm for January. It is often thirty-five degrees below zero here in the Uralsk." It gets colder at the suggestion. The three starting-bells ring, and everybody scrambles into the compartments. The express rolls onward down the Urals. You stroll back to the warm dining-room and idly watch the groups around. Across the way is an elderly mild-looking officer, whose gold epaulettes, zig-zagged with silver furrows, are the insignia of a major-general. He smokes endless cigarettes in company with another officer lesser in degree, a major, decorated with the Russo-Japanese service-medal, smart of carriage and alert of look. By the window beyond is a young German, gazing meditatively at the hills and the snow through the bottom of a glass of Riga beer. A rather bright-mannered dame, with rings on her fingers and long pendants in her ears, chats vivaciously in French with a phlegmatic-looking personage in a tight-fitting blue coat which buttons up to his throat like a fencer's jacket. A quietly-dressed gentleman, evidently in civil life, is reading one of the library copies of de Maupassant.

Outside, cut and tunnel, hill, slope, and valley, green forest, white drifted snow, and bare craggy rocks, the Urals glide past. The little track-wardens' stations beside the way snap back as if jerked by a sudden hand, and the telegraph-poles catch up in endless monotony the sagging wires.

The Tartar waiter goes from place to place, clearing off the ashes and the glasses, and getting ready for dinner. There is a table-d'hôte repast, the Russian *obeid,* a meal which starts with a fiery vodka gulp any time after noon, and tails off in the falling shadows of the winter sunset with tea and cigarettes. Or, if one wishes, he may press the bell, labeled in the Graeco-Slavonic lettering, "Buffet," and dine à la carte. "Il vaut mieux essayer le repas Russe," says the quiet reader of de Maupassant, joining you.

He is duly thanked for the advice, and we beckon to the aproned waiter. At once the latter passes the countersign kitchenward to set the meal in motion, and puts before us the little liqueur-glasses and the bottle of vodka. While we still gasp and blink over this, he has gotten the cold *zakuska* of black ryebread and butter, *sardinka,* salty *beluga,* and cold ham, and has started us on the first course. Then comes in, after the omni-inclusive *zakuska,* a big pot of cabbage-soup which we are to season with a swimming spoonful of thick sour cream. The chunky pieces of half-boiled meat floating in it are left high and dry by the consumption of the liquid. The meat becomes the third course, which we garnish with mustard and taste. "Voyons!" the Frenchman observes. "Of the Russian cuisine and its method of preparing certain food-substances one may not approve. Frankly it calls for the sauce of a prodigious appetite. But contemplating the *obeid* as an institution so evolved as to fit into the general scheme of life, it finds merit. The Russian meal is a guide to Russian character."

"What signifies this mélange of raw fish, eggs, and great slices of flesh, and mush of cabbage-soup?"

"Not that the Russian has no taste. It is that he sacrifices his finer susceptibilities to his love of freedom. A regular hour for meals would seem to him a sacrifice of his leisure and convenience to that of the cook. The guiding principle of the national cuisine is that all dishes must be capable of being served at any time that the eater feels disposed."

This is a problem to put to any kitchen, we allow. Napoleon's chef met it by relays of roasting chickens. But one cannot keep half a dozen fowl going for each household of the one hundred and forty million inhabitants of Russia. Thus sturgeon is provided, and sterlet, parboiled so that it tastes like blotting-paper; and the filet that is called "biftek," and the oil-sodden "Hamburger," that is dubbed "filet." These can be started at nine in the morning, and be removed at any time between that hour and nine at night, without any appreciable change in taste or texture. The cook of the restaurant, like his brethren of the Empire, has laid his professional conscience sacrificially upon the national altar of unfettered meals. If the *obeid* is not a triumph in culinary art, it is at least a signal example of domestic generalship.

We have advanced without a hitch to roast partridge, with sugared cranberries, which our friend washes down with good red wine from the Imperial Crimean estates. We get through a hard German-like apple-tart, and reach the last item of cheese.

When the mighty meal is over, we order tea, light cigarettes, and lean back in the armchairs to chat and note how our neighbors are getting through the time.

At the far end of the room a Russian has joined the French lady and her escort. They are celebrating some occasion that requires heaping bumpers of champagne. The babble of their conversation is in the air. It seems to refer to the comparative appreciation of histrionic talent in Rouen and Vladivostok!

Somebody is being treated to a dressing-down in the latest Parisian argot. "Ces sont des betteraves là-bas!" one hears scornfully above the murmurs.

Across the way some Germans are engaged with beer-schooners. One of them gets excited and brings his fist down upon the table. "Arbeit in Sibirien nimmer geendet ist; they always want more advice about their gas-plants."

In the lull that follows the explosion, a gentle English voice floats past from the seat behind us. "And so I told him that the station had nearly enough funds, but we needed workers, more workers." It is the English medical missionary on his way to Shanta-fu, discussing China with the American mining-engineer, bound for Nerchinsk.

The piano, under the corner ikon with its everburning lamp, tinkles out suddenly, and a man's voice starts up –

You can hear the girls declare,
He must be a millionaire.

He misses a note every now and then, which does not embarrass him in the least. Caroling gayly to his own accompaniment, he forges ahead. The crowd in the armchairs around the room, consuming weak tea or strong beer, and smoking, all join with an untroubled accord and versatile accents, French, English, and Russian, in the blaring chorus, "The man that broke the bank at Monte Carlo."

The train rocks faster on the falling grade; little by little the mountains drop away; gradually the mighty forests become dwarfed into scattered clumps of straggly birches, and the great trees dwindle into bushes; lower and still lower fall the hills, until all is flat. As far as the eye can see are the snow-covered wastes, treeless, houseless, lifeless. The lowest foothills of the Urals have been passed. It is the beginning of the great steppes.

Slowly the daylight wanes. The gray darkness deepens steadily; it seems to gather in over the gliding snow, and the peculiar gloom of a Siberian winter's night closes down. At each track-guard's post flash with vivid suddenness the little twinkling lanterns of the wardens of the road. Involuntarily conversation becomes less animated and voices are lowered; the spell of the sombreness is over all.

Soon the electric lamps are lighted, and from brazen ikon and sparkling glasses flash reflections of their glitter. Curtains are drawn, which shut out the enshrouding blackness. The piano begins tinkling again; the waiters come and go with tea and liqueurs; the babble of conversation rises; and the idle laughter is heard anew. Darkness may be ahead, behind, and beside, but within there is light—enjoy it.

The train slows for a halt. Station-lamps shine mistily through the brooding night. Lanterns bob to and fro on the platform as fur-capped trainhands pass, tapping wheels and opening journal-boxes. At each door a fire-tender is catching and stowing away the wood which a peasant in padded sheepskins is tossing up from his hand-sled below. It is Chelliabinsk, whose old importance as the clearing-house of the convicts has been passed on to the new city of the railroad. Here the just completed northern branch, linking Perm to Petersburg, meets the old southern line from Samara and Moscow.

A short stop and the train moves on again. The day is done and gradually each saunters into his own warm compartment, which the width of the Russian gauge makes as large as a real room. One can read at the table by the window, under the electric drop-light, or, propped in pillows, one can stretch out luxuriously on the easy couch that is nightly manoeuvred into an upper and lower berth. Practically always after crossing the Urals, the number of passengers has so thinned out that each may have a stateroom to himself.

Presently you push the bell labeled, "Konduktor." A uniformed attendant appears standing at the salute. "*Spate*" (sleep) is sufficient direction. The sheets and pillows are dug out and the transformation of the couch into a bed is effected. "*Spacoine notche*" (good-night) he says, and you fall asleep to the rhythmic throb of the engine.

Transport Across the Country
A.Rado

In such a vast country as the Soviet Union transport plays a part of extraordinary importance. The transport of raw materials from the outlaying districts to the industrial centres over distances of thousands of kilometres, requires an extensive and efficient network of railways. Under these circumstances, the economic life of the country was much handicapped by the state of the railways, to which the former Tsarist government had given but scant attention. Particularly in Siberia and Turkestan, there were tremendous stretches of arable land lying idle, because of the lack of transport facilities, and even in Europen Russia the railway system was far behind that of Western Europe. These circumstances aggravated the terrible wounds inflicted by the imperialist and, especially, the civil wars upon transport, thus influencing the entire economy of the country. The destruction during the three years of civil war alone, amounted to 21,250 kilometres of railway track, 3,672 bridges, 175,000 telephone and telegraph equipments and upwards of 10,000 telegraph posts. Fully 85% of the locomotives were badly in need of repairs, and about 65% of the locomotives were unfit for service.

By straining all its resources, the Soviet Government succeeded not only in repairing all the damage, but in some respects, even in taking a step forward. The total length of the Russian railways was actually increased as compared with 1913 (74,000 kilometres in 1924 instead of 58,000 in 1913). The railways are functioning with an efficiency which at times surpasses the pre-war standard.

The Strategic Dream
Sir Henry Norman, 1901

Since the Great Wall of China the world has seen no one material undertaking of equal magnitude. That Russia, singlehanded, should have conceived it and carried it out, makes imagination falter before her future influence upon the course of events. Its strategical results are already easy to foresee. It will consolidate Russian influence in the Far East in a manner yet undreamed of. But this will be by slow steps. The expectation that the line would serve at a moment of danger, or in pursuit of a suddenly executed *coup*, to throw masses of soldiers from Europe into China, is yet far from realisation. The line and its organisation would break down utterly under such pressure. But bit by bit it will grow in capacity, and the Powers which have enormous interests at stake in the Far East, if they continue to sleep as England has done of late, will wake to find a new, solid, impenetrable, self-sufficing Russia dominating China as she has dominated, sooner or later, every other Oriental land against whose frontier she has laid her own.

A Cure for the Insomniac
Harry de Windt, 1901

At 10 p.m., on January 4, we left Moscow in a blinding snow-storm, a mild foretaste of the Arctic blizzards to come, which would be experienced without the advantage of a warm and well-lit compartment to view them from. For this train was truly an ambulant palace of luxury. An excellent restaurant, a library, pianos, baths, and last, but not least, a spacious and well-furnished compartment with every comfort, electric and otherwise (and without fellow travellers), rendered this first "étape" of our great land journey one to recall in after days with a longing regret. But we had nearly a fortnight of pleasant travel before us and resolved to make the most of it. Fortunately, the train was not crowded. Some cavalry officers bound for Manchuria, three or four Siberian merchants and their families, and a few Tartars of the better class. The officers were capital fellows, full of life and gaiety (Russian officers generally are), the merchants and their women-folk sociable and musically inclined. Nearly every one spoke French, and the time passed pleasantly enough, for although the days were terribly monotonous, evenings enlivened by music and cards, followed by cheery little suppers towards the small hours, almost atoned for their hours of boredom.

Nevertheless, I cannot recommend this railway journey, even as far as Irkutsk, to those on pleasure bent, for the Trans-Siberian is no tourist line, notwithstanding the alluring advertisements which periodically appear during the holiday season. Climatically the journey is a delightful one in winter time, for Siberia is then at its best – not the Siberia of the English dramatist: howling blizzards, chained convicts, wolves and the knout, but a smiling land of promise and plenty even under its limitless mantle of snow. The landscape is dreary, of course, but most days you have the blue cloudless sky and dazzling sunshine, so often sought in vain on the Riviera. At mid-day your sunlit compartment is often too warm to be pleasant, when outside it is 10° below zero. But the air is too dry and bracing for discomfort, although the pleasant breeze we are enjoying here will presently be torturing unhappy mortals in London in the shape of a boisterous and biting east wind. On the other hand, the monotony after a time becomes almost unbearable. All day long the eye rests vacantly upon a dreary white plain, alternating with green belts of woodland, while occasionally the train plunges into dense dark pine forest only to emerge again upon the same eternal "plateau" of silence and snow. Now and again we pass a village, a brown blur on the limitless white, rarely a town, a few wooden houses clustering around a green dome and gilt crosses, but it is all very mournful and depressing, especially to one fresh from Europe. This train has one advantage, there is no rattle or roar about it, as it steals like a silent ghost across the desolate steppes. As a cure for insomnia it would be invaluable, and we therefore sleep a good deal, but most of the day is passed in the restaurant. Here the military element is generally engrossed in an interminable game of *Vint** (during the process of which a Jew civilian is mercilessly rooked), but our piano is a God-send and most Russian women are born musicians. So after *dejeuner* we join the fair sex, who beguile the hours with Glinka and Tchaikovsky until they can play and sing no more. By the way, no one ever knows the time of day and no one particularly wants to. Petersburg time is kept throughout the journey and the result is obvious. We occasionally find ourselves lunching at breakfast time and dining when we should have supped, but who cares? although in any other clime bottled beer at 8 A.M. might have unpleasant results.

* Russian whist.

Looking Backward to the Future
Lindon Bates Jr, 1908

When, on this seventh day, the train is winding up the Angara Valley toward Irkutsk, one may mentally look back over the country that has been traversed and estimate somewhat the meaning of the railway. The Urals formed the first landmark. As in the dominion of the blind the one-eyed man is king, so after the monotony of the plains, the Ural Mountains seem great and worthy of the name given by the old Muscovite geographer, the "Girdle of the World." By actual measurements, however, in their seventeen hundred miles of length, no peak rises over six thousand feet. Coming eastward from the Urals the line has cut through the southwestern corner of the old Tobolsk Government, has skirted the northern border of the steppe, has bisected the Tomsk Province, and after crossing the Yenesei River in Yeneseik has entered Irkutsk Province, and traversed the central highland region nearly to Lake Baikal.

Many who journey this way will have as their first impression, when the long winter ride draws to its close, a feeling of depression, almost of discouragement, so few are the settlements, so desolate seems all Nature. They see the single line of rails, without a branch or feeder in the mighty expanse from Chelliabinsk to Irkutsk, save for the stub put in for the ungenerous outlands of unlucky Tomsk. They calculate that for a territory forty times the size of the British Isles, and one and a half times as large as all Europe, the inadequacy of a railroad less in total mileage than the Chicago, Milwaukee and St. Paul, is manifest. Statistically-informed bankers sometimes shrug their shoulders at the mention of the Trans-Siberian. "Every year a deficit," they say. "Gross earnings but twenty-four million roubles, – one sixth of the Canadian Pacific Railway; one tenth of the Southern Railway. *Hudoo* (bad)!" One hears expressed not infrequently in Russia the opinion that the railway is a sacrifice justified politically by Russia's need for a link to the Pacific, but ineffectual to secure prosperity and advancement to the isolated land of mid-Siberia. It is deemed, like the Pyramids, a monument to colossal effort and achievement but of little service to mankind.

Their statistics are correct. But it is to the greater honor of the road that much which it has accomplished will never appear in credits on the account-sheets. Where the white stations of the Siberian Railway stand now were once the wooden prison-pens with their guarded stockades. Murderers and priests, forgers, profligates, and university professors, highway robbers and privy councilors, all together have tramped this way. It is its past from which the railroad has raised Siberia, the past of neglect and exile that this steam civilizer has banished to the far Yakutsk.

Closer study gives, too, a better appreciation of the railroad's economic significance. The line holds a strategic position as truly as does the Panama Canal. Though in Siberia proper there is the enormous area of nearly five million square miles, so much of this is in Arctic tundra, impassable swamp, forest, or barren steppe, that the really habitable and arable land narrows down to a tenth of this, which lies in general between the parallels of 55° and 58° 30 north, and is contained within a belt some thirty-five hundred miles long and two hundred to two hundred and fifty miles broad.

When it is noted that the tillable area of one hundred and ninety-two thousand square miles in Tobolsk and Tomsk, mostly along the Obi System, the stretch of twenty thousand miles in the steppe, and that of one hundred thousand in the Yeneseik and Irkutsk governments of eastern Siberia, are all in immediate proximity to the railroad, whose course is generally along the 55th parallel, the economic value of Russia's great enterprise takes a different perspective.

Its vantage is still more emphasized when the element of the north and south watercourses is considered. One after another the great Siberian rivers are crossed, – in the Tobolsk Gobernia, the Tobol, the Ishim, the Irtish; in the Tomsk Gobernia, the Obi and the Tom; in Yeneseik, the Yenesei; in Irkutsk, the Angara. Each of these reaches far up into the agricultural zone that lies north of the railroad, bringing the harvests to its cars by the cheap unfettered water avenues. Thus, to the part of Siberia that is capable of extensive development, the railroad is even now in a position to give great aid.

It is from such natural factors as these, not from financiers' figures, that one must weight the potentiality of this great line. Its direct value is enormous, its indirect commercial services greater yet. It may best be compared to a mighty river system such as that of the Mississippi. The latter's traffic has never directly returned a dollar of the millions that have gone to maintaining its levees and training-walls and channels. Yet indirectly the return and the value, as an asset to the American people, are so great as to be incalculable. From its controlling position in relation to the cultivatable land and the interior watercourses of Central Siberia, as well as in relation to the far eastern artery, the Russian railway is an empire-builder as important as has been the Nile.

The Rossiya Westwards
Paul Theroux, 1974

Afterwards, whenever I thought of the Trans-Siberian Express, I saw stainless steel bowls of *borscht* spilling in the dining car of the Rossiya [the train on which Theroux was travelling] as it rounded a bend on its way to Moscow, and at the curve a clear sight from the window of our green and black steam locomotive – from Skovorodino onwards its eruptions of steamy smoke diffused the sunlight and drifted into the forest so that the birches smouldered and the magpies made for the sky. I saw the gold-tipped pines at sunset and the snow lying softly around clumps of brown grass like cream poured over the ground; the yachtlike snowplows at Zima; the ochreous flare of the floodlit factory chimneys at Irkutsk; the sight of Marinsk in early morning, black cranes and black buildings and escaping figures casting long shadows on the tracks as they ran towards the lighted station – something terrible in that combination of cold, dark, and little people tripping over Siberian tracks; the ice-chest of frost between the cars; the protrusion of Lenin's white forehead at every stop; and the passengers imprisoned in Hard Class: fur hats, fur leggings, blue gym suits, crying children, and such a powerful smell of sardines, body odor, cabbage, and stale tobacco that even at the five-minute stops the Russians jumped onto the snowy platform to risk pneumonia for a breath of fresh air; the bad food; the stupid economies; and the men and women ("No distinction is made with regard to sex in assigning compartments" – Intourist brochure), strangers to each other, who shared the same compartment and sat on opposite bunks, mustached male mirroring mustached female from their grubby nightcaps and the blankets they wore as shawls, down to their hefty ankles stuck in crushed slippers. Most of all, I thought of it as an experience in which time had the trick distortions of a dream: the Rossiya ran on Moscow time, and after a lunch of cold yellow potatoes, a soup of fat lumps called *solyanka*, and a carafe of port that tasted like cough syrup, I would ask the time and be told it was four o'clock in the morning.

The Rossiya was not like the Vostok; it was new. The sleeping cars of East German make were steel syringes, insulated in gray plastic and heated by coal-fired boilers attached to furnace and samovar that gave the front end of each carriage the look of a cartoon atom smasher. The *provodnik* often forgot to stoke the furnace, and then the carriage took on a chill that somehow induced nightmares in me while at the same time denying me sleep. The other passengers in Soft were either suspicious, drunk, or unpleasant: a Goldi and his White Russian wife and small leathery child rode in a nest of boots and blankets, two aggrieved Canadians who ranted to the two Australian librarians about the insolence of the *provodnik*, an elderly Russian lady who did the whole trip wearing the same frilly nightgown, a Georgian who looked as if he had problems at the other end, and several alcoholics who played noisy games of dominoes in their pajamas. Conversation was hopeless, sleep was alarming, and the perversity of the clocks confounded my appetite. That first day I wrote in my diary, *Despair makes me hungry.*

The dining car was packed. Everyone had vegetable soup, then an omelette wrapped around a Weiner schnitzel, served by two waitresses – a very fat lady who bossed the diners incessantly, and a pretty black-haired girl who doubled as scullion and looked as if she might jump off the train at the next clear opportunity. I ate my lunch, and the three Russians at my table tried to bum cigarettes from me. As I had none we attempted a conversation: they were going to Omsk; I was an American. Then they left. I cursed myself for not buying a Russian phrase book in Tokyo.

2

THE RAILWAY

Siberia has been under Russian rule since the late sixteenth century, over-come by methods similar to the settlement of North America: war and threats of war with the Tartar rulers; treaties which placed *vast tracts* of land under at first the nominal and later the actual rule of Russia; settlement spreading out from ostrogs or fortresses which became towns and later cities; expeditions sent out to explore and claim possession of wider terri-tories; fur traders and merchants spreading the net yet wider.

Between 1719 and 1721 John Bell of Antermony, a Scottish physician, travelled from St Petersburg to Peking and back as doctor to the Russian ambassador sent by Peter the First to the Emperor of China. In his book *Travels from St Petersburg in Russia to Diverse Parts of Asia* he gave a very op-timistic account of Siberia:

> Considering the extent of this country and the many
> advantages it possesses, I cannot help being of the opinion that
> it is sufficient to contain all the nations in Europe; where they
> might enjoy a more comfortable life than they do at present.
> For my part, I think that, had a person his liberty and a few
> friends, there are few places where he could spend his life more
> agreeably than in some parts of Siberia.

Once dominated, Siberia had to be peopled by men and women who would colonize the vast area, pushing the indigenous tribes aside or assim-ilating them. Some people went voluntarily as immigrants, encouraged by promises of freedom and land; some went as missionaries; others were sent as convicts and political exiles to become virtual slave labour. Of these, when their sentences were completed, many were settled either as serfs or later as free men.

Count Muraviev-Amurski who, by the Treaty of Aigun in 1858, annexed the land north of the Amur and along the Pacific coast, settled ex-convicts there with these words: "Go, my children, be free there, cultivate the land, make it Russian soil, start a new life". Then, to these men, he gave

female convicts as wives, marrying them *en masse* as they stood in pairs on the banks of the Amur, saying, "I marry you, children. Be kind to each other; you men, don't ill-treat your wives–and be happy."

However, until the railway was built, travel to and across Siberia was slow and often painful. By horseback, *telega* (a sort of buck-board), *tarantass* (a sort of sprung, hooded carriage) or by sledge along the grandly named Great Siberian Post Road, with its many crossings of great rivers, the journey was hard. For the convicts who trudged all the way on foot it must have been terrible. The story of those who made the journey before the railway would fill another book.

The first proposals for a trans-Siberian railway were made in 1857 by an American, Perry McDonough Collins:

> A line of railroad striking the Amoor from Moscow via Nijne, Kazan, Ekaterinburg, Omsk, Tomsk, and Irkutsk to Kyachta, would be quite as manageable as some of our lines over the Allegheny Mountains or the more northern roads in Canada; and if the severity of the climate and the fall of snow as a hindrance to the building of a railroad from the head of the Amoor to the sea is all that is to be taken into consideration, and no other or greater difficulties presented themselves to be overcome, a railroad from Moscow to Pekin and the Pacific Ocean might be considered as a fact accomplished.

Count Muraviev-Amurski himself supported the scheme, quickly reporting to Collins on receiving his letter that:

> I have already sent your project of a railroad with a courier to St Petersburg, and I do not doubt that you will receive an answer to your proposal before your departure to America. I sincerely wish our government may give its consent to an enterprise in which I take a most lively interest, and in which I wish you all possible success.

Collins and Muraviev-Amurski were ignored. Various Englishmen and Russians made further proposals, including one using horse-drawn trams until such time as steam engines could be afforded. It took three decades of endless committees before, on 24 February 1891, ministerial agreement was at last reached and the great project could begin.

In this chapter the writers and travellers describe the railway and its construction. In 1897 James Young Simpson gave his understanding of the reasons for the building of the "Great Siberian Iron Road" and elucidated its beginnings. The official *Russian Guide to the Great Siberian Railway*, published in 1900, provides Tsar Alexander's instructions for its inauguration in 1893, and gives a picture of the complex bureaucracy behind the building of the railway and details of the immense task and its effects. James Simpson shows how the work forged ahead, and with hindsight, Simpson portrays the work on the line as he saw it in 1897. William Greener in 1902 was critical of its construction. Bassett Digby got closer to the local people than many of the travellers and he tells of the theft of a train. Eric Newby, who travelled the railway in 1977, gives the history of the do-it-yourself package that was made into the ferry *Baikal*. Sir Henry Norman, MP, talked to the British engineers who put it together and worked on it on Lake Baikal.

The Vast Enterprise
James Young Simpson, 1897

When in the years to come men review the greater undertakings of the nineteenth century, it will be hard to find a rival to the Trans-Siberian Railway. Winding across the illimitable plains of Orenburg, traversing the broad Urals, spanning the widest rivers, like the Irtish, Ob, and Yenisei, it creeps round the southern end of Lake Baikal, and mounts the plateau of far Trans-Baikalia. Thereafter, leaving behind it the Yablonovoi Mountains, the line descends into the valley of the Amur, exchanges it presently for that of the Ussuri, and ends at last in Vladivostok. Such is, in brief, the original course of this vast enterprise.

For long, Russia has been feeling her way towards the open ocean. It is as if she were being choked for want of air. The White Sea and the Arctic Ocean enchained in Polar ice, the Baltic similarly blocked for half the year, the Black Sea closed in yet another way, and finally the landlocked Caspian, cannot satisfy her. In face of this, she has been compelled to seek the shores of the Pacific Ocean. As early as the middle of the seventeenth century a handful of intrepid, though predatory, Russian pioneers had gained the barren Okhotsk shore and founded the town that bears that name. But it was only to find that here the same conditions prevailed as on their western Baltic, and the disappointed explorers involuntarily turned their eyes towards the kindlier south. Soon a party of Kossaks and hunters, passing through Trans-Baikalia, took possession of some land on the Upper Amur. Gradually the whole territory on the left bank of that river, and thereafter the region of the Ussuri, came into Russian hands, though it was General Muraviev who in 1854, during the progress of the Crimean war, played the greatest part in the work of annexation. About four or five years later dawned the appearance of Siberian railway effort.

The Trans-Siberian Railway scheme was probably but the development of sundry other lesser projects which had as object the providing of suitable means of communication in and with the newly acquired territories, so that they might be the more easily held, and, in addition, colonised. There are some patriotic individuals amongst ourselves who would have it kept in remembrance that no plan of Trans-Siberian conveyance appeared earlier than that of a certain English engineer. But this had better be forgotten. For when we learn that his proposal to carry a horse tramway from Nijni-Novgorod through Kazan and Perm to some port on the Pacific Ocean was unsupported by any estimate – his name was Dull – we do not wonder that the Government passed it by in silence.

But his was not the only paper scheme. More modest was that of Collins, an American, who wished to unite Irkutsk and Tchita by rail. In 1858 three English projectors – Morison, Horn, and Sleigh – offered to lay a railway from Moscow to the Straits of Tartary, but at the same time petitioned for such privileges as would have retained the exploitation of Siberia and the ensuing profit in other than Russian hands for a number of years. Hence these and all other like vague drafts, based on no preliminary surveys or careful investigation of the needs and trading possibilities of the districts they affected, went no further.

A mass of details, exact and inexact, had been collected as the result of the various preliminary surveys bearing on the future Siberian

Railway, and since no definite conclusion as to the direction of the route seemed possible under the existing circumstances, a Special Commission was sent out to the Urals and directed to make a final investigation of the question. Their orders were to let the requirements of the Ural mining industry bulk most largely in their deliberations: the Siberian transport trade, although to be kept in view, was always to yield to the other in importance. The principal outcome of this activity was the decision that these two interests were incompatible. Accordingly, for the time being, the idea of a local Ural Railway was preferred to that of a Trans-Siberian trunk line. Government surveys were conducted during 1872-74, and in 1878 the Ural line was opened as far as Yekaterinburg. Four years later it had been extended to Tiumen, through which town it was still felt that the future Trans-Siberian Railway must pass.

Meanwhile, within European Russia there had been considerable railway extension. Orenburg was now in communication with the general system, and if for the moment the idea of a Trans-Siberian Railway had slipped somewhat into the background in the West, yet in the far East no little attention was given to the project, and as early as 1875 there were petitions, *e.g.,* to unite Vladivostok and Lake Khanka by rail, if for nothing else than in view of future relations with China and Japan. The result of all this was, that in 1882 the subject of the Siberian Railway was taken up afresh, and as additional surveys and other considerations showed the inadvisability of continuing the line through Tiumen, the whole matter had to be gone into again from the beginning.

The Time has Come
Guide to the Great Siberian Railway, 1900

On a report drawn up in 1885-1886 by Count Ignátiev, then Vice Governor-General, the late Tsar-Pacificator, who was always anxious to further Siberian interests, traced with his own hand the following resolution, which so greatly influenced the decision of the question:

"I have read many reports of the Governors-General of Siberia and must own with grief and shame that until now the Government has done scarcely anything towards satisfying the needs of this rich, but neglected country! It is time, high time!"

The petitions of Count Ignátiev and Baron Korf presented at the end of 1886, for the construction of a railway line from Tomsk to Irkútsk, and from the Baikál to Srétensk, uniting by means of the Amúr the West and East Siberian navigation systems, together with the plan for connecting by rail Vladivostók and the post of Bussé, were submitted by Imperial command to a special Conference of Ministers under the presidentship of Actual Privy Councillor Abazá.

As a result of this Conference, a Special Commission was directed to make surveys along the Mid-Siberian, Transbaikál and South-Ussúri lines. His Imperial Majesty wrote the following decision on the report of the Minister of Ways of Communication presented to him on the 12 June 1887, in consequence of the data obtained by the Conference and from the surveys made:

"Quite right. I hope the Ministry will practically prove the possibility of the quick and cheap construction of the line".

This note of the Emperor's was made known by the Minister of Ways of Communication to the Board of Government Railways and to the Survey Commissions.

The Emperor showed a special interest in the execution of the surveys, which were carried on most successfully. Frequent reports as to their progress was presented to His Majesty by the Minister of Ways of Communication.

The Committee of Ministers, having taken the project of the Minister of Ways of Communication into consideration, issued the following order sanctioned by the Emperor on the 15 and 21 February 1891: 1) To approve the direction of the Ussúri line from Vladivostók to Gráfskaya station; 2) To commence the construction of the Miás-Cheliábinsk line in 1891; 3) To conduct surveys in the same year, from Cheliábinsk to Tomsk or some other point of the Mid-Siberian section, and from the terminus of the first section of the Ussúri line to Khabárovsk; 4) To carry out these works under the direction of the State; 5) The Minister of Ways of Communication to receive the sanction of the State Council for the necessary expenditure.

The Imperial Rescript addressed to His Imperial Highness the Grand Duke Tsesarévich on the 17th March 1891, finally and irrevocably decided the question of the construction of the Great Siberian Railroad.

This memorable document was made known by His Imperial Highness upon his again treading Russian soil at Vladivostok, on the 14th May 1891, on his way back from the Far East.

Your Imperial Highness!
Having given the order to build a continuous line of railway across Siberia, which is to unite the rich Siberian provinces with the railway system of the Interior, I entrust to you to declare My will, upon your entering the Russian dominions after your inspection of the foreign countries of the East. At the same time, I desire you to lay the first stone at Vladivostók for the construction of the Ussúri line, forming part of the Siberian Railway, which is to be carried out at the cost of the State and under direction of the Government. Your participation in the achievement of this work will be a testimony to My ardent desire to facilitate the communications between Siberia and the other countries of the Empire, and to manifest My extreme anxiety to secure the peaceful prosperity of this Country. I remain your sincerely loving

Alexander.

The question of the construction of the Great Siberian Railway, which for a third of a century had occupied the attention of the Government and society, was now settled, representing the most important event of the century, not only in our country, but in the whole world.

On the 19th May, at Vladivostók, His Imperial Highness the Grand Duke Tsesarévich, with his own hands filled a wheelbarrow with earth and emptied it on the embankment of the future Ussúri line, and then laid the first stone for the construction of the Great Siberian Railway.

Underway
Guide to the Great Siberian Railway, 1900

On the 14th January 1893, His Imperial Highness the Grand Duke Tsesarévich, the present Emperor Nicholas II, by a rescript of His Imperial Father was appointed President of the [special Siberian Railway] Committee.

At its first meeting on the 10th February 1893, His Imperial Highness the Grand Duke Tsesarévich addressed the following words to the members of the Committee:

"In opening the first meeting of the Committee for the construction of the Siberian Railway, I contemplate with emotion the grandeur of the task before us. But love of my country and an ardent desire to contribute to its welfare, have induced me to accept the commission from my beloved Father. I am convinced that you are animated by the same feelings, and that our joint efforts will bring us to the desired end."

After the decease of his Imperial Father, the present Emperor Nicholas Alexándrovich retained the post of President of the Committee of the Siberian Railway.

At the meeting held on the 30th November 1894, which was the first after his ascension to the throne, his Imperial Majesty addressed the following memorable words to the members of the Committee and of the Department of State Economy:

Gentlemen! To have begun the construction of the railway line across Siberia is one of the greatest achievements of the glorious reign of my never to be forgotten Father. The fulfilment of this essentially peaceful work, entrusted to me by my beloved Father, is my sacred duty and my sincere desire. With your assistance, I hope to complete the construction of the Siberian line, and to have it done cheaply and, most important of all, quickly and solidly.

The Trans-Siberian Railway

After having heard the gracious words of His Imperial Majesty, the Vice-President of the Committee, Actual Privy Councillor Bunge expressed as follows the loyal feelings of all the members:

> We are most happy that in accordance with Your Imperial Majesty's desire, the work of construction of the Siberian Railway will remain under Your Majesty's immediate direction. At the time of Your visit to distant lands, Your Majesty took the first step at Vladivostók towards the execution of the Siberian Railway. Upon Your Majesty's return, You were appointed President of the Committee for the construction of the Siberian line by the late Emperor, Who thus assured the fulfilment of the task entrusted to the Committee, which always was the object of Your constant endeavour. At present, Your Majesty having desired to retain the direction of this vast enterprise, which is to connect European Russia with the shore of the Pacific Ocean, we are convinced that this grand work bequeathed to Your Majesty by Your Imperial Father, will be brought to a successful end and constitute the glory of the late and present reigns.

In accordance with the desire of the Monarch Pacificator, this costly Siberian line was constructed exclusively by Russian engineers and with Russian materials.

During the achievement of this work, the principal attention was paid to the speedy and solid construction of the permanent way; the building of stations was to be effected gradually, with a view to economy, and to avoid the risk of useless expenditure, which might result from a false estimate as to the future traffic. The buildings for the accommodation of passengers and goods were to be constructed in proportion as they were called for by the actual requirements. Considerable modifications and technical simplifications were admitted in the construction of the Siberian Railway, with a view to a more speedy execution of the work and a reduction of the expenditure.

Working on the Line
James Young Simpson, 1897

We have already noticed the numbers of men who are engaged on this vast undertaking. In the heat of the midday sun it was assuredly hard work, and one was not surprised to see the somewhat deliberate fashion in which any particular task was carried through. The great majority of the labourers were toiling in white (or what had once been white) cotton shirts and pantaloons, barefoot, bareheaded. Some of their tools and implements were primitive – *e.g.*, the wheelless barrow shoved along a plank. One saw the evolution of the spade in a single party, for while some were employing long-handled wooden shovels, all of one piece, others had the edge of the blade protected with a thin binding of tin, while yet others had the ordinary one with iron blade. Another tool looked like half a pick, with the back of the head flattened hammer-wise. They also made use of giant sledgehammers of wood – a vast bole with a stout handle driven into it, making a very formidable weapon. Utilising a thick beam as a lever, they would prise up great lengths of rail attached to the sleepers, and so fill in more ballast. One noticed also the absence of what are commonly known as "chairs": the broad-based rails are simply laid on the notched sleepers, and held in position there by a small species of clamp on the inside only. Great care is being exercised in the regulation of this railway. Every hundred yards or so appear white boards indicating the gradients, which occasionally alter very considerably over quite short ranges.

Also at extremely short intervals are posted the usual men in charge of the line, green flag in hand, to signify that their section at least is clear. Throughout its length the line is continuously accompanied on either side by excavations of varying size, from which the soil was taken for its construction. At those points where over long distances the embankment remains a considerable height, these trenches increase greatly in breadth, but not so much in depth. The cause of this is simply that the ground is frozen at about 6 feet below the surface till towards the end of July, so that the upper stratum alone is workable. These broad ditches fill with water, and become the spacious nurseries of myriads of mosquitoes and other objectionable forms of insect life. Beyond these lie immense expenses of verdant plain, whose uniformity is interrupted at intervals by irregularly set thickets of stunted birch. Occasionally some Kirghize boy betrays our laboured progress by forging ahead of the train on his hardy pony. Shaggy, sure-footed, speedy, they are the true Siberian travellers; shrewd also, for when the sun has dipped below the western horizon and the evening air seems to exist for nothing but mischief-making mosquitoes and their inhuman clan, mark how by yonder small encampment in the lee of a birch coppice the patient burden-bearers stand beside the fire, facing the wind, and hold their heads in the smoke to be relieved from their pestiferous associates. Animal life otherwise is not much in evidence. Occasionally a startled hare dashes from his "form" too near the track of progressive man. Perhaps a mallard rises from some weeded brake, and overhead a towering hawk recks not but for his prey: save for these we are alone.

The Great Siberian Iron Road
James Young Simpson, 1897

By the 15th June 1895 one quarter of the line had been laid; in the autumn of the following year passengers were set down at Krasnoyarsk. The year 1897 saw the railway open as far as Nijni-Udinsk, and it is expected that by the summer of 1898, or at latest by spring of the succeeding year, not only will Irkutsk and St Petersburg be connected by rail, but steam communication will have been established between the capital and Vladivostok. That is to say, after crossing Lake Baikal by boat, the passenger will resume train as far as Srjetesnk, whence Khabarovsk, which is already joined by rail to the Pacific port, will be reached by steamer. Fourteen days is optimistically given as the duration of such a journey between the extreme points, which will be reduced to ten, or even nine, when everything is in working order and the Manchurian line completed. But it is difficult to see how the original plan can be carried out before 1903.

Remission through Labour
James Young Simpson, 1897

The question of criminal labour on the railway presents some interesting features that may be briefly narrated here. Once it was resolved to employ convict labour, the problem that presented itself to the Ministry of the Interior was how, out of the criminal prisoners from European Russia, the lazy local population of the Siberian prisons, and the political exiles, to form a disciplined army of railway workmen. It was, however, solved so brilliantly that the convicts working on the Mid-Siberian road by their labour and irreproachable conduct attracted the attention of the august President of the Committee of the Siberian Railway. Convict labour was at first directed to the construction of the Ussuri Railway, where, on the contrary, it far from verified expectations, and the convict party was soon sent back to the island of Sakhalin. On a larger scale the experiment was repeated in the construction of the Mid-Siberian Railway. In order to make the work attractive, and so include convicts of all categories, a regulation was made for those who came under the Governor-General of Irkutsk, that eight months' railway work should count as one year of imprisonment or hard labour, according to circumstances. For the exiles the term required to enable them to be registered as peasants was to be reduced, in return for labour on the railway, in the proportion of one year for two. For those who more than two years before had been transported for life, the period during which they should have to wait before permission would be granted to choose a dwelling-place was reduced by one half; and for those compelled to live in far Siberia, the term of deportation was to be shortened by counting one year as two.

It is difficult to estimate the enormous amount of labour that has been expended on this railway. Consider how, to begin with, all the sleepers have been sawn tediously by hand. The log rests at a considerable elevation upon two props; one man stands upon it, working the saw downwards to another man below. Then in the construction of any high embankment the supporting piles are driven in by a primitive contrivance, also of wood, in the form of a giant tripod, from the top of which there hangs a pulley. Over this runs a rope, to one end of which is attached a heavy stone, with level base, while the other end is led on to a wheel at the side, by means of which the weight is raised. This arrangement is fixed over *each pile* in turn, so that the descending stone may strike it: thus after a generation the pile is driven home to the required depth. Again, one was impressed with the extremely finished nature of the work: thus the side of the large brown embankment was often covered with an infinite number of small squares of turf, each of which was held in position by two little pegs of wood.

Good in Parts
William Oliver Greener, 1902

Much nonsense has been written respecting the "Great Siberian Railways." The lines have been over-praised; they have been ruthlessly condemned. There are poor sections; none is either very good or very bad; some are much better than others. Altogether, it is just a light railway – nothing more. The gauge is five feet; the rails weigh from forty-two to forty-eight pounds the yard; they are too light for the heavy engines and rolling stock of the State railways. They ought to be seventy-four pounds to the yard as was specified, and used on the eastern sections. Some, instead of being hard rail-steel, are soft, and the weight of a heavy train passing strains them beyond the point of elasticity and they do not recover, but remain sunk between the sleepers. On one curve, it is said that a certain rail is crushed every time the "express" passes, the buckling of the web of the rail renders it useless, and it has to be replaced by a new one each time, that is, four rails each week. Generally, the rails are just able to sustain the weight at slow speeds, and no more.

The embankments are too narrow and too steep, the cuttings the same, the sleepers too soft and too thin. As a narrow-gauge railway little fault would have been found, but its staunchest champions admit that it is inferior to the average railways in European Russia. There are sections which ought to be perfect, according to theory. That is to say, that by the engineering text-books the embankments are at the right angle, the sleepers are close enough together, and the rails strong enough to carry the weight. Everything has been accurately calculated; but everything, too, has been made just as specified in the calculated minimum, and no margin allowed for possible differences of soil and material. Consequently there are, and always will be, subsidences of the track, falls of loose earth in the cuttings, and spreading of the rails; therefore delays to the traffic which even the proposed re-ballasting of the track with broken stone will not prevent.

The speed of the trains can never be great. Short trains with a light load like the Siberian Express may be able to average twenty miles an hour; the heavier, ordinary trains do not often exceed twelve miles the hour, whilst the heavy goods trains rumble along like traction engines on a country road. The express is the safest train by which to travel; the long freight trains bring down the falls of earth and cause subsidences of the track, and so themselves sometimes come to grief. The expresses are merely delayed by having to wait for the track to be cleared. From these strictures certain sections may be exempted, as of a more solid character.

Before long many crudities of the existing trunk line will have been improved. It will not be necessary for the locomotives to take reserves of water in tubs on trucks; or for it to be pumped a half-mile, or more, to tanks; the line will be properly ballasted; there will not be falls of earth down the banks every time a train passes; with the settlement and subsequent drainage of the lands adjacent to the railways the subsidences caused by flood water will cease.

State railways may be expected to cost more than private undertakings, but then the work should be better done. Work of the best class is not conspicuous on the Siberian railways, but Americans, who remember the completion of the Union Pacific line, say that the track is no worse than the first put down in the United States, and that is the highest praise I heard from experts competent to form a just opinion. On the other side Russians are not slow to recount instances of jobbery in connection with the construction of the railway, of which the most flagrant instance perhaps is that of the contractor who made his embankment of snow instead of earth, so that when the thaw came, by which time he had been paid, the track subsided four feet throughout the length of his section.

Again, the whole principle of railway building is primitive and costly. For the greater part of its length the track runs across practically level ground, and the bank is raised by digging a ditch corresponding in depth and width to the embankment. When a cutting has to be made, the earth therefrom is piled on both sides of the banks, and not used to make the embankments. In fact such tools as excavators and tip-waggons do not appear to have been used at all, nor are they employed in the construction of the Eastern Chinese railway.

It is an all-Russian line, and if it has cost much more to construct than would have been the case had the work been given to foreign contractors, the Russians have gained what they needed badly, practical experience in carrying through engineering work of the first order. In this way, if in no other, the State benefits, but the value of the individual experience is to some extent lost to the State, owing to the fact that the continuation of the work of covering the East with a network of lines is entrusted to new hands. Instead of employing the men who have gained their experience at the cost of the State those now engaged are, with few exceptions, young engineers fresh from the technical colleges. On the other hand, it must be allowed that the railway presented no very serious engineering difficulties; severe winter weather was the most troublesome element. Nowhere has the line a long tunnel completed, or a bridge like that over the Kishta or the Forth; when it is not running on a dead level, it winds like a serpent.

The railway is staffed by 14,728 persons, and the official return gives the rolling stock as: 751 locomotives, 548 passenger and 7743 goods waggons, 33 mail-vans, &c., but the number of each has been increased by recent large additions; though it is hinted that on the stock-taking visits of the inspector, by altering with white paint the numbers on the trucks and sending them on ahead, whilst the inspector is detained, many have been counted twice or oftener.

The Siberia opened up to Russians by the railway is a land of much promise; it is not the Eldorado some picture it, nor is it the desolate waste Siberia is generally considered. Nowhere throughout its whole length does it cross or approach barren land. The Siberia of the railway, possibly the pick of the vast regions in Russian Asia, is just plain, commonplace country, such as one expects to find in any great British colony, and its like can be found far to north and south of the actual tract traversed. It must be admitted that the country does impress the beholder favourably. The neat railway settlements, composed of large immigrant homes, schools, picturesque churches – built out of the Alexander III. memorial fund – substantial and commodious dwellings, the mills, stores and station buildings are not properly representative of Siberia, but of the new better free colonies the Russian State is doing its utmost to plant all over the fertile regions of northern Asia. In time other railways will be wanted, but at present Siberia wants men and it wants those men badly.

Baikal's Lurid Past
Bassett Digby, 1928

Champagne came out in sealed ammunition cars. Such cars, right up to the time of the recent World War, had a nice little coloured painting on each side, of a bursting shell – flame, smoke, and all – to deter the illiterate soldiery from treating them roughly. Near Irkutsk, an hour's journey west of Baikal, an entire train was lost, to the extreme perplexity of the railroad administration. It was given the "all clear" by a signal box one night and told to proceed and wait on a siding until morning. But when morning came it had vanished. The next signal box vowed that it had not seen it. What had happened was that the locomotive was run on a few miles and diverted, by a few feet of specially laid rails, into a deep hole in the river. The "ammunition" cars were drawn by horses into the thick of the jumbled scores of sidings in a park of empty rolling-stock awaiting return to Russia and their identification marks changed. A ring of army officers who had been keeping a watchful eye on the consignment's progress ever since it had left Moscow, cleared about 100,000 roubles on the seven carloads of champagne that had been thus discreetly consigned to South Manchuria.

Crossing Lake Baikal
Eric Newby, 1977

Until the completion of the Circumbaikal Loop, Port Baikal on the north-west shore was the terminus of a ferry which carried the rolling stock across the lake to Mysovaya on the far shore. The contract for the first of these train ferries, which also had to be an ice-breaker, had been signed by Prince Khilkov, the then Minister of Ways and Communications, at the end of December 1895. The contractors were a British firm, Sir W. G. Armstrong, Mitchell and Company.

The *Baikal*, as she was later named, was a four-funnelled vessel, 290 feet long, with a beam of 57 feet. The hull was constructed with inch-thick steel plating, reinforced internally with two-foot thick timber sheathing. Propulsion was provided by three triple expansion steam engines, developing 3750 horse power, which drove two steel propellers and a bronze forescrew in the bows capable of breaking through ice up to four feet thick, and it had fifteen boilers which burned wood fuel. The engines, boilers, water-pumping machinery and some other items were made at St Petersburg.

The work of building the *Baikal* at Newcastle-upon-Tyne took a year and every part was stamped with an identifying number. When it was finally completed it was taken to pieces, packed up and sent to St Petersburg where all the components were again divided up, this time into 7000 separate packages, for the immense journey across European Russia and Siberia to the lake.

At Krasnoyarsk the great bridge over the Yenisei had not yet been completed and there the whole consignment had to be off loaded and shipped down the Yenisei and up the Angara by barge and sledge, a distance of well over 1000 miles, which involved unloading everything at the rapids and making portages.

The first parcels began to arrive at Listvyanka, a small port across the Angara from Port Baikal, towards the end of 1897, but piece-meal, so that parts of engines turned up before the keel. It was a miracle that nothing of importance was lost *en route*.

At Listvyanka a marine engineer and four foremen from the Tyne were waiting to rebuild the ship, together with a force of Russian workmen, some of whom had been sent from St Petersburg.

The *Baikal* was finally launched at the end of July 1899, almost four years after her keel was first laid at the British yard. Even then she still lacked her fifteen wood-burning boilers, which had been held up at Krasnoyarsk for two years awaiting the completion of the bridge. When she finally went into service, in April 1900, she had a displacement of 4250 tons and drew 20 feet. Meanwhile dock facilities had been built for her at Port Baikal and Mysovaya.

No one in Siberia had seen anything like this huge, slab-sided, gleaming white vessel. Three lines of track were laid on her main deck to accommodate the carriages of an entire train, or 25 loaded flat cars. There were staterooms, first and second-class cabins, deck accommodation for more than 600 third-class passengers, a sumptuous restaurant, crew accommodation and a chapel in which it became fashionable for Irkutskians to get married. Another, smaller, vessel, the *Angara*, had meanwhile been commissioned from the same firm and in the autumn of 1901 it too arrived at the lake in pieces and was re-assembled there. Unfortunately, the experts had miscalculated the depths to which the lake was capable of freezing and it was soon discovered that the only way in which the *Angara* could operate in winter was for the *Baikal*, which had to be without a train on board, to charge the ice ahead of her and force a passage. In severe weather both vessels became ice-bound and then the train passengers had to cross the ice in sledges. Even in the summer months the ships were often immobilized for days on end by fog.

In February 1904, while both ships were ice-bound in a temperature of − 40°F, the Japanese launched their surprise attack on the Russian Fleet at Port Arthur and it became imperative that the military reinforcements that were being rushed to the east, and which were piling up at Port Baikal, together with all their trains loaded with war material, should be able to continue their journey.

It was now that Prince Khilkov put into operation a plan that his Ministry had toyed with years before and then rejected, which was to lay a track across the ice, which that winter was five feet thick, using extra long sleepers to spread the load. An experiment was made using a test engine, which suddenly plunged into the depths owing to the existence of unsuspected warm springs beneath the surface. It made a hole in the ice almost five feet wide and more than 14 miles long. After this disaster engines were dismantled and, with their component parts loaded on to flat cars, were dragged across the ice by huge teams of men and horses, while the army marched, or travelled in sledges, if they were lucky – a seventeen-hour journey on foot across the ice with halts at huts set up at intervals. In this way thousands of men with their munitions, dozens of locomotives and thousands of flat cars crossed the 25-mile expanse of ice to Tankhoy on the southern shore of the lake, where they were able to resume their journey by the railway.

In the meantime the contractors and their huge, cosmopolitan labour force were working flat out in the – 40°F weather to complete the cliff section of the Circumbaikal Loop between Port Baikal and Kultuk; and in September 1904 they succeeded. It is true that the first test train to run over the route was derailed ten times in the 50-mile cliff section and took three days to cover the entire route, and that Prince Khilkov's inaugural train, which passed over it a week or so later, was also derailed; but the latter was only derailed once, and the whole work must be regarded as a triumph.

Criminals and Ice-Breakers
Sir Henry Norman, 1901

The firm of Sir William Armstrong, Whitworth & Co. has built upon Lake Baikal one of the most remarkable steamships in the world, to ferry the Siberian trains across the lake, and in winter to break the ice at the same time. The *Baikal* was brought out in pieces from Newcastle-on-Tyne, and put together by English engineers, who have been living in this remote and lonely spot for over two years. I found three of these hard at work, the chief, Mr. Douie, and his assistants, Mr. Renton and Mr. Handy, and spent some very interesting hours with them. They ought to be well paid for the fine work they were doing, for a more dreary exile can hardly be imagined. They lived at a little village called Listvenitchnaya, a nest of crime and robbery, crowded during the summer with innumerable caravans bringing tea from China. Every civilised person carries a revolver there, and two if he is of a cautious temperament. Nobody thinks of going out after dark, and every week somebody is robbed or killed. The whole population is ex-convict or worse. The boss of the labourers on the *Baikal* was in Siberia for outraging a child; the man who conducted me to where Mr. Douie and Mr. Renton were at work was a murderer from the Caucasus; a short time before my visit another murderer employed on the ship had tried to repeat his crime, and had been consigned to chains again; the very day I was there the police were looking for a man supposed to have obtained work in the yard, who was wanted for killing eight people, I was told, at one time. There are a few Cossacks at Listvenitchnaya, but they are wholly incapable, even if they have the desire, of coping with the turbulent place. It may be the best policy for the Russian Government not to hang its murderers, or keep its criminals in confinement, but to turn them loose in such places. There can be no excuse, however, for its failure to provide an adequate police force to control them, or for the preposterous tolerance which allows every man of these criminals to go about armed to the teeth. A few months before my visit they held up the mail-cart from Lake Baikal to Irkutsk, shot four of its five guards, and stole its gold. Some day they will hold up a train, and rob the passengers. Then authority will doubtless assert itself. I do not see anything to prevent such an act. In a place like this the English engineers have absolutely nothing to do or think about, except their work, and the long evenings of a Siberian winter, spent within fast-barred doors, must be inexpressibly dreary.

The *Baikal* is a magnificent vessel of 4000 tons, with twin engines amidships of 1250 horse-power each, and a similar engine forward, to drive the screw in the bow; for the principle of the new type of ice-breaker is to draw out the water from under the ice ahead by the suction of a bow-screw, when the ice collapses by its own weight and a passage is forced through the broken mass by the impact of the vessel. The *Baikal* has extensive upper works, and these contain luxurious saloons and cabins. Upon her deck she carries three trains – a passenger-train in the middle, and a freight-train on each side. Her speed is thirteen knots, and on her trial trips she has shown herself capable of breaking through solid ice thirty-eight inches thick, with five inches of hard snow on the top – such snow is much more difficult to pierce than ice – and has forced her way through two thicknesses of ice frozen together, aggregating from fifty-six to sixty-five inches. In summer her bow propeller should be removed, and large propellers

substituted for her smaller winter ones; but so far the railway authorities have taken no steps to build a dock upon the lake, without which
neither of these important changes can be effected, nor the steamer
herself repaired if any mishap should damage her hull. Lake Baikal is
frozen from the middle of December to the end of April, and there is
also talk of laying a railway across upon the ice, as is done each year
from St. Petersburg to Kronstadt; but probably all depends upon the
success of the ice-breaking steamer. If this accomplishes its purpose
another similar vessel will be built, for obviously the entire Trans-
Continental service would otherwise be staked upon one ship never
getting out of order the whole season. The *Yermak,* however – the ice-
breaker also built by Sir William Armstrong, Whitworth & Co. for
service in the Baltic – has been such a splendid success, forcing her
way through mixed ice twenty-five feet thick, that there is every reason
to presume the *Baikal* will do her work equally well.

3

THE TRAIN

The gauge of the Russian railway system is wider than most other countries: 5 foot (1,524 mm) as against the usual 4ft 8½ in (1,435 mm). At the borders on entering and leaving Russian territory, the bogies have to be changed and the huge trains are lifted up while one set of wheels is rolled out and another rolled in. It is an amazing feat, especially when, on the Chinese border, the task is done by slips of girls.

With a wider gauge the Russian engines and rolling stock are bigger than others–towering 17 foot 2 inches (5.23 metres) high and being 11 foot 2 inches (3.4 metres) in width. This makes travelling, in soft class at least, far more spacious than on any other railway system.

The high point of passenger comfort and opulence was the Paris Universal Exposition of 1900 when the Wagon-Lits carriages of the Trans-Siberian Railway were exhibited in all their glory, with gold-buttoned green plush seats and a Moorish-style smoking-room with armchairs garlanded in flowers. The dining car was the *pièce de résistance* with a diorama of the scenery between Moscow and Irkutsk unfurling past the windows. For three quarters of an hour portions passed at different speeds to represent fore-, middle- and background while "passengers" were served bortsch, caviar and sturgeon by an attendant dressed like a Tartar, before descending at a mock Chinese station at the end of the "journey".

But the trains are slow. Russian passenger trains are timed, at about 30 miles an hour, to fit in with the freight trains which dominate the system. Russian rail freight traffic is more than all the rest of the world's rail freight put together. There are approximately a quarter of a million loaded wagons dispatched along the system each day, and at every large station are huge freight yards.

Today the carriages on the trains are functional and roomy, at least in first and luxury class with 20 in a carriage. Second-, or tourist-class carriages take twice as many passengers, and in lounge or "hard" class there are berths for twice this number of local passengers. In the past some people travelled in virtual cattle trucks, prisons on wheels; others, after 1900, made the journey in sumptuous luxury.

Today the journey takes just over six days (165 hours including an overnight stop), although most tourists stop over at Irkutsk to recover their land legs. At the turn of the century the journey took twice as long–if you were lucky–but passengers normally allowed longer to take into account the delays caused by the frequent derailments along the way.

Gone now are the days when the restaurant car was the hub of social life on the trains. There is no liquor aboard today to loosen tongues and, as a foreign tourist with a group, meal times are likely to be fixed. In the past people had a very different tale to tell.

Karl Baedeker gave a factual account of Russian trains in 1914. Harmon Tupper describes the luxury train provided for first-class passengers and tells of the unveiling of these luxury carriages to the world at the Paris Universal Exposition in 1900: his later reports on the variations in the real service are revealing. Annette Meakin, the first Englishwoman to make the complete journey in 1900, visited the Paris exhibition with her mother to study the train before embarking on the journey. She found the reality to her satisfaction, as did Sir Henry Norman, MP, in 1901, although he also found much to criticize. The American Francis E. Clark, who travelled from Vladivostok in 1899, details the *train de luxe,* and in a later excerpt also describes the "fourth-class" carriages in Trans-Baikalia. The American duo, Digby and Wright, who travelled third class in 1910, found things very different from Annette Meakin's experience. Helen Wilson and Elsie Mitchell, who had come from America to work in a post-Revolutionary Utopia in Siberia, travelled only briefly on the train in 1927. Malcolm Burr experienced the "Bolshevik" train in 1930. Maurice Baring in 1905 enjoyed the tea, which is still served at regular intervals each day on the journey. John Foster Fraser in 1901 observed Russian eating habits and Eric Newby described the train as he found it in 1977.

Railways and Other Means of Communication.
Baedeker, 1914

Railways. The sale of tickets begins ½ – 1 hr. before the departure of the train. The traveller should reach the station in good time, and leave the purchase of his ticket, the registration of his luggage, and the securing of his seat to one of the numerous *Porters* (Nosilshtchik; fee

30-50 cop.), who are thoroughly trustworthy. The porter's number should of course be noted. A bell is rung 3 times before the departure of the train: the first time (pervi zvonók) ¼ hr. before, and the second (vtorói zvonók) 5 min. before, while the train leaves immediately after the third (treti zvonók). – The speed of the *Ordinary Trains* is very low, not exceeding 20-25 M. per hr., besides which they make long halts at the stations. The *Express Trains* attain a speed of 35-40 M. per hr. The trains are frequently late. On many lines there are only two trains daily in each direction. The gauge (5 ft. ½ in.) is wider than the standard of Europe (4 ft. 8½ in.). Most of the railways belong to the State. – The stations are usually at some distance from the centre of the towns. At Kiev, Moscow, Nizhni-Novgorod, St. Petersburg, Warsaw, and other large towns, tickets may be purchased and luggage registered in the town-offices of the State Railway (small commission charged). In many cases no one is allowed to enter the platform without a railway ticket or a platform ticket.

The chief railway and steamer guide (price 85 cop.), appearing twice yearly (April & Oct.) and obtainable at all railway stations. The local trains are dealt with in a separate section and are not shown in the tables referring to international or long-distance trains. The `Kursbuch für Russland', published in Riga by N. Kymmel (80 cop.), is sufficient for the more important routes, and gives the names of stations in both Russian and German. St. Petersburg time is given throughout, except in regard to the steamers, which are scheduled according to local time. – St. Petersburg time is 61 min. in advance of Central European, and 2 hrs. 1 min. in advance of Greenwich time; comp. the table at p. xxxii. The station clocks keep St. Petersburg time, and occasionally local time as well.

Order at railway stations is maintained by *Gendarmes*. Complaints may be registered in the Complaint Book, kept at every station for this purpose. – There are three kinds of employés on the trains: the *Head Guard*, who comes to examine the tickets; the *Guard*, who assigns the seats; and the *Provodník* or attendant, who gives out the bedding, makes the beds, locks the compartments at the stopping-places, and makes himself generally useful. This last, like the negro porter in Pullman ears, expects a fee for his services. The head-guard and guards are dressed in a uniform consisting of a black blouse with belt, wide trousers tucked into the boots, and a round fur cap; the head-guard may be recognized by his silver and red braid and shoulder straps.

The *Carriages* (1st cl. blue, 2nd cl. yellow, 3rd cl. green) are corridor coaches, with doors at each end; they are divided into compartments and are provided with lavatories. The Russian takes as much hand-luggage into the carriage as he possibly can. The traveller should provide himself with pillows, towels, and soap (comp. p. xiv). All the trains have carriages for non-smokers and for ladies. In winter double windows are universal. The carriages are steam-heated or are provided with stoves. – First-class carriages have compartments for two or four persons, with a lockable corridor-door, and broad upholstered seats without arm-rests; at night the back-cushion is hoisted up by the provodnik to form an upper berth. – Second-class carriages on the long-distance trains are fitted up in much the same style as the first-class, but are often overcrowded; there are also compartments for travellers without seat-tickets (p. xxiii), as on the ordinary trains. Passengers who wish to transfer from second to first class, buy a third-class ticket, which costs exactly the difference between the first and the second class fares. – Third-class carriages have a central corridor and wooden seats.

LUGGAGE. The allowance of free luggage is 1 pud (36 lbs.). Each additional 10 lbs. (Russian) is charged for according to the distance (comp. the table at p. xxii). In breaking the journey the traveller is entitled to obtain access to his luggage on production of a voucher, which has to be produced on again booking or registering his baggage. Luggage may be deposited in the Left Luggage Office for three days (fee 5 cop. daily for each article).

For EXPRESS TRAINS it is necessary to take not only *Supplementary Tickets* but also *Reserved Seat Tickets*. Early application is advisable (town-offices, see p. xxi). As the number of seats is limited, the traveller cannot count on securing one at an intermediate station. – Seat-tickets must be procured at the booking-office and not from the train-conductor. The charges are reckoned according to a zone-tariff: 1st and 2nd class up to 650 V., 1½ rb.; from 651 to 2250 V., 1½ rb. + 30 cop. per 200 V.; from 2251 V. to 4250 V., 3 rb. 90 cop. + 20 cop. per 200 V.; from 4251 V. onwards, 6 rb. 10 cop. Third-class seat-tickets cost half the above charges. Trans-Siberian Railway, see R. 77. When one passenger wishes to reserve a double compartment for himself, he has to take four seat-tickets. At the time of taking their tickets passengers must state whether they prefer a smoking, a non-smoking, or a ladies' compartment, and whether they prefer a lower or an upper berth. Bedding is obtained from the provodník for 1 rb.; the passenger is entitled to occupy his berth from 9 p.m. to 9 a.m. (local time).

SLEEPING CARS of the International Sleeping Car Co. run from St. Petersburg to Wirballen (Berlin), to Vienna (viâ Warsaw), and to Moscow & Sebastopol; from Moscow to Nizhni-Novgorod, to Warsaw, and to Siberia, and so on. By purchasing two supplementary tickets a passenger can secure the exclusive use of a first-class compartment; advance booking is necessary (¾-1 rb. for each ticket). – RESTAURANT CARS are run on a few trains (B. 35 cop., déj. 1¼, D. 1½ rb.), with sections for smokers and non-smokers.

On some lines the conductor collects the tickets in the evening, giving a receipt in exchange, and returns them the following morning.

Passengers who desire to BREAK THE JOURNEY at an intermediate station must on quitting the train present their tickets to the stationmaster to be stamped, and on resuming the journey must present them at the booking-office at least 10 min. before the departure of the train to be again stamped.

On most railways the RAILWAY RESTAURANTS at the chief stations may be safely recommended. The food is good and inexpensive; the prices, which are fixed by the Railway Management, are usually to be found on the dishes. Tea is procurable at any hour of the day or night (10 cop.). – Those who leave their compartment during a stoppage at any station should ask the conductor or the provodnik to lock it, or at least get a nosilshtchik (porter) to look after their belongings (fee 20-30 cop.).

The *Railway Book Stalls* of the larger stations generally offer a small assortment of English, French, and German books (not cheap), but foreign newspapers are seldom met with.

The Dream of Service
Harmon Tupper, 1965

In first-class sleepers, the compartments, or "coupés," would be limited to two persons, and, in second class, to four, with berths seven feet long. Each car would also feature a communal lounge with an over-stuffed sofa, comfortable armchairs, a table for cards and other games, and electric reading lights (power deriving from a steam-driven dynamo in the baggage car). In winter, the vestíbuled, double-doored and double-windowed carriages would be individually heated, each coupé to be equipped with adjustable levers for regulating the steam radiators. In summer, passengers would be cooled by electric fans and downdrafts from iceboxes under the roof. These last were not to be confused with the water tanks of live fish for cooking by the chef, who would make no charge for boiling milk, and but a nominal one for roasting wild game which could be purchased at stops along the way.

On every State Express, patrons could rely on a train chief of stationmaster's rank, omniscient conductors, attentive porters, multilingual waiters in evening dress and menus in French as well as in Russian, a barber, and a licensed "dispenser of medicines, competent to treat obstetrical cases."* In instances of serious illness, the train chief would telegraph ahead to the nearest section point with a doctor. His services would cost the patient nothing; if hospitalization were necessary, treatment and medicines were also on the house for a specified period. And all this for hardly more than a cent a mile! Even blasé Americans accustomed to the grandeur and pampering services in the Boudoir or Palace cars of Messrs. Mann, Wagner, and Pullman were becoming curious.

Despite the Boxer troubles that curtailed passenger-train service east of Moscow, the Trans-Siberian publicity campaign racketed into high gear at the Paris Univeral Exposition of 1900. Thousands of visitors at the Palace of Russian Asia in the Trocadéro gardens thronged round enlarged maps and photographs of mysterious Siberia; a gleaming scale model of the great train-ferrying icebreaker *Baikal;* stuffed seals and polar bears perched precariously on papier-mâché icebergs; reindeer-drawn sledges with fur-clad dummies of Ostyak hunters beside them; and rich, Oriental objets d'art from the private collection of the Emir of Bokhara, that same impolite potentate whose spiritual lord Mohammed, according to the offended Li Hung Chang, had been a convict chased out of China.

But the lodestone of the show was the spectacular prize-winning exhibit of the Sleeping Car Company. To demonstrate that travel by rail across Siberia was anything but "visionary and unworthy of serious consideration" (as a leading Parisian journal had once declared), the enterprising concern put on display four magnificent, fresh-from-the-factory coaches that would ostensibly be assigned to its own Siberian "Internationals." Standing on a track better laid than any in Siberian were two *wagons-restaurants* furnished in both "subdued modern" mahogany and richly ornamented Louis XVI light oak, and two *wagons-salons,* each containing four sleeping compartments with connecting lavatories, a palatial lounge, and a smoking room. In one of the carriages, furniture and décor were of the French Empire period, contrasting dramatically with the adjacent smoking room done up in vivid Chinese style. The lounge of the other car, in which an upright piano with hand-painted panels graced one end, might be said to be a turn-of-the-century version of a Louis XVI drawing room, with walls, chairs, and tables of white-lacquered limewood, a number of large plate-glass mirrors, a ceiling frescoed with diaphanously gowned nymphs and allegorical figures, and, framing the windows, fancifully embroidered valances and drapes. Not displayed at the Exposition but almost as breathlessly described by French publicists was the *fourgon,* a special baggage car with fire- and burglar-proof lockboxes for passengers' jewels and valuable documents; a hairdressing salon in white sycamore; a green sycamore bathroom noteworthy for a tub so ingeniously designed that water could not slosh out despite lurches on sharp curves; and the gymnasium, dignified by the name of "veloroom" because of the peddling machine it contained in addition to dumbells and other muscle-toning paraphernalia.

As a further draw to jaded travelers in particular, the company invited Exposition visitors to dine (at [5 francs] a head) in the stationary *wagons-restaurants* and view from the windows the "Trans-Siberian Panorama of a Journey from Moscow to Peking," a long, train-high strip of canvas said to have been painted by two master scenic-artists of the Paris Opera sent to Siberia especially to soak up local color. While the diners progressed toward nothing but an entrée after the soup, and fruit and coffee after that, they had only to look through the windows to imagine themselves deep in exotic Siberia, for the mechanized canvas, not twenty feet from their eyes, moved at a speed to convey the illusion that the cars themselves were passing by steppes, mountains, virgin forests, onion-domed churches in towns, and station crowds gazing in amazement at the smoke-belching iron monster and its splendid coaches. What with lyrical brochures, railway carriages "equal to the special trains reserved in Western Europe for the sole use of Royalty," and the sensational Moving Panorama, the Russians and the Sleeping Car Company had succeeded in projecting an entrancing image of a journey across Siberia on "the world's unique train."

Despite its ballyhoo, the Sleeping Car Company pursued a cautious policy for several years after it began Siberian operations, and … ran nothing so fine as the magnificent carriages at the Exposition. As for the State Express, this much-touted *train de luxe* comprised the familiar wood-burning locomotive, a baggage car, diner, one first-class and two second-class sleepers, and required eight days to complete the journey between Moscow and Irkutsk.

*In 1986 one of our group had a wound that needed treating. Each day a "dispenser of medicines" came abroad to care for him.

The Real Siberian Express
Annette Meakin, 1900

The Siberian Express, or *Train de Luxe* as it is called, leaves Moscow for Irkutsk every Saturday evening, whilst the ordinary post train leaves daily at 3 p.m. There is no difference in the speed of the two trains, but by stopping less time at the stations the express gains two days on the entire journey.

We took up our abode in the express on Saturday, May 12, and did not emerge from it till the following Wednesday evening, when we alighted at Omsk station after a journey of four days and four nights.

We shared a luxurious *coupé* with two other ladies. I retired at once to my comfortable bed and remained there for three days, after which time I was well enough to get up. Had I taken that journey, ill as I was, in a "sleeper" on the so highly praised Canadian Pacific, I might never have lived to tell the tale. Every morning I should have been forced to rise at an early hour and sit upright for the rest of the weary day on the seat into which my bed had been transformed. Above all, privacy, the luxury that a tired traveller covets most of all, would have been absolutely unattainable. The Siberian express is a kind of "Liberty Hall," where you can shut your door and sleep all day if you prefer it, or eat and drink, smoke and play cards if you like that better. An electric bell on one side of your door summons a servingman to make your bed or sweep your floor, as the case may be, while a bell on the other side summons a waiter from the buffet. Besides the ordinary electric lights you are provided with an electric reading lamp by which you may read all night if you choose. Time passes very pleasantly on such a train, and it is quite possible to enjoy the scenery, for there is none of that fearful hurry that makes railway travelling so risky for body and nerves in Europe and America. Our average speed was about sixteen miles an hour.

At one end of the cheerful dining car was a Bechstein piano, and opposite to it a bookcase stocked with Russian novels; doubtless it will contain plenty of French and English books in time. On the fourth day we had an agreeable concert. Amongst the performers were a gentleman with a good tenor voice and two lady pianists of no ordinary merit. Three portraits adorned the dining car walls – those of the Emperor and Empress and that of Prince Hilkof – while ferns and flowers gathered by the way gave a homelike appearance to the whole.

Variations
Harmon Tupper, 1965

During the first years of its Siberian operations, the Sleeping Car Company followed wait-and-see tactics and used ordinary first- and second-class carriages in its "International" trains that alternated with the State expresses on the Moscow-Irkutsk run. To the hard-headed

Franco-Belgians, it made little business sense to tie up highly expensive, ultra-luxurious equipment – identical in every respect to that displayed at the Paris Exposition – when no one could even guess if the Trans-Siberian would attract heavy spenders; and why risk staggering losses if the precious Louis XVI-French Empire palaces ran off the Russians' flimsy track and cracked up beyond repair? The company, for all its glamorous Orient and Riviera expresses, was nonetheless ever-practical, and found no reason to run anything better in Siberia than its regular *wagons-restaurants* and *wagons-lits*. Some foreigners said that they were superior to the Russian deluxe cars; others took the opposite stand, nationalistic prejudices undoubtedly influencing both views. But there was almost unanimous agreement that the food in the *wagons-restaurants* was as bad as that in the government *trains de luxe*. In those earliest years of the present century, the company did not particularly care, for it was losing money from low fares imposed by the Communication Ministry, as well as from predominantly Russian passengers who rode for relatively short distances and shunned first class, the company's main resource for profits. The management therefore continued to mark time until completion of Trans-Siberian improvements and of the Chinese Eastern Railway to Vladivostok and Port Arthur. Then, it would press hard for fare increases, run better *wagons-lits* and *wagons-restaurants,* and concentrate an advertising barrage on rich international travelers seeking pleasure or business in the Far East.

Finery and Faults
Sir Henry Norman, 1901

The Siberian Express is still a novelty in Russia, and people come to the station to inspect its luxurious appointments and witness its departure. The Siberian station is the finest in Moscow, with an imposing white facade – "God Save the Tsar" in permanent gas illumination over the entrance – spacious halls, an admirable restaurant, and a series of parallel platforms, which make one think sadly of certain great London termini. At the farthest of these stand five unusually large and heavy corridor carriages and a powerful engine. As always in Russia, a crowd of uniformed officials is on hand; a brilliant light pours through the little windows high up in the flat sides of the carriages; the locomotive is only purring softly, but somewhere in the train an engine is at work at high speed, for there is a cloud of escaping steam, a stream of wood sparks, and a shrill buzz; and a chattering, laughing, crying crowd is at each entrance taking long leave of those going far away. Three strokes of the bell, big men with swords kiss each other fervently, a whistle, a snort of the engine, an answering whistle, and the train is off into the night on its unbroken journey of 3371 miles, to the far confines of that land whose name was recently only a synonym of horror.

The Russians are very proud of their Siberian train. They told me at every chance that I could never have seen such a train – that there is nothing so luxurious and so complete in the world. This is a mistake of tact – it rather causes one to look for short-comings, and little failings look larger in the light of these boasts. Moreover, the Siberian Express needs no puff; from almost every point of view it is a marvellous achievement, though the train itself is not so wonderful as Russians think. It differs enough, however, from all other *trains de luxe* to be worth a detailed description. The first engine I noticed was built in France, all the rest were Russian, and some of these, with four large driving-wheels coupled together, were extremely powerful. These were freight engines; in fact, after the line enters Siberia all its engines are freight engines; the train is a very heavy one, the speed is low, and passenger engines will not come until the line is complete and a great effort is made to shorten the entire journey. Behind the locomotive comes a composite car, the forward part being the locked luggage compartment, and the after-section being the kitchen. Between the two is the electric-light plant, for the entire train, even to the red tail-lamps, is lighted by electricity. This plant is an illustration of the enterprise Russian engineers are showing in every direction. Steam is supplied by an ordinary upright boiler, but the dynamo is run by a tiny Laval steam turbine – the same Norwegian firm that makes the familiar milk separators – revolving at an enormous speed. This turbine makes the shrill note that is audible whenever the train stops after dark. The electric plant was not out of order for a moment during my double journey, and the trains were lighted magnificently.

The second carriage contains the sleeping quarters of the cooks and waiters, the pantry and the restaurant. This is a car which formerly served as a royal saloon, and it is in no way suited for a dining-car. It contains two leather sofas, a piano, three tables seating four persons, and certain absurd tables about eighteen inches square. In the front part of this car there is also a full-sized bath, with shower, and an exercising machine, something like the crank in our prisons, which you make more or less laborious by adjusting a weight. The third and fifth cars are second class, and the fourth first class.

Except in two points, there is virtually no difference between the two classes, although, of course, as elsewhere, or, rather, much more than elsewhere, you are less likely to find objectionable companions in the one than in the other. There is a through corridor at the side, and six compartments for four persons and one for two persons in the second class, and three larger compartments and one small one in the first class. One of the advantages which the first has over the second is that in the former the centre of the car is an open salon, with sofa, easy chairs, writing-table, a clock, and a large map of the Russian Empire. This, when it does not happen to be monopolised by a party playing cards, is certainly delightful, and I have seen nothing like it elsewhere, except in the private car of an American railway magnate. Both first and second class have one improvement over similar trains elsewhere, which cannot be too highly commended. All the upholstery is of soft leather, and all the walls are covered with a species of waterproof cloth, which is washed at the end of each journey. The difference between this and the cloth and plush upholstery of other trains, which soil you at every touch, and fling clouds of pestilent dust into the air, is indescribable.

The Siberian Express, however, shows more improvement than this. In the roof of each compartment are two electric lights, one of which is extinguished when you pull the curtain over it at night. There is also a table lamp hanging on the wall, which can be placed anywhere, and an excellent moveable table. With these two you can read and write in perfect comfort. Above your head are two levers: one admits fresh air, through wire gauze to keep out dust; the other turns hot water into the heating apparatus. There is a pneumatic bell to the restaurant and an electric bell for the servant. The beds are wide and very comfortable, and the whole of your luggage goes in the racks overhead. In the corridors are more ingenious filter-ventilators, and outside the windows are plate-glass flanges, so that you can look ahead without the danger of a spark entering your eye. Overhead, in the little central salon and in the dining-car, is an elaborate ventilator to be filled with ice from outside in summer, so as to admit cooled air. The corridor also contains a frame to hold a large printed card showing the name of the next station, the time of arrival, and the length of the stop. Finally, there is the other advantage which the first-class passenger enjoys. There are no brakes on his carriage! There is no hand brake, as on every other part of the train, and the Westinghouse passes underneath him in its pipe. He is thus undisturbed by the grinding and jolting which even the best-regulated brake produces, and can read and sleep peacefully through stoppages and down grades and hostile signals. This is surely the height of railway consideration. Such luxury, however, it is perhaps needless to add, speaks volumes concerning the speed on the Siberian Express... .

Russia has in this train gone somewhat ahead of herself, so to speak. It is not enough to build a fine train – you must educate in knowledge, and more especially in responsibility, the people who are to work it. The dining-car, for example, will not bear a moment's comparison with that of the Orient Express or the Riviera Express. We waited interminable times for our meals. One passenger sat at table fifty minutes, having had nothing but a plate of soup and being unable in all that time to obtain a bottle of beer. Then he left the car in disgust, and in a loud voice demanded the complaint book. Result: he was snowed under with apologies and waited upon like a prince. If the dining-car were properly arranged, it would hold all the passengers. As it is, one has to intrigue and struggle for a table. Again, not once after we left was one of the station and time cards put in the frame. All the pneumatic bells, too, were out of order, and no waiter could be summoned. When I ordered a bath I was told that the pipes were inexplicably stopped up. There are other matters I might mention, and it is only fair to add that some of the short- comings are the fault of the passengers themselves, who are not yet educated to the use of the facilities so lavishly provided for them. A needless inconvenience is that all the lavatory arrangements of the train are shared by the two sexes, with consequent delays and embarrassments.

The greatest disturbance, however, to the foreign visitor's comfort is that all Western mealtimes must be abandoned before a Russian's daily food-scheme. No Russian has an exact sense of time, the lack of it being probably attributable to the Orientalism in his blood. Nobody, indeed, could have one on this train, for the clock keeps the hour of St. Petersburg for a thousand miles or more of due eastward traveling, in order that its time-table may have some semblance of utility and conformity; then as the days pass the train itself grows ashamed of such a childish pretension, and after Chelyabinsk it leaps lightly to local time and hurls a couple of useless hours out of the window, so to speak – hours that make no record, either of weal or woe, against any of us – two sinless hours, two joyless, tearless little hours flung forth upon the brown Siberian steppes. As for a Russian's meal-times, he simply has none. If I had my tea early there would be the invariable nameless official in his dark-blue uniform piped with green or blue or magenta cloth, with crossed pick-axes or hammers or bill-hooks on his collar and cap, finishing a *hâchis* made into the shape of a cutlet – futile masquerade! – or thoughtfully spitting out the bones of a fried carp upon his plate while he selected a fresh mouthful with his knife. When we dined or supped they would be drinking tea, and once when we went into the restaurant-car for a sandwich about midnight a party of rugged-looking men – not officials, for once, but of occupations which their strange faces did not allow us to presume – were sitting round an empty *cafetière* drinking champagne from tumblers, a saucer in front of them piled high with the cardboard mouth-pieces and ashes of many dozen cigarettes. This habit of eating when you are hungry and eating whatever you may happen to fancy, instead of eating when the cook wills, and then only what custom severely restricts you to, is disorganising in its effects upon the refectory of the train. There is no time to sweep up and set tables; no time when the servants can feel free to rest, sleep, or eat; no time when the wearied kitchen fire can "go down" as it does at home. The result is great discomfort for Western passengers, and the authorities should certainly insist upon all meals being served at fixed hours, and at those hours only.

The Siberian Train de Luxe
Francis E. Clark, 1900

The Paris Exposition had made famous the Siberian *train de luxe*, with its moving panorama, its terminal stations at St. Petersburg and Peking, and its dinners at seven francs per head. The newspaper correspondent, too, who has seen it only in his mind's eye, as he sat at his own cosy fireside rehashing second-hand descriptions of its magnificence, has done his share to advertise it, until the wondering world has an idea that it is a veritable Waldorf-Astoria on wheels, before which all Empire State expresses on the American continent must hide their diminished heads. We read of library-cars and bath-cars, gymnasium-cars where one can make a century run on a stationary bicycle, elegant dinners, barber-shops where passengers receive a free shave every morning, pianos, and other luxuries too numerous to mention.

As a matter of fact, the Siberian *train de luxe*, at least as it started from Irkutsk on the 29th day of June, in the year of our Lord 1900, was a rather shabby vestibuled train of three sleepers, a diner, and a baggage-car. It was luxurious, indeed, compared with the fourth-class emigrant train on which we had been journeying, but it is still many degrees behind the best American trains. It should be remarked, however, that the best cars had been sent to Paris for the Exposition, and it is doubless true that the train we took is somewhat below the average of the Siberian *trains de luxe*. It is well worth describing, however, as an important link in the great chain that connects the Atlantic and the Pacific in this new way around the world.

First, and very naturally, comes the engine of Russian make, with a great flaring smoke-stack for burning wood. Next to it is the baggage-car with one end fitted with a bath-tub, where dusty travellers can enjoy a refreshing bath on payment of a rouble and a half (seventy-five cents), a very high price to be sure compared with the rate charged for transportation; but then the scarcest and dearest thing throughout Siberia we found to be cold water, either for drinking or bathing purposes.

Following the baggage-car was the dining-car, which was also divided into two sections, half being occupied with small tables that

seat two and four each, and the other half fitted with easy-chairs for
the smokers and provided with ample windows for observation. In the
smoking-room was a small library of, perhaps, fifty books in the
Russian, French, and German languages, but nothing in English,
except two or three discarded fifth-rate novels in paper covers, evidently contributed by previous travellers.

In the dining car, two *table d'hôte* meals were provided: a lunch of
two courses at one o'clock, which cost one rouble, and a dinner at six
of four courses, for a rouble and a quarter. At other times of day passengers could order what they pleased à *la carte* from a limited bill of
fare.

Behind the dining-car came a second-class sleeping-car, then a
first-class sleeper, and, last of all, another second-class sleeper.

These cars are all divided into compartments, or little staterooms,
holding two or four people each, with a window, a table, and a wide
and very comfortable berth for each person. The cars are all hand-
somely carpeted and upholstered in blue plush, covered, for the sake
of protection, with red-striped denim. In each stateroom were convenient racks and hooks for the disposal of clothes and baggage, and
in every way one could make himself as comfortable and have almost
as much room as in an ocean steamer's cabin.

For two friends travelling together, or for a small family of three,
as in my own case, this arrangement is far superior to America's more
promiscuous and public Pullman sleeping-car. For individuals travelling alone, the Pullman plan has some decided advantages, if one does
not care to be cooped up in narrow quarters for eight or nine days with
any chance stranger who may be assigned to the same stateroom. The
Pullman cars, too, economize space, for while from forty to forty-eight
people can sleep in a Pullman car when crowded, only eighteen can
find "lying-down room," in a Siberian sleeper.

One curiosity of this particular *train de luxe* was that the first and
second class cars were precisely alike in every particular. In amount of
room, fittings, upholstery, and comforts of every description, there was
not the slightest difference between the three sleeping-cars that composed our train, while the difference of price was nearly forty roubles
in favor of the second-class. One would think that, these being the
facts, the second-class cars would be overcrowded and the first-class

would be empty. Such was not the case of this train at least, for I found every cabin in the first-class taken, and was able to get a large four-berth stateroom in one of the second-class cars for little more than I would pay for two berths in the first-class car.

At the most, the fares in Siberia are remarkably cheap. For the whole stateroom I paid less than one hundred and twenty dollars from Irkutsk to Moscow, a distance of three thousand three hundred and fifty miles; this included four fares and the supplementary price of the *train de luxe*. For the same accommodations in a Pullman car across the American continent (a shorter distance) I should have paid at least five hundred dollars. The full first-class fare in the *train de luxe* is about fifty dollars, while the second-class fares are less than thirty dollars. By the ordinary trains a considerable saving is effected over these very cheap rates.

Each car has its porter, who can usually speak German or French in addition to Russian, but the specimens that we saw were very lazy and inefficient fellows compared with the deft and obliging "George" who attends to one's wants in a Pullman car. Our porters on the *train de luxe* never thought of sweeping or dusting the staterooms, and seemed to think it an imposition to be asked to thoroughly make up the berths for day travel, preferring to leave the beds made up by day that they might have less trouble at night. All day long the lazy porters would loll about on their seats in the middle of the car, doing as little as possible, and apparently begrudging that little. Twice a week the bed linen is changed. Ample washrooms, with a single roller towel, for all guests who do not furnish their own, complete the equipment of the Siberian sleeper.

My excuse for this somewhat minute description of these accommodations is that it will be welcomed by future travellers who have to spend at least eight and one-half days in their little room on wheels.

It must not be thought that for all its name and fame the "Siberian Special" is a lightning express. In speed it would be outstripped, during all the early part of the journey, by any "huckleberry train" in America. Fourteen miles an hour, including stops, was all it pretended to make during the first five days from Irkutsk. The road-bed is new, the rails are light, and as a consequence the train plods along at a pace which an able-bodied cowboy on his bronco would outstrip. In fact I saw, one evening, a race between our famous train and a Siberian "cow-puncher," in which, for two miles or more, the horseman more than held his own. Then he pulled up with a careless wave of his hat, as though he did not consider it worth while to race any longer with so slow a rival.

Third Class into Siberia
Bassett Digby and Richardson Wright, 1910

It is not as easy as you might suppose to go to Siberia with the Russians in the third class of a slow train. Manfully our *istvostcbik,* he who had driven us up to the Koursk Nijni-Novgorod station at Moscow, with a dashing carriage and pair, the courier of the Hotel Continental, and two white-aproned porters stood their ground and explained, with abundant gesticulation, that the thing was not done, was unprecedented, was out of the question.

However, we prevailed; and at half-past ten on Saturday morning, our long train pulled heavily out of the Moscow terminal of the Trans-Siberian railroad, bound direct for Tcheliabinsk, on the Asiatic side of the Urals, the gateway to Siberia, two thousand and sixty *versts* toward the rising sun.

The fault of the slow train in the Russian empire is not so much its modest speed – our train, on occasion, gathered the dizzy rate of fifteen miles an hour. What handicaps it is the unconscionable wait at each wayside station. There is a stop of ten to twenty minutes at the tiniest platform serving a group of rude log cabins, often without a single interchange of passengers. The stop is simply and solely for the passengers to get hot water for a brew of tea, or a snack of something to eat. The claim of the running schedule is utterly subordinated to the claim of the buffet.

Your tea is cheap and fragrant. At every station, the Government maintains a free boiling water depot for travelers on the railroad, and marks it with a conspicuous sign-board.

There was none of the conventional stiffness of demeanor on this train that you meet with in the Occident, nor was there the Oriental riot of squalor and filth that one has been led to expect from the tales that pass in America and England. Everyone fraternized. There was no expectoration, no drunkenness, no vermin.

The third class train to Siberia is more a suite of rooms than a series of railroad compartments on the European plan. From the wooden walls on every side folding back rests pull up or slide down into comfortable sleeping shelves. Each passenger, however humble, has his or her shelf, which, with a quilt, a camel-hair blanket or two, and a big, soft pillow, forms a lounge by day and a bed by night. You carry your own bedding on Russian trains. This applies to all classes. When the Russian gads about, he invariably takes with him, beside his entire family, half his household goods, which includes everything from blankets, sheets and pillows to scissors for cutting up sugar and to tea tumblers. Consequently our aisles were for the most part blocked with heaps of luggage. If one's legs got stiff and he craved exercise, he had little opportunity for it. He would invariably stumble against rolls of dirty blankets and dirtier pillows or kick over someone's tea kettle, an accident not without disastrous results and a prodigality of expletives. The *chainiks* [kettles] were always half full.

The days were gloomy. Though the sun shone in an unclouded sky, a keen wind, coming up from the southern steppes, raised blinding clouds of fine snow for fifty feet from the ground. There were few idle folks among us, however. By day, with one accord, we all brewed *chai*, carved and shared our snacks of food, and exchanged cigarettes. From eight o'clock in the morning until night-fall there was always a brew of tea near by, and, kettle in hand, a couple of dozen passengers bolted up to the *keepatok* or hot water tap, as we slowed into each successive station.

Our train did not boast a diner, but food you could buy at the buffets or at the row of booths in which the peasant women congregate. Every sixth or eighth station has its buffet, sometimes with a better selection of dishes than can be found in many a city terminal in our land. The food at the booths was good and cheap – newly baked, fragrant rye bread at three *kopecks* (1½ cents) a pound; baked fish tarts, each as big as a plate, at two cents each, containing four small trout;

whole roasted chickens for fifteen cents; nearly a quarter of a roasted goose, tender and well-cooked, for a dime; big jam turnovers for a cent. Small wonder that the train to Siberia was one great picnic party during our waking hours!

The picnicking waned when night fell. When it had become quite dark, one of the conductors would come through the train, fitting in the two flickering candles that lighted each room. The few of us who wished to play cards or read bought little stumps of candle from a friendly conductor and fixed them on to *five-kopeck* pieces, that we stood on our shelves.

Seventh Class in Trans-Baikal
Francis E. Clark, 1900

This road is not yet officially opened for traffic, and we were taken on sufferance, as it were. At least, most of those who take it have to suffer severely. Nor can they complain overmuch, for the government does not invite them to go or advertise any attractions. The best cars that are yet run, with the exception of the little *car de luxe,* are marked "fourth class," and are no better than they pretend to be. They have wooden seats of the hardest possible variety, and three wooden shelves, one above another, afford cramped opportunity for a man not more than five feet long to stretch himself out. Each of these cars, with three tiers of shelves, is supposed to afford accommodations for forty-three people. But these are the best, as I have said. Others, which might be termed fifth class, if the nomenclature of railway trains descended so far, are simply box-cars, with no seats, and marked on the outside, "to carry twelve horses or forty-three men." Into these cars there crowded, helter-skelter, pell-mell, higgledy-piggledy, Russians and Siberians, Moujiks and Chinamen, Tartars, Buriats and Englishmen, Frenchmen, Germans, and Americans.

If there were fifth-class cars, there were plenty of sixth and seventh class people – some in rags, and many in tags, but few in velvet gowns. Old Moujiks, with half a dozen half-naked children, filthy with a grime that has accumulated since their birth, and alive with unmentionable parasites, crowded every car, or, rather, human pigpen, as each car soon becomes. Odors indescribably offensive made the air thick and almost murky. The stench, the dirt, the vermin grew worse the longer the car was inhabited, and one simply resigned himself to the inevitable and lived through each wearisome hour as best he could.

Our non-Russian fellow-passengers, when they found the true state of affairs, made a desperate resistance to their fate, and after repeated remonstrances, objurgations, and even threats, which nearly came to blows, induced the station-master to put on another little car, which they could have for themselves.

Travelling Hard
Helen Wilson and Elsie Mitchell, 1927

Russian railway trains, like the boats, are divided into classes. The first and second class cars are divided into separate compartments and are upholstered. Hence they are called "soft," and to travel "soft," is looked upon as the height of luxury and extravagance. The great mass, who must economize, travel "hard." The "hard" cars are not upholstered, and are divided into sections like Pullmans, with very high divisions. There are three tiers; – the long seat running three-quarters of the way across the car, a solid wooden shelf fitting into the back and raised for sleeping constitutes the second, and a third narrower shelf is under favorable conditions used only for baggage, but when the car is crowded, as it most frequently is, can also be a bed. Across the aisle are two single seats, converted with their shelves into bunks too, narrower and shorter, running lengthwise of the train, and generally considered less desirable, but they assure a certain privacy for two people as it is an evident impossibility for a newcomer to squeeze in anywhere. We often took them when not assigned definite places. In each section there is a little shelf between the windows used as a dining table. Place cards are of two varieties, lying and sitting. The first, which is, of course, most desirable, guarantees the passenger room enough to lie down at night. It means that there may be only four and certainly will not be more than six people to a section. A "sitting" place card means that there may be eight people to a section, and that occupants of the lower seat cannot lie down, while those on the upper berths, which are close together, get no opportunity of sitting up except by exchange with some one below. This arrangement is endurable, but by no means comfortable.

Going down the financial scale we come to the "lower depths" of the "Maxim Gorky," aptly named after the Russian writer whose descriptions of life at the bottom are famous, and whose own name, – Maxim (maximum) Gorky (bitterness), – is so applicable to this style of transportation. The "Maxim Gorky" is a train made up for the most part, if not entirely, of innumerable worn-out cars, for which no place cards are sold and where there is no limit to the number of passengers. The overloaded engine puffs and snorts and slowly drags the endless length of packed cars across the wide steppe, while the passengers, mostly poor peasants, struggle on and off at the innumerable way stations, encumbered by baggage and children. The overcrowding is shocking and, as on the boat, we were always filled with amazement at the incredible numbers of poverty-stricken peasants and workers who, notwithstanding the almost intolerable hardships of such travel, still continue with patient and dogged endurance to wander up and down, back and forth, across the immense distances of their country. After all, not many generations ago Russia was a land of migratory peoples, and the instinct has not yet died out.

Each car is provided with a lavatory at one end and a toilet usually at the other end. In the better class trains the two are often combined, a not altogether desirable arrangement. In the "Maxim Gorky," the needs of the primitive and rustic crowds have been appropriately met by a room with no plumbing, the floor and walls lined with zinc, with an opening in a depressed corner. The whole place is flushed regularly by the *provodnik*.

The Bolshevik Train
Malcolm Burr, 1930

The Trans-Siberian was drawn up alongside the platform and it was with some curiosity that I looked at the famous train. It was made up of the sleepers of the wagon-lit company, special rolling-stock adapted for the broad gauge used in Russia. It had survived ten years constant use and neglect, yet the dining-car, with tables laid neatly and white folded napkins, seemed positively inviting. I looked forward with pleasure to spending the greater part of a week in this train on the journey halfway across Asia. I booked my seat for Irkutsk, and on the Saturday evening took possession of the cabin, which I was to share with Naum Moiseivich, a Jewish mining engineer and excellent fellow. The compartment was on the lines of an ordinary European sleeper, but the broader gauge gives more space, so it was more roomy, loftier, much more comfortable, and there was no difficulty in storing one's kit. As I was to spend the winter on the edge of the Arctic, mine was pretty bulky, but it stowed away easily in a big recess over the corridor. Another advantage is that the bunks are not arranged one on the top of the other, but the upper berth is placed longitudinally across the top of the window. This does away with that feeling of oppression inseparable from having a roof close down upon one's head.

My travelling companion was, I think, the only Russian in the train, for no citizens of the Soviet Union can afford the price of such a ticket, and there did not happen to be any official travelling. Of course, nobody travels for pleasure in Russia. The passengers were mostly Chinese students returning home and some Germans bound for Shanghai. I made friends with a Frenchman bound for Harbin, who had lived many years in Russia in the old days and was perfectly familiar with the character and language of the people. He had been a manager of the sleeping-car company, and it was with rueful expression that he examined the familiar old train that had once been under his charge. He was gratified when I praised the comfort and ingenuity of the various gadgets, for many of which, with pardonable pride, he claimed the credit of invention.

Chai
Maurice Baring, 1905

The comfort of travelling third class in Russia is that there is always tea to be had. One would need the pen of Charles Lamb to sing the praises of Russian tea. The difference between our tea and Russian tea is not that Russian tea is weaker or that it has lemon in it. I have heard

Englishman say sometimes: "I don't want any of your exquisite Russian tea; I want a good cup of strong tea." This is as if you were to say: "I don't want any of your soft German music; I want some nice loud English music." It is a question of kind; not a degree. You can have tea in Russia as strong as you like. The difference is not in the strength, but in the flavour and in the fact that it is always made with boiling water, and is always fresh. But if you put a piece of lemon into a strong cup of Ceylon tea and think that the result is Russian tea you are mistaken. Russian tea is an exquisitely refreshing drink, and I sometimes wonder whether tea in England in the eighteenth century, the tea sung of by Pope and of which Dr. Johnson drank thirty-six cups running, was not probably identical with Russian tea. It certainly was not Ceylon tea.

How the Russian Eats!
John Foster Fraser, 1901

That first night, with a single blinking candle for illumination, I lay on an improvised bed I made myself, listening to the regular jog-thud, jog-thud, of the carriages over the metals. Twice the conductor – a stout, black-bearded, mayoral gentleman in military kind of frockcoat, with a white and purple tassel on the shoulder – came with a couple of supernumeraries, thinner men, to open and shut the doors for him, and inspected my ticket. There must be an odour of large tips about the foreigner. Anyway, he received my ticket with a bow, examined it carefully as though it were the first thing of its kind he had ever seen, and then handed it back to me with another bow.

I was glad when the weary dawn arrived. I was gladder still when the train pulled up at a station, and I joined in the dash and the scramble towards the buffet, where scalding tea was to be had and mince-meat stuffed dumplings, satisfying, and most indigestible, to be bought for a trifle.

How the Russian eats! He has no fixed mealtime, but takes food when he is hungry, which is often. He has about six square meals a day. He has at least a dozen lunches, a little bit of salt fish or some caviare, a piece of bread and cheese, an onion and some red cabbage, a sardine and a slice of tomato, all washed down with many nips of fiery vodki. He never passes a station without a glass of tea – marvellous tea, with a thin slice of lemon floating in it. I got a fondness for Russian tea, and foreswore bemilked decoctions for ever.

Russians have a sufficient dash of the East in them to be careless about time. Whether they arrive at their destination to-morrow or next week is a matter of indifference. But the inner man must be attended to. So at every station there is a buffet, sometimes small, sometimes large, but always good, clean, and painted white. There are one, two, or three long tables, with clean cloths, with serviettes covering slices of white and Russian rye bread; plants are on the table, and are circled by rows of wine bottles, with the price written on the label. On a side table are hot dishes, half fowls, beef steaks, meat pies, basins of soup. There are plenty of waiters dressed as are waiters in Piccadily hotels. Everything is bright and neat. And this is at wayside stations with not a house within sight; with indeed, nothing but heaving dreary prairie around. It is the same all along the line. There is a difference in the size of the buffets, but never in excellence. I am enthusiastic about these Russian refreshment-rooms. And if ever the Muscovite thanks the Great White Czar for anything he should thank him for the food on the railways. Foreigners grumble about the slowness of the Russian trains. They are not particularly slow. The time is spent at the railway stations while the passengers eat. And while Russians have appetites in proportion to the size of their country those waits are not likely to be shortened.

Dragging the train on which I travelled were two engines, black and greasy, and with huge funnel-shaped chimneys. They consumed an enormous quantity of wood. But there was no scarcity, for at every station there are stacks of wood sawn into convenient chunks.

The Big Red Train
Eric Newby, 1977

We now took a closer look at our deluxe, "soft-class" compartment, which was one of nine such two-berth compartments in the only soft-class, two-berth car on the train… On this May morning in 1977 the compartment was almost as dank as the weather outside, but only because the heating had not yet had time to seep through the pipes to it from the furnace at the end of the corridor, which was fuelled with coal.

The compartment was clean and, apart from a brown tabletop and a strip of carpet similar to that in the corridor, remarkable for its lack of colour. The walls and ceiling were the palest of pale greys; the cotton covers on the upholstered back rests and the curtain on a rod, which obscured the view from the lower half of the window and kept falling down, were off-white, not because they were dirty but because this was their natural colour. All the metal fittings were of some pallid alloy. Altogether it was rather like looking at a photograph of a sleeping compartment that had been heavily over-exposed.

There was a ceiling light which could be dimmed to a sinister, frigid blue and a couple of well-meant but rather inadequate reading lights above what would be the beds when they were made up. These were side by side, opposite one another on the ground floor – no nasty little ladders leading to upper berths which make going to bed in the upper regions of a four-berth compartment on a train as dangerous as fooling about on the Eiger without a rope.

But there was nothing wrong with the design of the appurtenances. The folding table was a miracle of ingenuity. There was a water carafe, stable and heavy enough to survive a force 9 gale in the Bay of Biscay. There was sufficient space in the containers under the seats to take a folded corpse, as well as a large suitcase, and the seats had enough overhang to accommodate a couple of small suitcases behind one's feet. There was also a space in the bulkhead above the door ample enough to take a small trunk. At present it was occupied by our two sets of bedding: a mattress fitted with a sheet covering, a top sheet, two pillows and a blanket and two hand-towels, which had to last all the way to Novosibirsk, although we did not know this, two nights and two days to the east.

Between us Wanda and I disposed of two large suitcases, two small ones, not much bigger than document cases, a formidable black overnight bag which looked as if it might contain a brace of human heads, Wanda's handbag, as commodious out somewhat less sumptuous than a buyer's from I. Magnin, the cardboard telescope containing maps, a camera bag, and a pile of raincoats, windcheaters and sawn-off

Wellington boors, all of which had defied our efforts to contain them in any sort of portable container, plus the food-and-drink box. The various luggage depositories swallowed all these impedimenta quite effortlessly and with room to spare. I began to wish we had brought more.

There were two lavatories, one at each end of the car, and we inspected them with care, knowing that we were going to be stuck with them for the foreseeable future whether we liked them or not. There was however no cause for alarm – at least at this stage of the journey, when few passengers appeared to have discovered their existence.

The washbasins and the loos were clean and the basins both had plugs, thus rendering superfluous the black squash ball (a dog ball for the smaller sort of dog will perform the same function) which we had brought all the way from England to serve as a plug and which we had guarded with our lives. It had been a godsend in Moscow at the Ukraina Hotel where, if our first-class accommodation was anything to go by, there are more than 1000 plugless rooms.

On the deficit side there was no trap under the washbasin, so that if you dropped your toothbrush, earrings or contact lenses down the hole they would end up on Russian soil. These basins were also equipped with those devilish taps, which they also have on ships to prevent the user sinking them from the inside, that work only with the exertion of superhuman pressure, and when they do, finally and grudgingly, deliver either scalding hot or freezing cold water, but never at the same time.

The lavatories were huge, large enough almost to accommodate a Siberian mammoth, and fitted with seats. These mammoth traps came from the same factory as the taps, shooting up, when there was no weight on them, with a vicious and resounding clang, revealing two non-skid plaques on the pan itself, intended for those who, like me, prefer to stand rather than sit on strange, outlandish objects. On the other hand there was a big bar of pink soap, an adequate supply of tough paper and a 220-volt, two-plug socket for electric razors (of which there were more out in the corridor for those who like to shave in public). I have spent many a night in far worse places.

The Toilets
Deborah Manley, 1986

There are few descriptions of the lavatories and washing arrangements on these trains. On ours they were very basic. For soft-class passengers, this is not so serious: twenty, if one includes the two train girls, share two washrooms with lavatories. In hard-class the ratio is fifty to two.

The facility is reminiscent of an old-fashioned battleship, with grey walls, grey painted floor and pipes, and stainless steel fittings. The lavatory is a low-squat type about four inches off the floor with a wide wooden seat.

The washing facilities consist of a steel basin with no plug, and a cold water tap which has to be held in order to run. An electric shaver point gives an unexpected touch of sophistication. On a hook on the wall a toilet brush soaks in a tin of disinfectant which scents the air. Above it is an exploded diagram showing how the plumbing works, with numbered parts so that an amateur out on the steppes could mend a fault.

To aid those who like a strip wash, there is a bucket and a hole in the floor. The Siberian wind and thunder of the wheels whistles up this hole and anything one dropped would be gone forever. So a damp, dirty cloth is placed over it. Only much later, on the smart train which took us into Mongolia, did we discover that there should have been a plug for this hole; like all Russian plugs, it had gone missing.

Between the Carriages
Deborah Manley, 1986

Moving from one carriage to another for meals or visiting is quite an event. In winter one is wise to put on extra coverings.

You open the heavy indoor of your carriage and step into the no man's land where, in non-smoking carriages you can smoke – a real deterent. Then you open another, heavier, door and a thumping, metallic struggling bridge faces you. If you are alone, you must hang onto a handle and lean over this bridge, with flashes of rail and space below you and push open the far heavy door. Then you can step across the swaying bridge through to the next carriage. And then it all has to be done again between each carriage on the way back.

In pairs, the shared effort makes the whole thing far easier and I suppose braver or less imaginative people than me don't mind locking themselves between the heavy doors and walking casually across the hump-backed clunking bridge.

In winter (as I would find out on later journeys) with cold winds whistling through and ice on the metal and certainly in gloves, so your hands don't freeze to the hand rail, it would be a nightmare. Yet one of the jobs on the train is to push a large trolley of food and drinks along the train to offer succour to the hard class passengers. A slight, whey-faced girl in a dreary whitish uniform and headkerchief pushed the trolley, which is not light, through the gaps and back two or three times a day. We did not envy them.

4

Preparations for the Journey

How does one prepare for such a journey? Guide books have gathered many practical ideas: loo paper (I found it was normally there but better designed for writing letters and keeping Scrabble scores than for other purposes); postcards of your home town or country and badges to swap or give away; plugs for plug-free Soviet basins (a squash ball acting as a universal plug), maps, Scrabble and a fur or wool hat with ear flaps in the Soviet winter are among the list. Russians very sensibly travel in track suits, or the knickerbockers advised by the *Russian Year Book 1917* could be useful. *Baedeker* in 1914 recommended:

> The traveller should be provided with a pillow or an air cushion, linen sheets, towels, a small india-rubber bath and some insect powder ... High goloshes or "rubber boots" are desirable, as the unpaved streets of the towns are almost impassable in spring and autumn; in winter felt overshoes or "arctics" are also necessary. A mosquito veil is desirable in eastern Siberia and Manchuria during the summer. It is desirable to carry a revolver in Manchuria and on trips away from the railway. The hotels are almost invariably dear and indifferent. Bed-linen, soap, etc. should always be taken. A disturbing feature is the inevitable concert or "singsong" in the dining-room, which usually lasts into the night.

Despite this last problem, which sadly when we travelled no longer seemed to trouble one, he did not think to recommend earplugs. Bryn Thomas recommends various useful and up-to-date items.

Many travellers take a camera and lots of film, but it may still land one in trouble (as it would have in 1917) if you ignore Intourist's advice. William Oliver Greener found matters arranged better in 1902, but Peter Fleming in 1933 describes the same sort of problem travellers meet today. Books and magazines can still cause difficulties similar to those Murray warned of in 1893 and John Foster Fraser in 1901. The best thing to take

on the journey today is the latest fashion magazines–nothing will break down Russian reserve faster.

Visas are required, but the bureaucracy is as nothing compared with what *Murray's Handbook for Travellers* described in 1893, although internal passports were required by Soviet citizens.

Police and Passports
Murray's Handbook for Travellers, 1893

The Russian police regulations are formal and minute beyond any thing known in other European countries; but to the traveller, unless he prefers doing everything himself to having it done for him by his *valet de place,* they are by no means troublesome or annoying; though certainly far more expensive than in any other country that I have visited. "For an Englishman bound to Russia, an English passport, obtained either from the Foreign Office, or from some British minister abroad is now absolutely indispensable." – H.L. No traveller can enter the Russian dominions by land unless his passport bears the signature of a Russian minister or consul; nor will he be permitted to secure a passage on board any steam-vessel bound for a Russian port without producing this all-important document similarly authenticated at the packet-office, whether at Lubec or Stockholm. Immediately you are settled in your hotel your passport is taken to the police office for the "quartal" district, and registered; the next day it is returned to you, and you must take it yourself to the alien office, to procure a billet of residence: each day's delay subjects you to a fine, of 5 rubles which is seldom, if ever, enforced, but it will be advisable to comply with the regulation as soon as possible. You must appear at the two distinct branches of the "Adres Kontòr," or alien office; at the first you give up yourpassport, and after answering the usual questions – Where were you born? Have you ever been in Russia before? What is the object of your present journey? Have you any letters to bankers, merchants, &c.? If so to whom? – you receive a small ticket from the officer, which you take to the office situated in the square of the great theatre, and receive in exchange for it a billet of residence, containing a true and faithful picture of your size, features, &c., for which you pay five or *ten* rubles each. Nobles* receive their billet gratis, and are not required to have their features described: all others are treated as merchants or traders. Having once obtained this document you may remain unmolested in St. Petersburg for three months, and even extending your rambles to Tsarskoe Selo, Peterhoff, and other places in the neighbourhood, without having occasion to apply again to the police; but if you visit Moscow, Archangel, or any other Russian city, you must have a new passport, the cost of which is about 5 rubles. Before you can quit Russia your name must be duly advertised in three successive gazettes, which process cannot be accomplished in less than nine days. If, however, you can procure some person of known respectability to be surety for the payment of all debts you may have left unpaid to any Russian subject of his majesty the Tsar, you will be allowed to depart on producing your surety, and the advertisement will be inserted afterwards. In addition to this you must present a petition to the governor, but you are not required to appear before him in person. This has to be signed and countersigned by sundry police officials, and at length the all-important paper by which you effect your escape to a land that knows neither passport or secret police is forthcoming, for which you pay in the ordinary course of things about 25 rubles; but if you give bail for your debts, and depart before announcing to the Russian capital the important news that a person bearing a name which no man living could recognise in its Russian dress is about to quit them, perhaps for ever, the expense falls but little short of 60 rubles …

The precaution of advertising, adopted to prevent people defrauding their creditors, is in reality of little avail, as you are allowed to remain three weeks after your name has appeared in its Russian disguise in the gazette, – a period simply sufficient to contract debts to any amount; and instances are repeatedly occurring of debtors getting clear off, in despite of all these regulations; one of these escapes was much talked of when we were at St. Petersburg.

* "Persons of title, military and naval officers, clergymen, or any one whose passport shows him to be in the service of the crown, are all, according to Russian ideas, *noble* i.e. gentlemen." – V.

Essential and Useful Items
Bryn Thomas, 2007

A money-belt is essential to safeguard your documents and cash. Wear it under your clothing and don't take it off on the train, as compartments are very occasionally broken into. A good pair of sunglasses is necessary in summer as well as in winter, when the sun on the snow is particularly bright. A water bottle (2 litre) which can take boiling water is essential as is a mug (insulated is best), spoon and knife.

The following items are also useful: a few clothes pegs, adhesive tape, ball-point pens, business cards, camera and adequate supplies of film (or memory cards for a digital camera), a torch (flashlight), folding umbrella, games (cards, chess – the Russians are very keen chess players – Scrabble etc), lavatory paper, calculator (for exchange rates), notebook or diary, penknife with corkscrew and can opener (although there's a bottle opener fixed underneath the table in each compartment on the train), photocopies of passport, visa, air tickets etc (keep them in two separate places), sewing kit, spare passport photographs for visas, string (to use as a washing line), the addresses of friends and relatives (don't take your address book in case you lose it), tissues (including the wet variety), universal bath plug (Russian basins usually do not have a plug), washing powder (liquid travel soap is good), and hand soap. Some people take along an electric heating coil for boiling a mug of water when staying in a hotel. A compass is useful when looking at maps and out of the window of the train. Earplugs are useful on the train and in noisy Chinese hotels. Don't forget to take a good book. It's also a very good idea to bring things to show people: glossy magazines (the more celebrity pictures the better), photos of your family and friends, your home or somewhere interesting you have been. Everyone will want to look at them, and will often get out photos of their own to show you. This is a great way to break the ice when you don't speak much of the local language.

The Russians are great present givers and there's nothing more embarrassing than being entertained in a Russian home when you have nothing to offer in return. Cake and chocolates can be bought locally, or better. Bring things that are harder to get, such as postcards or souvenirs of your country, foreign coins and badges are also good, as

Russia is full of collectors.

It is essential that you have things to share when you are on the train, such as chocolate biscuits, sweets or other snacks. If you are trying to impress a Russian with chocolate it has to be good, since Russian chocolate, the Red October brand in particular, can be excellent. Red October's Gold Label has been on the market since 1867.

Life on the Train
Bryn Thomas, 2007

Most people imagine they will get bored on so long a journey but you ay be surprised by how quickly time flies.

Don't overdo the number of books you bring: *War and Peace*, all 1444 pages of it, is a frequent choice, although I know of only one person who actually managed to finish it on the trip. There are so many other things to do besides reading. You can have monosyllabic conversations with inquisitive Russians, meet other Westerners, play cards or chess, visit the restaurant car or hop off at the stations for a little exercise.

"Time passes very pleasantly on such a train," as Annette Meakin wrote in 1900. It is surprising how the time drifts by and even though you do very little, you won't be bored. Having said that, the Russian man who bought the Tetris electronic game at the Manzhouli Friendship Store quickly became everyone's best friend.

Clothing
Russian Year Book, 1917

The traveller should take ordinary clothing – with the exception that a black morning coat is absolutely necessary, dress suits are much less worn than with us. A lady should take no thick underclothing except a pair of warm knickerbockers to wear out of doors, a fur or fur-lined coat, a golf jersey (very useful to wear under a fur coat) or else an undercoat of wadded material, a small fur toque, a motor veil to wear on cold days to protect the ears, snow-boots, fur gloves, and goloshes.

From the point of view of warmth, travellers may wear exactly the same underclothing, &c., as they wear at home, but a fur coat is essential. A walking coat thickly wadded and with a fur collar will be found very useful; it is advisable to have the collar made so that it can be turned up to reach above the tips of the ears. Pockets should be made in the length of the coat to allow the hands and wrists to be well submerged in their depths.

Travellers in Russia are especially warned that, in the matter of wearing furs and keeping their coats buttoned up, "Discretion is the better part of valour." Britishers especially are apt to imagine that they can play with the climate, and disregard the natives' advice born of experience, with the result that many of our countrymen have met their death here prematurely. There is no more treacherous climate in the world than one meets with in Petrograd. It is more variable than Moscow owing to its proximity to the Gulf of Finland. Rain and thaw will sometimes succeed 14-20 degrees of frost.

Photography
Russian Year Book, 1917

Tourists are permitted to carry cameras and use them as long as they do not attempt to photograph fortresses.

If the tourist means to stay long in Russia, he should obtain a permit from the Prefect of Police in order to avoid the annoyance caused by police interference. The best plan, however, is to join the Russian Photographic Society. Membership entitles to free photography throughout the Empire.

For the Benefit of Photographers
William Oliver Greener, 1903

A lavatory [on the train] is converted into a dark room fitted with ruby electric lamp, for the benefit of photographers, who may also have the use of a cabinet of trays, measures, fixing-baths, and other apparatus free of charge.

Taking Photographs
Peter Fleming, 1933

In 1931, I remembered, there had been some formality with regard to photographs. What was it? ... Oh yes. Instructions had been passed along the train that we were to give up all films exposed on Russian soil. The young Australian had one in his camera, to which he instantly confessed. But there was an interval before the collection of the films took place, and, not without trepidation, he adopted my suggestion that he should show up an unexposed film, rewound. This daring and elaborate ruse we carried out successfully. The Australian kept his film.

It never occurred to me that the procedure might have been altered, the regulations tightened up. The proud possessor of (as far as I know) the only photographic record of a derailment on the Trans-Siberian line made by a foreigner, I took no steps at all to hide the films in which it was embodied. They lay, side by side, plain to be seen by anyone who opened my dispatch case. I awaited the customs officials with composure.

They came on me suddenly: five large inquisitive men, command-ing between them about as much English as I knew of Russian. It was instantly apparent that they meant business. My suitcases were sys-tematically disembowelled. What was the number of my typewriter? Had I a permit for my field-glasses? Above all, had I any cameras or films?

But yes! I cried, I had indeed. I thrust into their hands a tiny Kodak, still rusted with the waters of the Amazon. I heaped upon them an assortment of unexposed films, whose virginity they tested by removing the tropical packing. I was playing for time.

Anyone can play for time with words, but my vocabulary was too limited for effective obstructionism. To decoy them into the subtler irrelevancies of debate was impossible, seeing that everything I said was either redundant or incomprehensible. This they quickly grasped. They were men of action. They ceased to listen to me. And all the time their search brought them nearer to that dispatch case, which lay on the end of the seat furthest from the door.

Words failing me, I fell back on inanimate objects. The train, I knew, must leave within a certain time. Every minute that I could delay them would make the closing stages of their search more perfunctory. So I showed them my shoes and my books. I made them all in turn sniff at my hair-oil. I pressed aspirins upon them, and potted meat. I demonstrated the utility of pipe-cleaners, and the principles on which sock-suspenders are designed. But the search went on. They were not to be fobbed off. Under the seat they had found the discarded packing of a film; they felt – and rightly – that they were on to a good thing.

It was very hot. My coat hung on a peg. And in the pocket of my coat (I suddenly remembered) was that photostat copy of Ian's letter from Stalin. I took the coat down and produced the letter.

It had no great success, though it checked them for a moment. A few polite exclamations and the search was resumed. But in the meantime I, with an aggressively careless gesture, had flung down the coat upon the dispatch case, and the dispatch case was no longer in sight. Presently, with a great parade of exhaustion and impatience I sat down heavily, sighing, upon the coat, the dispatch case, and the films.

Nothing would move me. Defiantly anchored, like a brooding hen, I watched the hounds draw blank. I signed the forms they gave me to sign. I handed over, protesting loudly, one partially exposed film containing photographs of my grandmother. The officials were puzzled, suspicious. They had seen everything there was to see? Yes, I said firmly, they had seen everything there was to see. Still puzzled, still suspicious, they withdrew. The train started. I had had them with me for three-quarters of an hour.

Photography
Extract from Intourist booklet, 1986

Coming to the USSR you will certainly find many interesting things you would like to film or photograph. You will doubtlessly take back home a multitude of landscape, genre or documentary photos or cine pictures.

We advise amateur photographers and cameramen to study the rules cited below, in order to avoid possible misunderstandings.

While travelling in USSR on Intourist routes, foreign tourists may photograph, film and make drawings of architectural monuments and buildings: cultural, medical and educational institutions: theatres, museums, recreation parks, stadiums, streets and squares, houses and landscapes. When taking pictures of individuals, please remember that some people do not like being photographed without their consent.

It is PROHIBITED to photograph, film or make drawings of all kinds of military hardware and military objects, seaports, large hydro-engineering works, railway junctions, tunnels, railway and motor bridges, industrial enterprises, scientific research institutes, design offices, laboratories, power stations, radio beacons, telephone and telegraph exchanges.

It is PROHIBITED to take pictures from planes, to take long-range overland pictures and make drawings within the 25km border zone.

At industrial enterprises, state and collective farms, government offices, educational establishments and public organisations, photographing, filming and drawing can only be done with permission of the managements of the said enterprises, establishments and organisations.

Film shooting in the USSR is allowed exclusively for persona! (non-commercial) purposes.

Literature
Murray's Handbook for Travellers, 1893

Of course nothing like liberty of the press is known in Russia. There is in fact hardly any press, in the common acceptation of the term as the only newspapers are published by the government, and no periodical literature of at all a political character exists in the Russian language. A strict censorship as to all books imported from abroad is estabhshed to prevent the introduction and diffusion among the mass of the people of any dangerous doctrines or unwelcome pieces of news; but our books were not even opened at the frontier, and in the Nevskoi Prospect I was offered several books which are prohibited throughout the whole of Germany, on account of their-ultra liberal doctrines, and are with difficulty procured even in the free city of Hamburg. Their entire vigilance seems to be exerted upon English newspapers.

The only English newspaper permitted in St. Petersburg is the *Morning Post;* all others are absolutely forbidden. At the Library of the English Factory the newest publications may be obtained, however liberal their tendency, and few English can complain of the censorship. Though an Englishman may receive books from England which *are* generally prohibited in Russia, *yet it* is with the understanding that they are not to be placed in the hands of Russian friends; and indeed it would be a gross breach of faith were this rule to be infringed. The best class of Russians may without difficulty obtain permission from the censor to receive any work published in Europe; and I know several Russians who have received that privilege.

Blacked
John Foster Fraser, 1901

You get the English papers in Moscow about a week late. Should there be anything interesting about Russia, which, of course, you particularly want to read, you will find the column smeared out with the toughest of blacking. I have friends who confess to making periodic attempts to wash that blacking. They are never successful. The cartoon in Punch is frequently obliterated by a black smudge. A lady I know received a London illustrated paper. A halfpage picture was blotted. Her innate feminine curiosity was aroused. She did her best to obliterate the obliteration. She failed. She was happily acquainted with an Englishman in diplomatic service who received his newspapers uncensored. She hastened to look at his paper. Her inquisitiveness was thereupon instantly appeased. The picture was an advertisement of the Czar receiving, with open hands and undoubted satisfaction, a box of much boomed pills manufactured in the neighbourhood of St. Helens, Lancashire!

Russian Custom-House

Murray's Handbook for Travellers in Russia, Poland and Finland, 1887

Travellers should be particularly careful not to change foreign coin for Russian paper money before they enter Russia. In order to prevent the introduction of forged notes, not only is the importation of paper money forbidden, but if any is found on the person or baggage, it is liable to confiscation, and the owner to fine and imprisonment. This does not apply to silver money, but the exportation of it is equally illegal. Sealed letters, lottery tickets, playing cards, books subject to the censorship, articles of dress which have not been worn, and poisonous drugs, come within the category of prohibited articles; so that a medicine chest is liable to seizure; but it will, of course, be returned, on assuring the authorites that the rhubarb is not intended for his Imperial Majesty's liege subjects, but for your own sweet self. Books, and even maps, will also be set aside to be examined by the censor; these are sometimes made up into a parcel and sealed with lead, and then delivered to the owner, who engages, by signing a paper, to send them to the censor. The penalty for breaking or losing the lead seal is twenty-eight silver rubles, about *4l.* 10s. If a stranger should have any objectionable work with him, for instance, Byron's Don Juan, it will be retained; but, on application, returned to the owner on his leaving Russia. The search is, generally speaking, strict; each article of dress is taken from the portmanteau or imperial, and contemplated with a degree of earnest attention that awakens the most lively anxiety as to its future destination. To ladies this ordeal is peculiarly trying, and a fair author thus feelingly and indignantly alludes to these annoyances:

A black-looking being, with face like a bull-dog and paws like a bear, fumbled and crumbled a delicate *garde-robe* without mercy – stirring up large and small, tender and tough, things precious and things vile, ruthlessly together, to the unutterable indignation and anguish of the proprietor. To witness the devastation of an English writing-desk was a curious sight to an uninterested spectator. First, the lock excited great anger, and was a convincing proof that little was to be done with Bramah by brute force; and, this passed, there ensued as striking an illustration of the old adage of a bull in a china-shop as could possibly be devised. Every touch was mischief. They soiled the writing-paper and split the ink; mixed up wax, wafers, and watercolours.

Trans-Siberian Excess
Chris Moss, 2007

Guidebooks, brochures and trainspotters tend to paint a romantic picture of life on board Russia's big train. Many Russians handle the four to seven day ride by getting wasted. At any time of the day, men (and only men) skulk out of their compartments with vodka-blasted eyes, groaning and blithely ignoring all those vast steppes. Officers in the military sleep all the way. Chinese teenagers chat on their mobiles.

Loos are, at best, cleanish. There are no showers and little space for a sponge down. Buffet car food is basic and doesn't change, so after a couple of stroganoffs you'll end up doing as locals do and heating up pot noodles at the samovar. You will be sat down half the time and lying down the rest – standing becomes a chore. Cabins are communal, and if you are in the lower bunk, your bed becomes a dinner table. Some *provodnitsas* (coach attendants) are polite; some are as cold as Siberian permafrost. If you don't speak Russian, you can't talk to them anyway.

Put all these factors together and do the whole seven-night epic from Moscow to Vladivostok and, rest assured, you will arrive looking awful, with your bowels shot, your hair insane and your energy sapped.

Of course, it all depends who you're travelling with. What can seem like an ordeal when you're on your own becomes a laugh with a group of friends. And couples should definitely consider upgrading to a two-berth carriage for the privacy and romance. And even on your own, there's always the view. And the chug-chug of the train and eternal wilderness. The view is ... Russia. On the European side, this is flat, grey, forests blasted apart by settlements, power stations and factories built here precisely because the train runs nearby.

Siberia is prettier, sunnier, shapelier, but it is repetitive. China comes as a relief if you take one of the Beijing routes. That said, borders are excruciatingly tedious – up to ten hours to cross directly to China, and if you go via Mongolia, you've got two to cross.

There is a sort of exception. The No 9 and 10 "Baikal" trains runs between Moscow and Irkutsk only and have sliding cellophane loo-seat covers, DVD rooms, regular vacuuming, and, apparently, a shower - if you ask. This is as luxurious as it gets short of taking an Orient Express-style charter service.

Tips are: take heaps of books, magazines, music, fruit and chocolate - the latter for barter as well as pleasure. Take booze other than vodka and introduce yourself to everyone. Sooner or later an Anglophone will appear. Learn basic Russian and try Chinese. Get off at every station and do silly walks. And accept the invitations to have firewater and cold fish – monosyllabic conversations will ensue, then a rapid sequence of 40-degree, throat-singing shots, and soon you'll be back in bed. The train goes at 45mph, but time flies when you're asleep.

5

REVOLUTION AND WAR

It was the threat of the Russo-Japanese War of 1905-6 that speeded up the completion of the railway around Lake Baikal and across Russian territory into Trans-Baikalia. But revolution was already stirring in Russia and, as Maurice Baring found as he returned from reporting the war in the east in 1906, it had its effect on the railway. Then, during and after the Revolution of 1917, as Lesley Blanch describes, terrible battles raged for possession of each section of the line:

> Roughly plated with iron sheeting, railway carriages became armoured cars. Within, supreme commanders planned their campaigns from these ambulant GHQs.
>
> Often, a briefly appointed leader would live out his whole command from one, never reaching the scene of battle, his route hampered by snow and blocked by mined tunnels. The carriages became Martial courts and execution cells too as they rolled across the country, slowing down or accelerating, attacked or attacking, carrying their secrets within their steel walls.
>
> In Siberia, battles were lost or won on trains rather than in the field, where diminishing numbers of soldiers sometimes waited forlornly for reinforcements that never came – that had perished, en route, when their train was dynamited; or they deserted, one by one, dropping from the train as it headed for battle. Thousands of such deserters, growing more and more uncertain of what they were fighting for, made their getaway from the troop trains and took to the *taiga,* on the run, as once the escaping convicts had done.

By 1918-19 the Red armies had taken over most of Siberia, but in that winter the Whites, with the stolid assistance of Czech troops trapped in Russia by the country's withdrawal from the First World War, drove the Reds back into Russia proper. But the Czechs were reluctant allies, eager to return home via the eastern seaboard; in a curiously little-known

moment of history, British and other allied forces were sent, in the spring of 1919, to train and equip the White Russian forces raised in Siberia. Brian Horrocks, later General Sir Brian Horrocks and well known through television as a historian, was sent as a member of this British military mission.

Eventually they failed, and Horrocks was taken prisoner as refugees struggled eastwards to escape from the advancing Reds. A young Englishwoman, Doreen Stanford, who had been living with her parents in Siberia, was swept up in this exodus.

Then in the changing scene after the Revolution, another strange piece of history unrolled: a group of idealistic Americans came to Siberia with the idea of helping the new regime. With them were two women, Helen Wilson and Elsie Mitchell, who, when the group dispersed, set off on their own "vagabonding" through the Soviet Union, and witnessed the damage caused by civil war to the railway. In 1939 the writer Noel Barber saw a great armoured Soviet train, ready for another war.

Pause for Revolution
Maurice Baring, 1906

My return journey from Harbin to Moscow was entirely uneventful until we arrived at Samara. At Irkutsk I had got a place in the Trans-Siberian express, which was crowded with all sorts and conditions of men: officers, merchants, three Germans, three Americans who had returned from working a mine in Siberia, a Polish student, and some ladies.

The first hint I received that a revolution was going on in Russia came to me in the following manner. We had crossed the Urals and had only been travelling thirteen days. We had arrived at Samara, when the attendant, who looked after the first class carriage, came into my compartment and heaved a deep sigh. I asked him what was the matter. "We shan't get farther than Tula," he said. "Why?" I asked. "Because of the unpleasantnesses" (*niepriyatnosti*). I asked, "What unpleasantnesses?" "There is a mutiny," he said, "on the line." We passed the big station of Syzran and arrived at the small town of Kuznetsk. There we were informed that the train could not go any farther because of the strike. Nobody realised the extent of the strike, and we expected to go on in a few hours. By the evening the passengers began to show signs of restlessness. Most of them telegraphed to various authorities. A petition was telegraphed to the Minister of Ways and Communications, saying that an express train full of passengers, over-tired by a long and fatiguing journey, was waiting at Kuznetsk, and asking him to be so good as to arrange for them to proceed farther. There was no answer to this telegram. The next day a sense of resignation seemed to come over the company. Although every evening, towards dinner-time, one heard innumerable complaints such as "only in Russia could such a *bezo-brazie* (literally an ugliness, i.e. a disgraceful thing) happen," and one passenger suggested that Prince Khilkov's portrait, which was hung in the dining-car, should be turned face to the wall ...

The passengers spent the time in exploring the town, which was somnolent and melancholy in the extreme. Half of it was a typical Russian village built on a hill, a mass of brown huts; the other half, on the plain, was like a village in any country. The idle guards and railway officials sat on the steps of the stationroom whistling. Two more trains arrived: a Red Cross train and an ordinary slow passenger train.

The passengers from these trains wandered about the platform, mixing with the idlers from the town. A crowd of peasants and travellers, engineers and Red Cross attendants, soldiers and merchants sauntered up and down in loose shirts and big boots, munching sunflower seeds and spitting out the husks till the platform was thick with refuse. A doctor who was in our train, and who was half a German, with an official training and an orthodox official mind, talked to the railway servants like a father. It was very wrong to strike, he said. They should have put down their grievances on paper and had them forwarded through the proper channels. The officials said that was waste of ink and caligraphy. "I wonder they don't kill him," said my travelling companion, and I agreed with him. Each passenger was given a rouble a day to buy food with. The third class passengers were given checks, in return for which they could receive meals. But they deprecated the idea, and said that they wanted the amount in beer. They received it. Then they looted the refreshment room, broke the windows, and took away the food. This put an end to the check system. The feeling among the first class passengers deepened.

Something ought to be done, was the general verdict; but nobody quite knew what …

On the morning of the fourth day after we had arrived the impatience of the passengers increased to fever pitch. A colonel who was with us, and who knew how to use the telegraph, communicated with Penza, the next big station. For although the telegraph clerks were on strike they remained in their offices conversing with their friends on the wire all over Russia. The strikers were most affable. They said they had not the slightest objection to the express proceeding on its journey, that they would neither beat nor boycott anybody who took us, and that if we could find a friend to drive the engine, well and good. We did. We found a friend, an amateur engine-driver, and an amateur engine, and on the 28th of October we started for Penza. We broke down on the way. The engine-driver was supported by public contributions. The moment the engine stopped work all the passengers volunteered advice as *to* how it should be mended, one man producing a piece of string for the purpose. However, another stray engine was found, and we arrived at last at Penza.

We arrived at Moscow at eleven o'clock in the evening and found the town in darkness, save for the glimmer of oil lamps. The next morning we woke up to find that Russia had been given a Charter.

The first thing which brought home to me that Russia had been granted the promise of a Constitution was this. I went to the big Russian baths. Somebody came in and asked for some soap, upon which the barber's assistant, aged about ten, said with the air of a Hampden, "Give the *citizen* some soap" (*Daite grazhdaninu mwyla*). Coming out of the baths I found the streets decorated with flags, and everybody in a state of frantic and effervescing enthusiasm. I went to one of the big restaurants. There old men were embracing each other and drinking the first glass of vodka to Free Russia.

To War by Train
General Sir Brian Horrocks, 1919

Brian Horrocks arrived in Vladivostok in 1919 and soon set off westwards to join the military mission in Omsk whose task it was to equip the White Russian army and train it in the use of the new equipment.

We were fourteen British officers and a platoon of British soldiers on a train with twenty-seven wagons full of shells. We officers were due to report to the British military mission, but our first job was to deliver these wagons intact to the town of Omsk, just over 3,000 miles away.

The fourteen of us lived in one box-car, called a *terplushka*, sleeping in double wooden bunks, and it was cold enough for us to be glad of the stove which burned continuously in the centre of the wagon. Captain Moore, my new-found Uncle Charlie, was in charge of the train, and as he was pretty good on banjo the evenings passed cheerfully enough. The snow had almost gone but immediately after the winter this Siberian landscape is very bleak and desolate; miles and miles of bare country, small stunted trees, and no undergrowth at all.

As we rumbled steadily westwards at eight to ten miles an hour, the monotony of the journey was broken by our arrival at stations and small wayside halts. For in Siberia the station is the centre of the social life of the district. People come from miles around and there were always dozens of small, shaggy and incredibly tough Siberian ponies tethered at the back of the building, while their owners, male and female, paraded up and down the platform. The arrival of a train was the great moment in the day, and the platform very quickly developed into a small market.

Up to now we had been passing through a comparatively peaceful region but west of Lake Baikal the country had already gone very Red and Bolshevik bands were constantly raiding the railway. So each night we spent in the sidings of some station, protected by soldiers of the White Russian Army.

We were soon involved in one of these raids. In the middle of the night we were awakened by rifle and machine-gun fire coming from all round the perimeter of our small station. I climbed pessimistically to the flat roof of our sleeping wagon which was my alarm post in an attack.

There was a great deal of noise and bullets were flying overhead, but most of the shooting seemed to be wild. Suddenly I spotted the dark shape of a figure in the branches of a tree a couple of hundred yards away, outhned by the arc lights which surrounded the station. I fired fifteen carefully-aimed shots, but, to my disgust, without any apparent result.

Then all at once the firing died down as suddenly as it had started, and we returned to bed. Next morning I discovered that my fifteen rounds had been fired at a large disused lamp, but even this, I must admit, showed no ill effects from my marksmanship.

In spite of these incidents, on the 20th May we pulled proudly into Omsk station, and handed over our twenty-seven ammunition trucks intact to the British authorities. It had taken us just over a month to complete the three thousand miles journey. Not bad going in the circumstances!

But my final destination was Ekaterinburg, now called Sverdlovsk, some 800 miles farther west, a charming place complete with gardens and a lake – very different from the normal, dusty unattractive Siberian town. It was here that the Tsar and his family were murdered and I used to pass the house every day on my way to work.

In Ekaterinburg I got to know the Russian soldier, for I was second in command of an N.C.O.s training school attached to the Anglo-Russian brigade. If was planned *to* form a brigade *of four* battalions, each of which had about seven British officers and twenty senior British N.C.O.s while all the rest were Russian. When this scheme had originally been put forward it had received the enthusiastic approval of the Russian authorities from Admiral Koltchak downwards, but, as we soon came to realise, there is all the difference in the world between approval in theory and practical help. In fact, every conceivable difficulty was put in our way... Orders were received from the United Kingdom that the experiment was to cease and the British officers were to return home.

Horrocks and Hayes were left behind to act as liaison officers with the 1st Siberian Army.

In our new job Hayes and I owned a small railway train of our own, consisting of three wagons. We lived in one, our Chinese servants and Russian groom in the other, and in the third we kept our horses. If we wanted to go anywhere, all we had to do was to ring up for an engine.

Our main task was to keep in touch with the situation on the front which was worsening rapidly, and report back daily to the chief of the British military mission, General Knox, at his headquarters in Omsk, 700 miles farther east.

As the only way to visit units was on horseback, I used to ride off with my Russian groom, and was often away for up to a week at a time, spending each night in some small Russian village many miles north of the railway line.

Prisoner of the Bolsheviks
General Sir Brian Horrocks, 1919

Things were getting steadily worse and the Reds were advancing against very little opposition. The trouble was that as soon as a White Russian battalion arrived at the front – having been trained and equipped by us – it almost invariably deserted *en bloc* to the Red workers' paradise on the other side of the lines.

One day even the army headquarters to which I was attached was attacked by a Red battalion. 1 sat on the roof of my wagon watching the Reds advance, and trying to decide when was the last possible moment for me to destroy my precious cipher book – all my messages to H.Q. were sent in code – which must at all costs be prevented from falling into enemy hands. It was a difficult decision, because if I destroyed it unnecessarily, it meant going back 700 miles to get another one.

I never had a better view of any battle in my life. In front of me were lines of Red infantry advancing steadily towards us, while the White officers and cadets were hurriedly dashing into defensive positions. Luckily for me and my cipher book, the attack was beaten off within 400-500 yards of our train.

But the writing was on the wall, and we were soon heading eastwards to Omsk. I did not like the look of the situation at all. Hayes and I were a lone English rearguard some 3,000 miles from Vladivostok, our base. Most of the people inhabiting the country in between sympathised with the Reds, and were hostile to us; in fact the only troops who could really be relied upon were the Czechs and some Polish units. Both loathed the Reds and were busy withdrawing to Vladivostok themselves.

To make matters worse, it was now October, with the winter closing in, and the cold of a Siberian winter is almost unbelievable, with temperatures down to forty degrees below zero. It was not a bright prospect.

We got back the 700 miles to Omsk without much difficulty, but then our troubles really started. The front disintegrated, and we were told to make our way back to Vladivostok as best as we could. Omsk itself was a seething mass of terrified people, all mad to get away from the Red terror spreading eastwards.

A mass retreat is one of the saddest and most despairing sights in the world. Most of these people were quite destitute. Families became split up, and the walls of the stations were covered with pathetic little messages such as: "If Maria Ivanovna should see this, her parents passed here on 10th October, making for Irkutsk." There were only two ways of escaping from the Red tide which rolled inexorably eastward, by train, or by sleigh along the tracks which ran parallel to the two railway lines.

On arrival in Omsk, we were lucky enough to join up with Major Vining and a dozen other British officers and other ranks, who belonged to the British railway mission which had been helping the Russians to run their railways. We were fifteen all told. They were now frantically trying to deal with the chaos in the station-yard, and to get trains moving east.

Vining had secured a couple of wagons on which he had painted *the* Union Jack. These immediately became the rallying points for all sorts of people who claimed British nationality – Persians, Russians with English names who could not speak a word of English, Indians, and goodness knows who else. We came to realise how very wide-flung was the British Empire. Unfortunately there were a number of women among them. This was the sort of situation where we would have gladly done without the female sex because the journey in front of us was likely to be tough and not the sort of thing for women at all. But we had no alternative and they were all packed in somehow.

On 13th November we pulled out of Omsk in one of the last trains to leave. The Red Army was approaching rapidly. We were attached to a train full of Polish soldiers, and we travelled on the right-hand track which was usually reserved for up-trains. To start with we made good progress, passing a ribbon of stationary trains on the left, or down-track. In fact, we arrived in Novosibirsk, 550 miles away, only one week later.

But from now on things became very difficult. Both lines were blocked with trains standing nose to tail, moving on perhaps a few miles at a time, then remaining stationary for hours. There was no water for the engines, so at frequent intervals we turned out and formed a human chain passing baskets of snow up to the engine. Not much fun this in the bitter cold of a Siberian night, but unless we kept up steam our chances of escape were nil.

The people were now getting desperate. At Tiaga, 150 miles farther east, Czechs, Poles and Russians were fighting for engines and the station echoed to the continuous rattle of machine-gun fire. I managed to wriggle my way into the station-master's office where I was handed a message from Vladivostok. It read: "If the situation seems to warrant it, do not hesitate to take complete control."

Could anything have been better? At this particular moment, it would have taken at least a division of well-trained British troops to have sorted out the situation. But the message did serve a useful purpose: it caused great amusement.

We managed to keep fairly cheerful in spite of the endless tragedies which were going on. Always that steady stream of sleighs pulled by Siberian ponies, with their pathetic burdens, old and young, women and children, some starving, many of them ill, but somehow clinging on desperately to the top of the few possessions which they had managed to save. The sick just fell down and died in the snow – there was nothing anybody could do about it.

Things were going from bad to worse. The Reds were now only thirty miles away and our engine was finished. We managed to get the women and children into one wagon on another train manned by the Russian railway battalion, which we knew had a better chance of getting through than any other. Having seen them depart, the men of the party decided to take to the sleighs.

It was the night of 15th December. We had been retreating for nearly a month, and we had had practically no sleep for seventy-two hours. It was almost dark when I heaved myself wearily on to the top of the loaded sleigh which had been allocated to me. The cold was frightful and the going terrible. Every now and then I was flung off into the snow and had to run to catch up again. But we were forced to walk and run pretty often, because of the intense cold.

And so the journey went on, riding, walking, falling off, running, hour after hour and day after day. The only time we were really warm was at night which we usually spent all packed together into one room in some village.

After five days on the sleighs we crossed the railway line again at a small station. The Polish commandant here told us that the line to the east was much clearer now, and then we suddenly saw, standing in the yard, the wagon containing our women and children – a most re-markable coincidence. They felt rather lonely and begged us to rejoin them. So we all crowded in, some forty-two people in a wagon meant for sixteen. However, it was warmer than on the sleighs.

Finally, we came to a longer stop than usual, some eight miles west of the Siberian town of Krasnoyarsk. Then, all around us, we saw offi-cers and men throwing away their arms. It appeared that the Red Army had done a wide encircling movement and had captured Krasnoyarsk four days before. The date was 7th January. We had now been retreating for six weeks and had covered nearly 1,000 miles, but this was the end. It was infuriating to think that all our efforts had been in vain. Here we were, cluttered up with women and children, almost exactly in the middle of Siberia in the depth of winter. We saw no Reds, there was no shooting – nothing. So, working on the principle "When in doubt, feed," we decided to have supper.

Then into our carriage came a soldier with a huge red cockade in his fur cap. He was followed shortly afterwards by a couple of officers, one of whom said he was the Red battalion commander. We were now their prisoners but, having discovered that we were British, they beamed with delight and asked us whether they might join us for supper – a truly Gilbertian situation.

Journey to the East
Doreen Stanford, 1919

On 31 December, 1919 Doreen Stanford, her father and mother and her fox terrier, Mimi, set off eastwards from Krasnoyarsk.

We now saw for ourselves what we had heard about, and had personal experience of the chaos which ruled on the railway. A surprising number of railwaymen stuck to their posts and did their best to keep traffic moving. Engine-drivers took long turns of duty until they could no longer do without sleep and had to abandon their engines and rest, rolled in their sheepskin coats, at some wayside halt. Engines broke down from continual use and usually could not be repaired. The possession of any rolling stock still serviceable was disputed by Czechs, Poles, assorted Russian forces, members of various Allied Missions who were leaving their hopeless task, and every conceivable variety of civilian refugee. The spread of disease could not be controlled. Sanitary conditions were only bearable because all refuse froze at once and the next snowfall covered it. We could imagine what the tracks would be like when the thaw came.

We had no means of knowing facts, and heard a variety of rumours, often contradictory. The one salient point was that the Reds were advancing steadily from the west into Siberia and pushing forward. The heterogeneous mass of people on the railway had one idea in common – to escape to the east. Now that we were committed to the journey, we felt the same urge. We too wanted to get away, somehow, somewhere, while it was still possible.

When we boarded the hospital train, it was believed that the main Red force was at Achinsk, some hundred miles away, but advancing fast, by road as well as rail, driving before them the remains of the White forces.

On January 3 our train began to move. It had been standing in the station at Krasnoyarsk for several months, before it was commandeered by the Czechs for a hospital train. Piled snow had frozen round it. It took a gang of men more than a day to dig the rails clear of snow. Several attempts to start the train failed, the coupled engine straining unavailingly, but a second engine was put on in front and a third behind, and at last there was a series of jolts and section by section the train was pulled to the main station, ready for its turn to use the eastward line...

We were relatively comfortable. We had a four-berth compartment to ourselves in a corridor carriage, other compartments being occupied by Czech orderlies and a few convalescents. Our carriage had been a second-class coach in passenger service when the railway was running normally, and was clean and no hardship to live in. We had our own bedding and such of our possessions as had not been abandoned in Minusinsk or discarded in Krasnoyarsk, including cutlery, kitchen utensils and a spirit-stove. We were to buy our midday meal from the train kitchen which supplied the troops and manage breakfast and supper for ourselves. We had bought a ham and a leg of mutton, both kept frozen until required, also a sack of potatoes, another of flour, several loaves and a keg of honey. We had an essential, plenty of tea, and some supplies such as milk and eggs could, we were told, be bought at stations along the line, if one was quick enough and had enough roubles. We were all right for the moment, and the whole coach was warmed by hot-water pipes – an important factor in a Siberian January. Even Mimi soon settled down to her new life.

It was slightly disconcerting to find that the only lavatory anywhere near us could only be reached through the office of the doctor in charge of the train, and that both he and his orderly jumped to their feet, clicked their heels and saluted each time Mother and I went through the office – both on the outward and inward journey. Mother and I were not sure of the correct way of acknowledging this courtesy, but we wanted to be equally polite, so bowed graciously. But the ceremony appealed to our sense of humour.

Had we known it, we got away only just in time. The advancing Reds were much closer than we realized and occupied Krasnoyarsk on the evening of the day we left it. Sir Brian Horrocks, who, as a young officer attached to a British Mission, was taken prisoner there just after our departure, has described conditions under the Reds; crowds, hunger and rampant disease; the prison camp where Whites were dying at the rate of 200 a day, and the fanatical attitude of the Bolshevik commissars. We had had a very narrow escape indeed. Our actual start was rather alarming, as we were so used to abortive efforts to move the train that my father had gone off to see friends elsewhere in the station, and Mother and I were alone in our compartment when the train left the platform and began to get up speed. I rushed to the window and thought I saw a familiar figure take a flying leap into one of the rear coaches, though the outside of the window was half-frozen over and it was hard to see clearly. However, to our vast relief, he came along the corridor to join us. Any form of separation in those days could become permanent.

Our progress, though fairly steady, was slow. The train steamed a short distance eastwards and stopped in a siding, where we got hot water from the station and took Mimi for a run. She gave no trouble throughout the journey; however odd she thought our present way of living, as long as she was with us she was content. She was also rather an asset, as the Czechs liked dogs and had many in their trains, also bear cubs and other pets. Mimi was known as "the English dog" and had many admirers. Like all fox-terrier bitches, she enjoyed being made a fuss of. She got her full share of the liberal rations which we drew from the Czechs and which we enjoyed: hot, well-cooked stews and soups which helped to guard against the very cold weather and kept us all healthy.

We heard appalling stories of what happened to some refugees. An officer of a British Mission stayed on our train for a day or two and was delighted to meet fellow-countrymen. He had been on a Russian hospital train when the Reds caught up with it. Anyone who could move had fled on foot and he looked back through the trees to see the glare of the burning train, set on fire by accident or possibly on purpose. As he hurried away, he could hear the cries of the helpless cases as the flames advanced.

The bitter cold, too, added to the hardship. We were told of abandoned trains where fuel had failed and the carriages were full of frozen corpses, sitting or lying as they had been when the cold overcame them. Even if there had been anyone to do it, the ground was too hard to bury the dead unless fires were lighted to thaw it. Bodies were stacked in heaps like timber, pending the spring. In some cases corpses – and not always only corpses – were pushed into the rivers through holes in the ice. Summer would bring even more disease.

At another station the American Railway Corps was still installed. Two unmistakable Americans were standing on the platform, and we spoke to them. We found on this and other occasions that the standard American greeting in those days was 'Pleased to meet you – would you like a bath?' *Would* we! *Did* we appreciate hot water, friendly faces and almost always a good meal! Blessings on those hospitable Americans.

Another group of British officers overtook us and left us. They had been on the roofs of box-cars in danger of frost-bite; they had forced themselves into carriages already crowded to the doors; sometimes they had travelled in relative comfort, but more often quite the reverse. They had learnt to tip engine-drivers to shunt a commandeered carriage and attach it to a train due to move, once to the fury of a Polish colonel who had a contingent of troops in a train which was already overloaded, and who threatened to shoot his allies. We even met Danes serving with the Red Cross. Our compartment was seldom without a visitor and Mother cooked bacon and eggs on her spirit-stove – luckily we had plenty of fuel for it – and fed our guests in order of rank, colonels first. It was an odd existence.

But anxiety deepened as time went on. The Czech safe-conduct which we had been given in Krasnoyarsk only ensured us a passage as far as Irkutsk, where we hoped to find some British authority who would help us to get to Vladivostok. There was no chance at all of travelling by the conventional means of buying a ticket, as no passenger services were running. All our hopes rested on a British Railway Transport Officer – if there was still one there, when we got to Irkutsk. And behind us, like a great storm cloud, came the advancing Reds.

At last the train really started and travelled two-thirds of a mile before the engine broke down. There were forty-six coaches attached to the train, all more or less frozen up, so we appreciated the difficulties. We were blocking the main line between stations, so something would have to be done about it. The engine was towed away for repairs and we settled down to wait again. An excellent string orchestra was practising at one end of the coach, and friendly Czechs came to talk to us, some of them in a word or two of English. They did not think much of the Russians on the whole. They had had extraordinary adventures, between their service in the Austrian army, their surrender to or capture by the Tsarist forces and their sojourns in prison camps, which had ended with the formation of the Czech Legion.

Eventually our engine was repaired and sent back to us, and towed the long train into a tiny halt called Zabituy. It was then uncoupled and vanished, and two weary days passed. My father boarded every train which stopped there to see if we could get transport. One commandant offered us a corner in a Red Cross carriage which had two typhus cases and a man with smallpox in it. He said there were still some vacant berths and he was prepared to take us. Another offered room in a horsebox – with horses in the other half of the accommodation. We would have preferred the horses to the typhus patients, but there was no heating at all in the horsebox, not even an iron stove, and we already knew what living like that would be like. They were genuine offers and well meant.

Our prospects for the journey now looked promising. Captain Carroll [a British officer in charge of transport] commandeered a railway coach with hot-water pipes, a cooking stove at one end, a lavatory and six compartments. He plastered the outside with Union Jacks and we moved in, having a compartment to ourselves with a door we could shut! We were joined by a very mixed bag of refugees with some call on British assistance: two Americans, one a YMCA man, the other working for the American Red Cross, and their Polish servant; a Polish officer and his wife and two other couples of vague nationality who had some claim to be assisted – probably Captain Carroll's kind heart had a lot to do with it.

Captain Carroll filled the coach with stores left by the American Red Cross. 'No use leaving them for the Reds,' said he, and we were given tins of meat, tinned milk, packets of tea, flour and sugar, and cakes of soap – riches!

That night my father and I had a tussle with the heating system and it looked as if we would have to confess that we had let the pipes freeze during our first night of occupation. We made up the fire, raked out the fire-bars and pumped vigorously, turn about, to keep the water circulating. Mother woke up and came along to take her turn at pumping, then the two Americans joined us and chased 'the ladies' away. (We didn't feel very ladylike, black with coal dust, at that time of night.) But we found out the trick of the heating, which was to keep the water at boiling point and to have plenty of coal and clean fire-bars; no pumping was needed. So we drew up a rota of stokers and kept the car warm.

On 1 March after two full months on the railway we halted in a big station, seeing some British and American friends and the French Mission train in the distance – without an engine. Our coach was now attached to a train bound for Harbin on what passed for a regular passenger service, and we spun along over the desert until the track began to climb the Hingan Mountains up and up a curving track, with two engines hauling the heavy load. After running through a long tunnel, the train went down an equally steep descent, the line looping like some railways in Switzerland. The construction of the railway was a considerable engineering feat. We flew down with a switchback movement, going faster and faster. In the brilliant moonlight we again saw the sinister shapes of wrecked cars, but the descent was too exciting to worry about the possibility of accidents. Our axles were red-hot when we stopped at last, and burning waste was pulled out of an axle-box.

The country now looked different and the climate was warmer, with only occasional patches of snow. The population was mainly Chinese and we saw men in blue quilted clothes driving bullock carts. The duties of station guards seemed to be shared by Chinese and Japanese troops: the former bigger men and looking good-tempered, but slouching and untidy; the Japanese very spruce and efficient but disagreeable.

We left Harbin at last, our coach coupled behind General Beckett's, and therefore in a reasonably strong position to remain as part of the train. We shot away at most unusual speed, the coach rocking and swaying, but we were on the move again and we were glad.

Next day we were still travelling hard through wild mountain scenery. My father had not been in our compartment for some time, but we knew he was somewhere on the train and everyone visited everyone else. He came back at a small station, very pleased with himself. He and two Americans had had the idea of riding on the front of the engine on the platform which all Trans-Siberian engines had to accommodate a look-out – during the Revolution a fully-armed soldier. This way of travelling had thrilled my father and he very kindly fetched me to share it. Mother protested faintly but I hurried along the platform and my father helped me up the high steps. I braced myself against the rail and hung on for all I was worth, while the big train went swooping down the mountain line. Presently the engine shut off steam and swung downhill on our own momentum. It was no use wondering whether the brakes were in use or whether there were any brakes. The crisp air stung our faces, the wind whistled past our ears. It was a long swaying rush like the flight of a huge bird. Our engine swung round curves, flashed over bridges. Chinese signalmen popped out here and there with green flags, though I strongly suspected that we could not have stopped if they had been red ones. Their impassive faces flashed into grins at the sight of passengers on the engine. It beat any switchback.

Once down from the mountains the train slackened speed and we stopped at a little station. A railwayman came and asked us politely in Russian if we would return to our coach, as the next stop was a big depot and 'passengers on the engine were not authorized'. Even in a revolution some of the conventions must be observed – some-times. We had our fun, so we climbed down and returned to our compartment.

On the evening of 20 May 1920 the last accommodation ladder was hauled up [in Vladivostok], there was a blast on the siren of *Keemun* and the deck quivered under our feet. The ship turned slowly and steamed down the harbour. The Czechs, in orderly ranks stood at attention. Gulls wheeled overhead against the sunset and the hills of the mainland showed dark in the fading light. First the Czechs sang their national anthem, then a requiem for their comrades who had died in Russia. It was deeply moving for us as well as for the men whose strong voices rang out over the water.

A bell rang in the engine-room and the beat of the engines quickened. We turned to go below. For us, too, it was farewell to Siberia. The engines throbbed and the ship began to roll a little, heading for the open sea.

After the War
Helen Wilson and Elsie Mitchell, 1927

We had already traveled a good deal by rail and knew only too well what we had to look forward to. The railway service of Russia was utterly demoralized by the long years of war, and the destruction of rolling stock was appalling. On our long trip across Siberia from Vladivostok to Kemerovo we ourselves had seen innumerable cars and engines lying beside the roadbed, derailed and wrecked. Once, while our dilatory train was side-tracked, and we were wandering about the railway yard in search of diversion, we discovered what appeared to be simply an unusually large freight car, but which actually was an armored car (made in America!!) housing a heavy cannon which had, no doubt, been responsible for some of the destruction we had seen.

Hardly any of the bridges had escaped damage to a greater or less extent. By tremendous efforts, however, all had been repaired, either permanently or by heavy temporary trestles of logs, except the great bridge over the Amur of which one span was missing. This immense steel span has since been restored, – an achievement to be proud of, – and the Moscow-Vladivostok expresses now run on schedule time as smoothly as before the Revolution and World War. But on the sidings and in the repair yards of every large town may still be seen such a collection of battered and war damaged engines and freight and passenger cars, broken, splintered, burned, shot to pieces, as fairly baffles description. Each year the work of salvage goes on, reducing the evidences of this orgy of destruction for which the allied powers (America included) were so largely responsible through their agents, Kolchak and Denikin and the rest.

Much has been done to repair this damage, and the through trains on the main lines have now for some time been running regularly, are clean, well-managed and reasonably comfortable though always crowded. But in spite of big purchases of new rolling stock and repair of the old, there are not yet enough locomotives and cars to accommodate the traffic. Inevitably the branch lines and the slower, cheaper trains which carry the poorer people suffer most. Travel by water is much pleasanter, and much more comfort is possible on the boats, for the same expenditure, than on the trains. Owing to these conditions, boarding a train in Russia is always a strenuous and exciting business. The trains are inevitably jammed and late comers fare badly. Every passenger is loaded to the limit of human endurance with baggage, and the crowd surges and pushes around the narrow car steps, shouting, exclaiming, shoving and scrambling until it seems as though serious accidents must occur. A Russian crowd is, however, good natured; there is no real violence, and in due course everybody, – or nearly everybody, – succeeds in getting on, breathless, exhausted but triumphant. We were unusually successful at the Omsk station and emerged from the mêlée in possession of a comfortable corner section of a third class car.

Railway Defence
Noel Barber, 1939

It was that late night that we saw suddenly in a station siding a great Soviet armoured train.

In its way it was one of the most impressive things I had seen for a long time. It was in three parts – two armoured coaches, bristling with guns, and an armoured engine in the middle. We looked at it for about ten minutes or quarter of an hour. One of the coaches had a heavy gun peeping through an armoured side, and the other had a battery of four machine-guns pointed upward. Skilfully resting on the armoured platforms were rail sections and half a dozen steel sleepers – obviously there to mend torn-up tracks.

I asked Alexandrov if he really thought an armoured train could be of much value in modern warfare – it seemed to me that a track was far too vulnerable these days, and that one well-placed bomb could immobilize such a train simply by stopping it from going forward to the battle line.

He shrugged his shoulders. 'I think they can be useful,' he said. 'Particularly in winter. You have seen the sort of country we have been travelling through. Roads blocked up – in some parts no roads at all. Then the armoured train comes into its own, I think. It has drawbacks, of course – it can be made stationary very quickly, but our shock workers on armoured trains can mend bomb-smashed railways very quickly.'

I was still sceptical, but since I got back armoured trains seem to have done some excellent work in the defence of Leningrad – notice, in *defence*. That, I think, is probably their primary function. They have been moving round and round Leningrad, mounting very heavy guns at a time when it would have been quite impossible, because of the weather, to move heavy guns by road.

Of course, the Russians were really the originators of modern armoured trains in the civil war. I believe there was one classic case in the civil war when two armoured trains actually met in battle on the Trans-Siberian track. Each side scored a direct hit on the other train, and the result was declared a draw.

Many of those early armoured trains were improvised affairs, because in the times of the Revolution the roads were in an appalling condition in Russia – they are not too good now, but they are all A.1 compared with what they were twenty-five years ago. The Russians simply mounted cannon and machine-guns on ordinary goods trucks, because they could not transport them over the roads. They made some attempt with steel plate to armour the trains and give some protection to the gun crew, but it was not very much.

But the train that I saw that night was very different. Here was a scientifically constructed instrument of war, specially built to get over the problem of winter communications, when railways are often the only means of transport left open. Yes, it was very impressive.

6

SIBERIANS, TRAVELLERS AND WORKERS

"Being sent to Siberia" was certainly not a Soviet invention. It was a Russian way of life for centuries, as revealed by Digby and Wright's description of how the population of Siberia expanded before the Revolution and how people reached Siberia to colonize it. Lindon Bates Junior met an ex-convict in 1908 and Francis E. Clark observed with interest the people who came to the stations to watch the passing train – the one excitement of the day in Trans-Baikalia in 1900.

With the railway came the tourists: John Foster Fraser in 1901 and Digby and Wright in 1910 travelled third class; Morgan Phillips Price, later a Labour MP, met businessmen on their way to Siberia; Maurice Baring, going to report the Russo-Japanese War in 1905, talked war to his travelling companions, and observed Russian literary tastes. Paul Theroux in 1974 suffered the most undesirable of room-mates. Bob Geldof's companions in 1978 were other tourists. Christopher Portway in 1970 met up, by happy chance, with an engine driver and learnt much about the life of the train staff.

Settling Siberia
Bassett Digby and Richardson Wright, 1910

On the immigrant train you see what purports to be civilized humanity at its lowest level. You may not quail at the housing and surroundings of the black races, but you will be unprepared for this degree of degradation among whites.

The first car behind the engine had a sinister aspect. Its windows were heavily barred and a Cossack with a bayoneted rifle stood on the platform at each end. There were hands held out to us from the windows of that car, hands that did not reach far because they were manacled. And the faces behind them – some were young and hopeful, some were hard and dead, it was an *arrestante wagon*.

One cannot travel a day on the railroad of the Kingdom of the

Little Father without encountering these prisons on wheels. Sometimes they form entire trains. This is not be wondered at since thousands of prisoners are shifted about each day. According to conservative offical data, those in transportation in all parts of the empire on one day, February 1, 1909, numbered 30,000.

Before the coming of the railroad the exiles to Siberia were obliged to tramp the entire distance. They and their women folk toiled wearily along the post road. The journey from Tcheliabinsk to Irkutsk and beyond Baikal took, in those days, all of two years. Now it is only a matter of a week or so before they reach their destination.

It was not pleasant to linger beside the *arrestante*. Moreover, the guards were growing uneasy at our presence.

On this immigrant train there were cars for families and cars for single men. The former were simply stables on wheels. In them, three human generations – grandparents, the man and his wife in their prime, the children – and the population of their little farm-yard back in Russia. Three cows and half-a-dozen sheep lie in straw and knee-deep filth, munching hay and green stuff. Bales of hay and straw are stacked to the roof, the home of the wandering fowls and turkeys and ducks. A couple of big lean dogs crouch in a corner.

A Russian log hut has not much furniture. All there is fits comfortably into a box car, even when cows and sheep, backed by a small haystack, swell the family circle. Goods and chattels are disposed here and there, chairs are placed around the rude table, a lamp and even a pair of religious prints hang on the wall. Baby is installed in her swinging cradle at the end of a spring. The peasant cradle in Siberia is like a meat scales and bounces up and down.

The single men's quarters were populated by an intimidating band of ruffians, bare-headed, bare-footed, shaggy-bearded creatures with flat animal faces and wild, bloodshot eyes, one's conception of a shipwrecked crew after ten years on the desert island.

Toward the tail of the immigrant train was a coach of dazzling white – the hospital, a very necessary adjunct to a journey taken under the conditions and lasting from one to three weeks. Through the open door we caught a glimpse of a brass and white enameled bed, a spotless white counterpane across it, and surrounded by all the dainty fittings of a private room in a good metropolitan hospital. The uniformed nurse sat by the window embroidering.

The clean, white, little room; the bleeding, shaggy brutes among their cattle in the filth of the dark, miasmatic box cars next door!

The first people who went out to settle Siberia did not go of their own accord. They came from the town of Uglitch, and against them was the charge of having enraged the Tsar by testifying to the murder of Tsarevitch Dmitri. With them was exiled a bell that had persisted in ringing when the Tsar demanded silence. It was ordered to be flogged, its ears chipped off, and thus mutilated, it was banished to Tobolsk to "do time" with the talkative inhabitants of Uglitch. That was in 1593. There is significance in the incident because it is typical of one of the methods Russia had employed in settling her territory in Asia.

Between 1823 and 1898, according to figures given in Wirt Gerrare's (William Oliver Greener) "Greater Russia," 700,000 exiles accompanied by 216,000 voluntary companions were sent into Siberia. In the same period 187,000 criminal convicts with 107,000 companions went out. Since that time, between 1898 and 1912, 157,000 were exiled to penal settlements in North Russia and Siberia. This, of course, includes the host of *politicals* banished for participating in the Revolution of 1905, though it does not include those who served their sentences in jails. The total number of exiles in 1909 to all parts of the kingdom amounted to 74,000. These are the figures of the Russian police. Ninety per cent of this aggregate went to Siberia. Those in exile in Siberia at this writing number about 40,000. Four thousand were sent into banishment in 1911-12. Alien supporters of the bureaucracy and those who see the country from the windows of the Trans-Siberian express will be apt to dispute these figures. The fact remains, however, that political exiles by the hundreds are to-day being shipped out to a living death. You cannot go down the rivers, the Irtish, the Angarar, the Yenisei, the Amur or the Lena, without seeing barges crowded with exiles *en route* to the prison settlements in the Tobolsk and Yâkutsk Governments on the verge of the Arctic circle.

Russia is offering, at present, great inducements to those of her peasants who will settle in Siberia. It costs nothing to emigrate thither though you do not journey as a convict. Upwards of some quarter of a million peasants come out every year, in consequence, an annual immigration bulking many times larger than that to Canada from England, yet passing unremarked by the rest of the world. A Russian peasant to-day can receive free transportation for himself and family, his flocks and his herds and everything that he hath, from his native village to a settlement in faraway Siberia. And there he will be given land and loaned a grant for a year's farming expenses.

The general attitude of the Siberian toward the convict is that of charity. There are societies to investigate cases of prison abuse and organizations to provide food and little comforts to those confined in jails. So long as a prisoner is in chains under a heavy guard, the Siberian will speak of him as a "poor fellow" and throw him a handful of *kopecks*, but once he is out of custody, he is a "bad man" and in general odium.

The *politicals*, on the other hand, form a nucleus of the best people in Siberia. If they survive their sentences, they come to the towns and settle, opening shops, or studying, and entering into the commercial and social life. The other inhabitants are not inhospitable to them. Few of the intelligent upper middle class families in the Russian Empire are without one or two relatives whose views are reactionary [that is, reacting against the official view] and who have undergone imprisonment for them. For this reason, when they have finished their sentences they are treated kindly by the others.

From this motley collection of immigrants, convicts, nomadic tribes, political and religious malcontents, the Russian Government hopes, in time, to build a united people. There will be Christian and Jew,

Buddhist, Mohammedan and Fire-Worshipper. There will be white folks and yellow, and the tawny of skin, many tribes and many tongues. Siberia is to be to Russia what the West is to the United States and Canada to Great Britain, part of a unified country.

That Siberia to-morrow may take her place in this dream of empire, the Government is tapping its riches and bringing them to the markets of the world by railroads constructed at enormous expense. She is sending out missionaries and building churches to lead the scattered tribes into the fold of the Greek Orthodox Faith and to inject into her own people at least a modicum of respect for the fundamental decencies. She is planting schools and fostering the new generation of those who go thither. She is erecting barracks and establishing troops throughout the land to remind the man in the street that "Russia is for the Russians" and that his will must be the will of the State.

Yet the day is very far off, indeed, when Siberia will take rank among the foremost colonies of the world.

Once a Convict
Lindon Bates Jr, 1910

"How long to Irkutsk? Seven days now, seven years when last I came." The bearded Russian standing in the doorway of the adjoining compartment in the corridor-car of the Siberian Express gazes thoughtfully at the fir-covered slope, whose dark green stands in sombre contrast to the winter snows. The train is slowly climbing the Ural Range, toward the granite pyramid near Zlatoust, on opposite sides of which are graven "Europe" and "Asia." Neighbors with easy sociability are conversing along the wide corridors, exchanging stories and cigarettes, asking each other's age and income in naïve Siberian style.

Regarding the burly occupant of the next stateroom one may discreetly speculate. From sable-lined paletot and massive gold chains you hazard that he voyaged with the traders' slow caravans in the days before the railway – that he was a merchant.

"A merchant? *Optovii?* No, I did not come with the caravans."

From the triangle of red lapel-ribbon, the rank-bestowing decoration, you venture a second guess.

"Perhaps the *gaspadine* made the great circuit to oversee the local administrations? He was a government inspector – *Revizor?*"

"*Chinovnik niet navierno,*" he answers. Most decidedly he was not an official. The suggestion causes him to smile broadly. "I was with the convicts," he says.

Beside the line of rails curves the old post-road winding like a ribbon through the highlands.

"It was by that road we marched. Seven years of my life lie along it."

The train swings through a cleft hewn in the living rock, steep-sided as if the mountain had been gashed with a mighty axe. It rumbles around the base of an overhanging crag while you look clear down over the white valley, with the miles of rolling green forest beyond.

"Was not seven years a long time for the march?" you venture.

"For a traveler, yes; for convict bands not unusual. We went back and forth, now northward a thousand versts as to Archangel, now west as to Moscow, now south as to Rostov. Again and again our troop would split, and part be sent another way. New prisoners would be added, from Warsaw, Finland, Samara. New guards would take charge. Some groups would go to the West Siberian stations, some east to the Pacific and Sakhalin. 1, who was written down for ten years at the Petrovski Works beyond Baikal Lake, with a third commuted for good behavior, had finished my term before I got there."

"Why did they wander so aimlessly?"

"It seems truly as a butterfly's flight, but you others do not know the way of Russia. Very slowly, very deviously she goes, but surely, none the less, to her goal. We each came at last to our place."

At the Stations
Francis E. Clark, 1900

The costumes of the people who flocked to the railway stations were most picturesque and interesting. Red was decidedly the favorite color with the women, and red of every shade and hue. Dull red and bright red, Turkey red and blood red, crimson, magenta, scarlet, and crushed strawberry. Often several, if not all, of these colors were combined in the same costume in a way which, I suppose, would have set the teeth of our fashion-plate ladies on edge, but which, after all, was undeniably picturesque.

The men were usually clad in a loose blouse, belted around the waist, and loose trousers tucked invariably into huge top-boots that reached nearly to the knee. Many times these boots looked to be by far the most expensive feature of the costume. As a Mexican peasant will often wear a sombrero, it is said, worth as much as his coat and trousers and boots, mule and saddle – in fact, the whole outfit combined – so the Siberian peasant clothes the other end of his anatomy with equal care, and even if he must go in rags, will bankrupt himself on his boots.

At all these stations the military were strongly m evidence, as is not unnatural, since this is a military road and the large places are all military headquarters. Everywhere, in the cars and out, officers and soldiers were to be seen. At least every other man you met seemed to be in uniform. But they, too, were invariably polite and showed nothing of the haughty arrogance and devil-may-care air often exhibited by the soldiery of Germany and other army-ridden countries. In fact, I was struck on this railway ride, and on all my other journeys in Siberia, by a certain quiet, dignified, self-contained air that the people displayed. The hucksters are not insistent on your buying their wares. The cabmen are not vociferous. The few beggars are not obtrusive. It is as though the vast, lonely stretches of their homeland had somehow impressed themselves upon the character of the people. The broad reach of upland and prairie, the noble hills, the wide stretch of blue heavens above them, the long, serious winter, the strenuous conditions of their life in this virgin land, have developed a national character, which seems never to have acquired the noise and bustle and artificial "hustle" of city-dwellers. On the whole, it is a pleasing, restful, and, I should think, likable type of character to which these surface indications point. I felt that I was back in the early days of New England, among the Pilgrim fathers and mothers of a new empire, as 1 looked into these earnest, frank, and serious faces, and as I looked I had large hope for the empire they are founding.

The parish priest is also a picturesque and interesting factor of village life. He often came to the station to take part in the one excitement of the day, the arrival of the daily passenger train. He was usually clad in flowing robes of black, with a close-fitting purple cap, while a huge gold or silver crucifix dangled from his neck. His hair is always long and curly. Whether the Greek priests were chosen for their curly hair or indulged in the use of curling-irons when preparing their morning toilet was a question which interested the ladies in our party. They seemed to mingle with their people on terms of benevolent equality, and their kindly and gracious presence shed a benediction even upon the railway platform. They were not averse to having their pictures taken, and the camera enthusiasts "snapped" the holy fathers with the greatest freedom.

The kodak is not unknown in Siberia, but it is evidently much more of a novelty than in the west, and always attracted crowds of staid peasants who wanted to look into the "finder" and see the resultant picture. Some were quite disappointed that the completed picture could not immediately be taken out of the camera and shown to them. One gorgeous railway official, much be-braided and be-spangled with gilt, insisted on having his blackbearded face transferred to the sensitive film. He posed with his most radiant expression, without any exhortation to "look pleasant."

Fellow Passengers
John Foster Fraser, 1901

At one end of the train was the post-waggon, with two brass horns ornamenting its outer panels, and a green painted letter-box, bearing a picture of a sealed letter hanging outside. In other lands the mail is sent by the fastest trains. In Russia it is sent by the approximately slow.

All the other cars were for passengers – one car painted blue for first-class passengers, two painted yellow for second-class, and seven painted green for third-class passengers.

So the majority were third-class, a higgledy-piggledy community of decent-looking artisans and their wives and hordes of children wandering East to settle, and a fair sprinkling of harum-scarum young fellows, always smoking cigarettes and diving into every buffet and shouting for *pevo* (beer), and making mock attempts to pitch one another out of the window.

The mass, however, of my fellow travellers were the *moudjiks*, shaggy men with big sheep-skin hats that gave them a ferocious air wearing rough-spun cloaks and often with sacking tied around their feet instead of boots. The women were fat and plain, though the colours of their dresses were often startling in brilliancy. Gaudy orange was popular.

The lavatory accommodation, even in a first-class car, was limited and as it was for the joint use of both sexes it was a cause of frequent embarrassments.

Ablutions had to be performed singly, and for two hours each morning there was a little crowd of unwashed and semi-dressed men and women standing about the corridor, all smoking cigarettes women as well as men, and each eyeing their neighbour with side glances of distrust lest there was some underhand move to get possession of the lavatory first.

Among the provoking things of life is the way Russian hotels and lavatories on Russian trains supply you with water to cleanse your self. There is no tap to turn on the water, but there is a button which, on pressing with your hand, releases a trickle. The moment you cease pressing the button the supply is cut off. When you are actually pressing the water trails along your elbow and soaks you shirt sleeves, or douses your clothes and boots. The only refuge is selfishness.

So I plugged the basin outlet with a cork and held the button up with a lead pencil till the basin was full. Then I washed. Thus the water supply soon gave out, and I picked up several expletives in Russian from my fellows. And after all, perhaps, they didn't mind Before the end of my journey I came to have a liking for the Russians But in the course of my vagabond life I have been in over thirty different countries and I've never met a people who get along so well on a minimum amount of water for washing purposes as do the Russians.

All the third-class cars were grimy. The woodwork was painted drab inside, but there was not a vestige of cushion.

I spent hours among these emigrants and found them interesting They were horribly dirty, and as they liked to have the window closed, despite the temperature, the cars reeked with odour. They carried all their worldy possessions with them, some foul sleeping rugs and some bundles of more foul clothing, which was spread our on the hard seats to make them a little less hard. Bread, tea, and melons was the chief food. There were great chunks of sour black bread, and at every halt kettles were seized, and a rush made to the platform, where the local peasant women had steaming samovars, and sold a kettleful of boiling water for a half-penny and a water melon as big as your head for a penny.

Besides bread-eating, and scattering half of it on the floor, and munching melons and making a mess with the rind, and splashing the water about when tea-making, there was the constant smoking of cigarettes. A peasant might not be able to afford a hunk of bread, but he had a supply of cigarettes. They are tiny, unsatisfying things, half cardboard tube, provide three modest puffs, and are then to be thrown away. You could smoke a hundred a day and deserve no lecture on being a slave to tobacco.

The emigrants were happy – there was no doubt about that. Though the faces of the men were heavy and animal, guile was not strong about them. The cars rang with their coarse laughter.

Late one night I visited them. At the end of each car was a candle flickering feebly. The place was all gaunt shadow. The men lay back loungingly, like weary labourers caught with sleep in the midst of toil. On the seat beside the man, huddled up, with her face hid in her arms, was the wife. Lying on the floor, with a bundle of rags as pillow, were the children. I had to step over a grey-whiskered old man, who was curled up in the gangway – a feeble, tottering creature to emigrate. Close to the door was an old woman, her face hanging forward and hidden, and her long, bare, skinny arms drooping over her knees. It was all very pathetic in that dim, uncer-tain candle flare. There was no sound but the snore of deep-sleeping men and the slow rumble of the moving train.

I stood looking upon the woeful picture and thinking. Then a child cried, and its mother turned testily and slapped it.

Fellow Passengers
Bassett Digby and Richardson Wright, 1910

The young engineer student took out his paper-covered book of quadratic equations – that bugbear of youth! – and buried his nose in it.

Two huge, fur-capped soldiers strummed away on their instruments, one a *balalaika* – a kind of mandolin with a triangular base – and the other a homemade, three-stringed, barrack-room fiddle. Eventually they came to "Yip-Ai-Addy," to which the Russians have a fearsome set of their own uncouth words, without a single lone "Yip" in the whole thing. The cosmopolitanism of "Yip-Ai-Addy!" The villagers of Holland were reveling in it when we had passed through a few weeks previously, and it had been a high favorite in Antwerp's Shrove Tuesday carnival that spring.

A Tartar woman, clothed like her Russian sisters, but, being a Mohammedan, with a thick white veil from brow to foot, crouched into the corner by her lame husband and young son. Next to them a dreamy-eyed man of thirty with hair five inches long; a man who moved gently and passed much time studying the faces of those about him. There was a sailor of the Russian navy, a linguist who could say "allri" – that convivial password! – and approved of our cigarettes. A bronzed old man, gray-headed but tall and big and active, with the physique of a Klondike miner, was there. With his two young daughters he was returning to Omsk, he told us, from a visit to relatives at Syrzan. By his side sat a veritable Pied Piper of Hamlin. You will recollect his costume in the picture books – a conical green felt hat, a long, pinkish sheep-skin coat, a neck cloth flaming with scarlet and pink and salmon and orange, great pink felt boots to the thigh, boots embroidered with trailing red flowers.

Peasant women, dumpy and uncouth of figure, shawls over their heads, short-skirted and with felt boots to their knees, rubbed shoulders with modernized Russian women who wore hideous military jackets, fur toques tilted over the brow, and with execrably hung skirts. A pair of dwarfs, man and woman, bunched up in sheepskins and gayly tinted shawls, neither of them bigger than a child of twelve, seemed to have walked straight out of a gnomish page of Grimm. By candlelight a tall, mop-headed student, his flat blue cap tilted rakishly over his ear, passed the time teaching a little fellow of ten to learn and repeat, *viva voce*, marked passages in a book of poetry. Such were our fellow passengers.

Businessmen
Morgan Phillips Price, 1911

Mr Phillips Price was, unlike many of the people who wrote about the railway, in Siberia on business and interested in commercial potential.

In the second class of the Siberian express, which runs twice a week from Moscow to the Far East and has every conceivable comfort on board, including a restaurant and a library, the traveller can always find interesting company, if he is that way inclined. Russian officers returning to their regiments in Eastern Siberia are frequently met with. These gentlemen are generally very proud of themselves, nor do they let that pride suffer from lack of advertisement; but they are always most polite and courteous, like ail Russians, and if you treat them like ordinary individuals they will show that under their uniform is a humanity which differs very little from your own. They are sure to tell you all about themselves, and their bravery and their personal contributions to the glory of Russian arms. But they are particularly fond of getting together in the corner of the library on the train in little coteries to enjoy a glass of cognac and a cigar. The place is soon filled with clouds of tobacco smoke and a perfect babel of voices is heard. Language pours forth in such torrents that not only does one fail to understand one word, but one marvels how any human being can manufacture at such a rate even reasonably grammatical sentences. Under such circumstances the Slav is a most communicative creature and bears strong resemblance to other races of the Continent, more particularly to those of Southern Europe. A stolid Englishman, unless he is accustomed to such social gatherings, is out of it. But he can soon become accustomed to them, if he is willing, after he has been in Russia for a short time.

European commercial travellers are generally to be found on the train, usually German, but sometimes a few Enghsh businessmen. The German shows considerably more adaptability to his Russian surroundings than the Englishman, who gives one the impression that he is wishing to be back in England again. But the German is much more at home. He rarely is seen in Russia unless he knows the Russian language more or less thoroughly: he never stands aloof in discussions with Russian fellow-travellers, or dines at a lonely table as if half in fear of contact with them. The Englishman seems to keep himself in the background as much as possible, a failing which is reflected in his order-book.

The Russian commercial men are generally of a free and easy character, altogether more talkative, and, I should think, rather less shrewd than the German type. They are usually the representatives of Moscow or St Petersburg business houses dealing in tea, cotton, goods, wool, hides, etc., visiting their Siberian branch offices or agents at the different trading centres along the railway. I remember talking to one who was travelling for a firm at Irkutsk. He was over middle age and told me that he had done the journey from Irkutsk to Moscow twenty times in his youth, travelling by sledge in winter and cart in summer. In those days the great post road along which everyone travelled followed the line of the present railway. All eastward-bound traffic except the mails went by the river system from Tiumen and Tobol to Tomsk and even up to the Altai by water route alone.

"Siberia," he said, "was an even more isolated region m those days than it is to-day. It was more truly Siberian, and the bureaucratic influence of St Petersburg was less, though," he added, "it must be confessed, we suffered more in those days under irresponsible Government officials who enjoyed almost arbitrary powers. Now, however, the dead hand of St Petersburg is on Siberia. It is becoming Russified and absorbed into the bureaucratic vortex; but how can St Petersburg officials know our wants here? Siberia is for the Siberians." As I listened, I seemed to hear echoes of similar denunciations by Canadian patriots at Ottawa concerning the actions of Downing Street politicians in London.

He seemed despondent about Russia's future, feared the corrupting influence of bureaucratic government, and only smiled when I suggested that possibly they were merely passing through the intermediate phase which might bring better conditions in the end. "If it has done nothing else," I suggested, "autocracy has surely held Russia together, while its evils are diminishing with the march of progress and reform." But he did not reply. Mankind, it seems, is ever ready to see the dark side of a change, and I have often noticed amongst Russians generally, something more than an innate conservatism. A passive apathetic fatalism, characteristic of Eastern minds, dominates them, and, as it were, overshadows their public spirit. And small wonder, when one thinks of the monotony of the country, with its endless plains and melancholy groves of stunted birch, and of the heavy hand of bureaucracy which so effectually stultifies individual effort.

Reading Together
Maurice Baring, 1905

Sometimes [the soldiers] read aloud from some volumes of Gogol and Pushkin I had with me. They began anywhere in the book and stopped anywhere, and always thought it interesting. One of them pointed out to another the famous letter in Pushkin's *Eugenie Oniegin* and said that it was very good. I asked him to read a poem called *Besg,* which is about the little demons that lead the sledge-driver astray in a snowstorm. He said it was good because one could sing it.

The soldiers had not read much. They have no time; but the book I found that they had nearly all of them read was Milton's *Paradise Lost.* When two years ago a schoolmaster in the Tambow Government told me that *Paradise Lost* was the most popular book m the village library I was astonished, and thought it an isolated instance. At a fair at Moscow, during Passion Week last year, I noticed that there were five or six different editions of translations of Milton's poem, with illustrations, ranging in price from 12 roubles to 30 kopecks, and while I was looking at one of them a *muzhik* came up to me and advised me to buy it. "It's very interesting," he said. "It makes one laugh and cry." I now understand why Milton is to the Russian peasantry what Shakespeare is to the German nation. They like the narrative of supernatural events which combine the fantasy of a fairy tale and the authority of the Scripture – the schoolmaster in Tambov also told me that the peasants refused to read historical novels or stories because they said they were mere *Vydumki* (inventions) – some of it makes them laugh, and the elevated language gives them the same pleasure as being in church. It is possible to purchase *Paradise Lost* at almost any village booth. I bought an illustrated edition at a small side station between Harbin and Baikal. Another English author who is universally popular, not among the soldiers but with the officers, the professional and upper and middle classes, is Jerome K. Jerome. He has for the present generation become a popular classic in the same way as Dickens did for the preceding generation. It was possible to buy a cheap edition of his works at every railway station where there was a bookstall between Moscow and Harbin.

Conan Doyle's books were also universally popular. I never came across an officer who had not heard of Sherlock Holmes. The officers used to take in a great quantity of magazines. These magazines consisted largely of translations from the English; from the works of Jerome, Wells, Kipling, Conan Doyle, Marie Corelli, and Mrs. Humphrey Ward. Officers used often to ask me who was the most popular English author. I used to answer that I thought it was Rudyard Kipling. This used to astonish them as they considered him rather childish. But then his stories lost their salt in translation. Mrs. Humphrey Ward, they used to say, was a really *serious* author. Translations of Wells and Conan Doyle used to be running as serials in several magazines at a time.

The Train Staff
Christopher Portway, 1970

Back in my own compartment my new companion turned up trumps. I had heard him ask the attendant my nationality and for a period we sat engrossed in a kind of optical sparring match, looking for an opening. Russians are less inhibited than the British and he got in first. Things began with the usual cross-examination in a *pot pourri* of languages until we found our common denominator to be German. He was not just an engine-driver but an engine-driver *de luxe*. He was going right through to Vladivostok to take over a west-bound Trans-Siberian Express on a steam section of its journey. He was amazed and delighted at my interest in the workings of the line, and though we frequently got bogged down by misinterpretation we had all the time in the world to hammer out the sense of the discussion. In spite of the fact that he was a hero of labour or something equally formidable I found myself liking himself immensely. The coach attendant treated him with great respect, bringing him (and me) copious glasses of tea, despite the fact that he barked at her unmercifully.

From him I learnt the routine of the Trans-Siberian staff. Coach attendants, dining-car waiters, guards, cooks and the like do a full nine-day stint. They then have a week off alternately in Moscow and Vladivostok. The pay is good and so it should be, for they work like beavers. Though there are two attendants to each coach – one off duty and one on – the young girls never let up. At least three times a day they vacuum-clean the compartments and corridor, rub down the walls, and at every halt nobody is allowed off the train until the door handles and brass handholds have been thoroughly wiped clean. Furthermore, there are the never-ending pilgrimages to attend the samovars which, throughout Russia, are coal or wood fired and various additional duties that are thrust upon them at stations. In the crowded dining-car the waiters were on their feet morning, noon and night. They were not very refined, and none too clean, but were always pleasant. I got to know one of them quite well and frequently passed him an English cigarette, which he appreciated greatly. One of their more unpleasant duties was the attempted removal of Russian youths who hogged the tables for card-playing and beer-drinking. Rows were frequent and loud arguments often rent the air. Sometimes the arithmetic of the waiters when they were compiling the bill was, to put it kindly, original. Everywhere in Russia – whether it be on a train, or in the most sophisticated hotel, shop or restaurant – a calculation has to be carried out on an abacus. I could never understand how the thing worked and as they flicked the beads up and down the runners at great speed I think they knew this, and so erred to their advantage! However, I was to learn this to be a very general Russian weakness, and I held it against those long-suffering waiters least of all.

Undesirable Company
Paul Theroux, 1974

Another day, another night, a thousand miles; the snow deepened, and we were at Novosibirsk. Foreigners generally get off at Novosibirsk for an overnight stop, but I stayed on the train. I would not be home for Christmas, as I had promised – it was now the twenty-third of December and we were more than two days from Moscow – but if I made good connections I might be home before New Year's. The tall pale man changed from pajamas into furs, put his equations away, and got off the train. I cleared his berth and decided that what I needed was a routine. I would start shaving regularly, taking fruit salts in the morning, and doing push-ups before breakfast; no naps; I would finish *New Grub Street*, start Borges' *Labyrinths*, and begin a short story, writing in the afternoon and not taking a drink until seven, or six at the earliest, or five if the light was too poor to write by. I was glad for the privacy: my mind needed tidying.

That morning I spent putting my thoughts into order, sorting out my anxieties and deciding to start my short story immediately.

The door flew open with a bang and a man entered carrying a cloth bundle and several paper parcels. He smiled. He was about fifty, baldness revealing irregular contours on his head, with large red hands. He had the rodent's eyes of someone very nearsighted. He threw the cloth bundle on his berth and placed a loaf of brown bread and a quart jar of maroon jam on my story.

I put my pen down and left the compartment. When I returned he had changed into a blue track suit (a little hero-medal pinned to his chest) and, staring through the eye-enlarging lenses of a pair of glasses askew on his nose, he was slapping jam on a slice of bread with a jack-knife. I put my story away. He munched his jam sandwich and, between bites, belched. He finished his sandwich, undid a newspaper parcel, and took out a chunk of gray meat. He cut a plug from it, put it in his mouth, wrapped the meat, and took off his glasses. He sniffed at the table, picked up my yellow sleeve of pipe cleaners, put on his glasses, and studied the writing. Then he looked at his watch and sighed. He monkeyed with my pipe, my matches, tobacco, pen, radio, timetable, Borges' *Labyrinths*, checking his watch between each item and sniffing, as if his nose would reveal what his eyes could not.

This went on for the rest of the day, defeating what plans I had for establishing a routine and eliminating any possibility of my writing a story. His prying motions made me hate him almost immediately and I imagined him thinking, as he tapped his watch crystal between sniffs of my belongings, "Well, there's thirty seconds gone." He had a little book of Russian railway maps. At each station he put on his glasses and found its name on the map. There were about fifteen stations on each map, so he dirtied the pages in sequence with his thumbs before the train moved to a new page, and I grew to recognize from the jam smears and thumbprints on his maps how far the Rossiya had gone. He read nothing else for the rest of the trip. He didn't speak; he didn't sleep. How did he pass the time? Well, he yawned: he could sustain a yawn for five seconds, sampling it with his tongue, working it around his jaws, and finally biting it with a loud growl. He sighed, he groaned, he sucked his teeth, he grunted, and he made each into a separate activity that he timed, always looking at his watch when he had completed a yawn or a sigh. He also coughed and choked in the same deliberate way, studying his eructations, belching with disgusting thoroughness as he exhausted himself of wind in three keys. In between times he looked out the window or stared at me, smiling when our eyes met. His teeth were stainless steel.

I find it very difficult to read and impossible to write with another person nearby. If the person is staring at me over a quart of jam and a crumbling loaf of bread, I am driven to distraction. So I did nothing but watch him because there was nothing but that to do. He was odd in another way: if I glanced out the window, so did he; if I went into the corridor, he followed; if I talked to the boy next door, whose father lay dying among empty champagne bottles, the zombie was at my heels and then peering over my shoulder. I couldn't rid myself of him – and I tried.

Fearing that I would be left behind, I had not gotten off the train at any of the brief stops. But when this haunting creature parked himself in my compartment and shadowed me everywhere, I conceived a plan for ditching him in Omsk. It would be a simple duffilling: I would get off the train and lead him some distance away, and then just as the train started up I'd spring over and leap aboard, pausing on the stairs to block him from gaining a foothold. I tried this in Barabinsk. He followed me to the door, but no further.

Omsk, three hours later, was a better opportunity. I encouraged him to follow me, led him to a kiosk doing a brisk trade in buns, and then lost him. I entered the train at the last minute, believing he was duffilled, but found him back in the comparment sniffing over his maps. After that he never left the compartment. Perhaps he suspected I was trying to ditch him.

He had his own food, this simpleton, so he had no need of the dining car. His meals were extraordinary. He surrounded himself with the food he had brought: a fist of butter in greasy paper, the bread loaf, the hunk of meat and another newspaper parcel of pickles, the jar of jam. He tore off a segment of bread and slathered it with a jackknife blade of butter. Then he set out a pickle and a plug of meat and took a bite of each in turn, pickle, bread, meat, then a spoonful of jam; then another bite of the pickle, and so forth, filling his mouth before he began to chew. I could no longer bear to watch him. I spent more and more time in the dining car.

Fellow Tourists
Bob Geldof, 1978

The train journey from Siberia through Mongolia and across the Gobi Desert down into China had two great advantages apart from the obvious romance and mystery of so epic a trip; it would take me to places where nobody knew me and because it was a holiday, an expedition organized by an international travel company, my only responsibility would be to relax.

I flew with Paula to Moscow to join the rest of the party of travellers. It was like stepping into an Agatha Christie novel. There was a dapper little German with a very clipped haircut who was a senior officer in the West German police force. He and his wife had fled East Germany before the end of the war, leaving behind her entire family. There was a fat American lady, who informed everyone that her name was Verna and added almost immediately that she had been divorced a few times. She spoke constantly of her relationship with her psychoanalyst lover and, within half an hour, had told the entire party what her husband used to do to her and what she did to him. There was a tall middle-aged British gentleman in khaki shorts and sandals called Maurice. His hobby was train-spotting. There was a burly, crew-cut American Army colonel called Dick who had fought in World War Two, Korea and Vietnam and who now ran a military academy; with him was his wife, Lou, a war bride from Manchester. She had adapted to the USA with gusto, as her blue chiffon dresses and diary on the doings of their two poodles testified. There was a young Californian man travelling on his own in orange dungarees and a bad temper. There was an attractive brunette who was a stewardess with Air Canada. There was a very tall young Englishman named John who was a doctor and there was the feckless Paddy pop star and his gorgeous journalist girlfriend. As a travelling party we looked suspiciously like a film-maker's idea of a perfect cross section of humanity. Failing a Murder on the Trans-Mongolian Express the very least we could expect was to be stranded for weeks without food in the Gobi Desert and be forced to draw lots who should be eaten first.

From the beginning the members of the party each exhibited national characteristics to the point of caricature. We dubbed the German Cecil after Cecil B. DeMille. There was never a moment when he was without his cameras. Once I found him filming a brick. He was punctilious, frowned heavily and always complained in a prissy high-pitched voice whenever I was late, which, playing the devil-may-care Irishman, I usually was. Maurice, the train-spotter, was always leaning out of the window and taking notes with schoolboy enthusiasm. Verna, the fat lady, had her entire trunk filled with different brands of patent medicines and nerve tonics. Dick, the colonel, was constantly taking pictures of sand dunes in the belief that there would be a radar station lurking behind one of them, while Lou fretted about the well-being of the two poodles, Esther and Julie, one of whom was due to have her glands done.

7

INTO RUSSIA AND ONWARD FROM
MOSCOW

Some foreign travellers on the Trans-Siberian railway fly to Moscow and
start their journey there. Others travel all the way by train as travellers did
in the past. Baedeker described the routes from England to Russia in 1914:

Routes from England to Russia
Baedeker, 1914

The quickest route from London to St. Petersburg is that followed by
the *Nord Express*, starting from Charing Cross station. This train runs
daily as far as Berlin (viâ *Ostend*, Brussels, Cologne and Hanover), and
twice a week (daily service projected) goes on to St. Petersburg (carriages changed at the frontier-station of Wirballen), taking just under
two days for the whole journey (1745 M.; fare 14*l*. 1s. 8*d.*; ticket from
Sleeping Car Co.). Other routes (change at Wirballen in all cases) lead
viâ *Ostend*, Brussels, Cologne, Magdeburg, and Berlin; viâ *Flushing*,
Wesel, Dortmund, Hanover, and Berlin; viâ *Calais*, Lille, Brussels,
Cologne, Hanover, and Berlin; and viâ *Hook of Holland*, Rotterdam,
Utrecht, Hanover, and Berlin. On Tues. (Mon. from London) the *Nord
Express* connects at Berlin with a train to Warsaw (carriages changed)
and Moscow, which is reached from London in 2 ½ days (1937 M.;
through-fare 14*l. 6s. 3d.)*. Other trains to Moscow (change at Warsaw),
taking 2½-3 days, travel viâ Ostend, Boulogne, Flushing, or Hook of
Holland. The fares by these trains are somewhat lower.

    STEAMERS. To *St. Petersburg* direct from *London* by the *St.
Petersburg Express Line* viâ the Kiel Canal, once weekly in 4 days (fares
7*l*. 10*s*. 5*l*., including meals); direct from *Hull* by the Wilson Line once
weekly in 4V2-5 days (fare 7*l*. 10s.).

    To *Riga* from *London* by the *St. Petersburg Express Line* viâ the Kiel
Canal, once weekly in 4 days (fares 6*l*. 15s., 5*l*., inch meals); during

the winter, if Riga is closed by ice, the service is maintained between London and *Windau* (same fares). From *Hull* by the Wilson Line once weekly in 4 days (6*l*. 15s.).

To *Libau* from *London* by *Det Forenede Dampskibs-Selskab* once weekly (fare *5l*. 15s); from *Hull* by the *Wilson Line* once weekly (fares *5l*. 15s., *2l*. *5s.*).

To *Odessa* from London by the *Westcott and Laurance Line* about every 3 weeks in 28 days, viâ Malta, Alexandria, Piraeus, Salonica, and Constantinople (fares 15*l*. 15s., including food).

Annette Meakin's excitement on reaching Moscow in 1900 is a delight; John Foster Fraser saw a very different place from the city we know today.

The real Trans-Siberian journey as described by Baedeker in 1914 starts at the Yaroslavl Vokzal, the terminus of the Trans-Mongolian, Trans-Manchurian and Trans-Siberian trains. And it is from here that the travellers from the past really make the journey come to life.

The other would-be travellers changed little from those John Foster Fraser described in 1900. Leo Deutsch's departure in 1884 was very different; and Esther Hautzig's train (as far as she knew) did not pass through Moscow in 1941. Once on their way the travellers reported their journeys in many different ways. John Foster Fraser went slowly in 1901; Shoemaker's gloom about eastern Russia in 1902 could be repeated today. As the train crosses the Urals, most travellers, like Shoemaker, are disappointed by the range. Sir Henry Norman, MP, thought little of the Europe-Asia boundary post, describing it as 'a little uninspired monument, some ten feet high, in yellow freestone. It is a simple base with a stone-built, pointed column on top – the sort of thing you may find behind some trees in a park of a nobleman, raised to mark the last resting-place of his favourite fox-terrier.' George Kennan had understood it better in 1897.

Not long after passing the boundary post, Sverdlovsk brings terrible memories, hinted at by Eric Newby, involving P. Gilliard, the Tsarevitch Alexander's tutor, and described by Noble Frankland. The journey settles down with Peter Fleming in 1931; Malcolm Burr's train lost its dining car in 1930; Michael Myers Shoemaker explained the strange train times which still exist today.

139

Life on board the train becomes all important, as John Foster Fraser in 1901 and Digby and Wright described in 1910 – broken for them only by the constant ticket inspections. Some travellers get left behind; a few explore beyond the stations. Digby and Wright found excitement in Omsk – as we soon come to expect from them. Tomsk had been bypassed by the railway and in 1900 Annette Meakin had trouble reaching it. Digby and Wright stayed out later than most travellers and so saw more of Tomsk life. Samuel Turner, like others, had trouble with the hotels, and Lesley Blanch's dressmaker had trouble on the train. Morgan Phillips Price found Krasnoyarsk colourful in 1910, and after the River Yenisey Malcolm Burr and Annette Meakin all found pleasure in the scenery.

To Moscow with Love
Annette Meakin, 1900

The night express from St. Petersburg to Moscow is the best train in Russia; it carries only first-class passengers and is always full no matter what the season of the year. We had secured a sleeping *coupé* by telephone, but a gentleman had bribed the conductor to give it to him instead. A dispute which took up an hour and a half of our journey had to be gone through before we could get possession of it and retire for the night. As it was we owed our victory to a gaily dressed officer who spoke French and came to the rescue. He asked if he might introduce to us a friend of his from St. Petersburg, who was also on the train, "an Englishman, and very rich." After the introduction had taken place the Englishman came and chatted with us in our *coupé;* he had seen from our official letter that we were going to Siberia, and his interest was aroused.

"Siberia is a dreary place," he said. "Are you sure it is wise to go there – two ladies alone?" And then turning to me he said, "It is a venturesome thing under any circumstances, but to start in your state of health is madness. You ought to be shut up in a warm room and not leave it for a week." I felt the truth of these remarks, but it was a case of "a purpose once fixed," and we were already a week late in starting.

Our *coupé* was cold and draughty, but about midnight it began to get warmer, and was too hot to be pleasant when we woke at about five the next morning. Pulling up the blinds we looked out on the most exquisite snow scene it had ever been our lot to witness. Snow was falling in large flakes and must have been coming down steadily for hours. The branches of fir trees, intermingled with those of others still more yielding, were loaded with snow and drooped gracefully under its weight, whilst every few seconds we saw some branch bent right downward and its load scattered and dropped through the lower branches like soft powder. I felt as if I must be Hans Andersen's little girl in the *Ice Queen* travelling through forests of snow! One breath of ice-cold air in that heated carriage would have made it a reality, but this was not to be had, and I fell asleep again with the feeling that I had seen some fairy panorama...

We found Moscow enjoying a regular April day of alternate sun and drenching rain, and people were quite surprised to hear us speak of snow. Moscow is a typical city of the old times and a more picturesque one I never saw. From our hotel windows we looked out on a vast array of coloured roofs, red and green predominating, whilst above all towered many glistening golden cupolas. "These cupolas are always bright and shining," said an English resident, "and yet I never see any one polishing them."

Those who are interested in Moscow should read the late Dean Stanley's beautiful letters written on the occasion of the Duke of Edinburgh's wedding. We all appreciate the wonderful charm of the old Russian capital, but it was Dean Stanley who had the power to bring its beauties before the eyes of those who could not come so far.

> Farewell, dear Moscow; I shall come again
> When I have traversed half the earth and more.
> Tis time to hasten now, for summer's heat
> Too soon might pass, and ice, which half the year
> Doth bind the rivers wide, impede my course.
>
> Farewell.

Moscow
John Foster Fraser, 1901

Now the train had stirred to speed, and with a thump-clang, thump-clang thundered over the metals. Everyone was at the window, with body half hanging out to catch the last gleam of sunlight on the cupolas of the gilt and bedizened Greek churches in wonderful Moscow, the great city of the plain, ancient capital of Muscovy, now blend of garish Tartar and drab European.

St. Petersburg is too modern, too cosmopolitan to please eyes fond of the picturesque. The buildings are usually imitations of something else, and the marble, not infrequently, is painted plaster. There is a T-square arrangement of thoroughfares which is useful, but not pretty. There are the palaces to be seen. But palaces are the same the world over – the same endless galleries, with the same giant vases and gilt bedsteads and slippery floors. Palaces must be uncomfortable to live in. You cannot put your feet on the chairs, and you would probably be decapitated if you dropped cigar ash on the floor.

Moscow is far better. Here you get the clash of east and west. It is a city with distinction and individuality. It is crowded with churches, and the bells, beaten with wooden hammers, boom the day long. The style of the churches is Byzantine, with spiral flowers m flaming reds and greens and yellows. There is the Kremlin, amazingly attractive and strange, with old-time grotesqueness.

As I strolled round the Kremlin, I seemed to slip back to the fantastic architecture in story book pictures, when I believed fairy tales. Had a fair lady appeared with a candle-snuffer hat twice as high as herself and tilted back, and trailing yards of muslin, I would have accepted it all as perfectly natural.

But dovetailing into and wrapping about the Tartar city is the strictly modern. There are horse tramcars in the town, and in the suburbs are whizzing electric cars that shriek as they tear along. There are charming gardens where, beneath the trees and in the candlelight, you may have dinner. You lounge and dawdle and puff your cigarette and imagine you are in the Champs Élysées. You understand the slow tread of civihsation, however, when the orchestra plays "There will be a hot time in the old town tonight" – a belated air, but reminiscent of home.

The Start from Moscow
John Foster Fraser, 1901

The bell in the big stuccoed and whitewashed Moscow station gave a clang. Thereupon brawny and black-whiskered men took off their caps, put their arms about each other's necks, and gave a brother's kiss upon the lips.

There was uproar. The train for Siberia was starting. A bunch of officers, well-set young Russians, in neat white linen jackets with gold straps on the shoulders, crowded a window and laughed goodbyes to friends.

From the windows of the next car were the uncouth faces of peasants, their hair tangled and matted, their red shirts open at the throat. They were stolid and brutal. They were the *moudjiks* emigrating to the mysterious, evil-omened Siberia. On the platform stood their wives – dumpy, unattractive women, in short skirts, and with gaudy handkerchiefs about their heads. They did not understand the language of farewell. With eyes tear-red and with quivering lips they looked upon the hulking hairy men with the sleepy animal faces. But they said nothing.

Three mechanics, drink laden, came reeling along, bumping everyone with their kits. Their eyes were glazed, and they grinned slobberingly and lurched like coal barges beating up against a gale.

The bell clanged twice. Everybody must get aboard now. Once more the brother's kiss. From the car window the young fellows got long and ardent hand grips. They were in the blush of life, and off to Siberia with laughter in their hearts.

Standing a little back was an ordinary soldier, a fair-haired lad, slim and beardless. He was at attention, his heels clapped, his arms taut by his side. He was more than head and shoulders taller than the wizened little woman, her tanned old face all seared with care, who was clutching at him, and kissing him on the tunic and dulling its whiteness with mother's tears. And she was praying a mother's prayer.

Clang, clang, clang! Three times, and all aboard now.

There was a shrill whistle. The cars creaked and moved. Everybody, in the train and on the platform, made the sign of the cross. The perilous unknown was ahead of them.

Some husky shouts of farewell were thrown from the windows, and there was some dimness of eyes. Even a scampering foreigner felt the solemnity of the occasion. But in a few seconds we were in the sunshine of a blazing afternoon, and the train was lumbering on its way to Siberia. It was Thursday afternoon, August 22nd, 1901.

This was not the famous Siberian Express about which so much has been written and which starts twice a week from Moscow, "the fairest jewel in the crown of the Czars," for the far-off city of Irkutsk in Central Siberia, a continent away indeed, 3,371 miles, and which is reached in exactly eight days. The Russians are an enthusiastic and credulous people, and in all the world they think there is nothing so magnificent as this Siberian Express. They come in their hundreds to the Moscow station every Tuesday and Saturday night, the grandees in their furs and their pearls, the red-shirted, matted-haired moudjiks, and the shaven-chinned, American felt-hatted commercial men who have the spice of the West in their veins, and they all stand and gaze at the people Siberia-bound as most of us will look at the first traveller to Mars. Siberia is a long way off. Has anybody ever returned from Siberia? Hearts grow big and words choke. Tears stain many cheeks. Yet laughter and merriment rings over sorrow.

The rich speculators, engineers, Government officials, Germans searching for trade, to build a bridge or to open a store, all travel by this train. It is invariably crowded. You have to sleep four in a *coupé*, two on the seats and two on the improvised bunks above. To be sure of a place you must book weeks ahead.

I had no desire to travel like this. I am a vagabond fond of taking things slowly. So what did it matter if I took eight or eighteen or twenty-eight days to reach Irkutsk? I had no mining concession. It was the last thing in my mind to open a store. Mine was but a mission of curiosity. I wanted to see Russia; I wanted to see the poor, crushed, depraved Russian peasants; above all I wanted to see Siberia. So I did what no wise foreigner had ever been known to do before. I travelled by the ordinary daily train that jogs along slowly, stopping at the wayside stations, picking up *moudjiks*, putting *moudjiks* down. It took very much longer, but there was a charm about that. Besides, it was much cheaper and it required only a very small bribe pressed into the hand of the black-whiskered, astrakan-capped conductor to get a carriage to myself. I spoke four words of Russian, and I carried all my belongings in a couple of bags.

Off to Siberia!

There is something uncanny in the phrase. The very word Siberia is one to make the blood run chill. It smells of fetters in the snow. You hear the thud of the knout of the shoulders of sickened men. For generations, to whisper Siberia in the ear of a Russian has been to make the cheek blanch. No one ever went there but in chains. The haggard men that ever came back told tales that made listeners breathe hard.

We have all supped on Siberian horrors. We shudder, cry out for their ending, but have a gruesome satisfaction in reading about them.

Yet Siberia, the land of criminals and exiles, is pushed into the dusk when we think of Siberia with its millions of miles of corn-growing land, minerals waiting to be won, great tracks of country to be populated.

Siberia is the Canada of the eastern world.

Departure and Farewells
Leo Deutsch, 1884

Our journey began on a beautiful morning in the middle of May when spring had just made its appearance in Moscow. The sunshine was bright and warm, and the scent of spring was in the air. Our mood was by no means in consonance with this aspect of outward things; but most of us elected to go on foot to the station. Our procession must have been an odd sight. Convicts with fettered feet and grey prison garb marched along beside other men and women in ordinary clothes. Most of us were quite young; few had reached middle-age. Of the twelve women in our party three were voluntarily accompanying their husbands to Siberia.

The last violent scene* had depressed us all, and we traversed in silence the quieter streets of Moscow, where the few passers-by paused to look at us, and here and there faces stared from the windows. The station, which we reached after a short tramp, had been cleared of people; only some gendarmes, prison officials, and porters were on the platform. Police were keeping guard all round, and nobody who had not a special order was allowed through to the train reserved for us. When we "politicals" were established in the places assigned to us, a few persons – relations of the prisoners – arrived to say good-bye. The gendarmes would not let them come near to the carriages, and we had to shout our farewell greetings.

"Good-bye! Good luck! Don't forget us!" sounded from the barred windows.

"Keep up your courage! We'll meet again soon!" came back the response.

"Let us sing something together," called out somebody. We had formed a choral society in prison, and now started a song of Little Russia – "The Ferryman." Slowly the train was set in motion, and as we glided away the affecting strains of the beautiful melody accompanied us. Many could not restrain their tears, and sobs were heard which the rattle of the train soon drowned. With faces pressed against the bars of the windows we gazed back at Moscow as long as it could be seen. Then came the outskirts, and then our eyes were refreshed by the sight of broad meadows.

When we halted at the next station there were a good many people on the platform – peasants and workmen. Many of them came up to the carriage windows unhindered, and seemed to be offering things to us.

"Here, take it, in the Virgin's name!" said a voice close by me. I looked out, and was aware of an old peasant woman who held out a kopeck to me.

"I don't need it, mother; give it to someone who does," I said; and felt my heart warm towards this kindly old woman of the people.

"Take it, take it, my dear!" she insisted.

"Well, as a remembrance, then," I agreed and I kept the little copper coin for a long time before I eventually lost it.

* When, told they were going for a medical examination to exempt them from travelling on foot when they reached Siberia, the convicts were forcibly held down while a barber shaved half their heads and the blacksmith riveted on their fetters.

Cattle Truck to Siberia
Esther Hautzig, 1941

Esther Hautzig's journey started in north-eastern Poland.

The car stank of animals and the sun that was shining so benignly over Vilna had made a furnace of this place. Four small square holes high up in the corners of the car and the slivers of space between the filthy slatted walls were all that provided light and air. However, to be fair, cattle on their way to the slaughterhouse did not need a well-appointed car. Even in that twilight, one could see the scars on the floor made by those other beasts as they shuffled uneasily during their journey.

And now we shuffled, some forty of us, as we looked around us. Stood, huddled in the middle of the car, shuffling from foot to foot. No one talked.

There wasn't much to see. The car had been divided in half, leaving a passageway between double rows of makeshift bunks. I was soon to discover that these wooden slabs were to be our beds, our tables, our chairs, our quarters.

No one knew what to do. My father took upon himself the job of leading this bewildered, shocked group of people. A gentle man, yet with a great capacity for making his presence felt and his orders obeyed, he now directed the older people to take the lower bunks and the young ones to climb to the uppers.

The crowd sighed. Victims of tyranny, they needed someone in authority, someone to tell them what to do. They began to select their bunks with a minimum of confusion; no one was in a mood to be fussy. Although Father had told me to climb a rickety ladder to an upper bunk, I stayed below to take a look at our travelling companions, our fellow capitalists. Possibly I imagined that by studying them I would uncover the secret of our own villainy, bring some sanity, however harsh, to this insanity. What I saw only added to my bewilderment; peering out from behind one of my braids, 1 saw nothing more villainous than peasants – women in shawls, men in cotton jackets and trousers that resembled riding breeches. I saw Polish peasants, not a rich capitalist among them; yanked from their land, they had toted their belongings in sacks, in shawls, in cardboard boxes. I saw reflected in their stricken faces our mutual shock.

In what was to be the perpetual twilight of this car, I could see that all the peasants were eating. I looked to see if there were any other children, but the youngest among them were m their late teens. There was no more weeping, but no one was talking either. The only sounds were the smacking of lips, the creaking of the boards, the squealing of the wheels on the rails, and the chugging of the engine. Someone sneezed and never did a sneeze sound more human.

Although it was early morning, the car was hot and the air had become still more foetid, impossible as that seemed. Forty human beings – many of them not recently bathed – were not improving the animal smells. The heat and the stink would become worse and worse.

At last the train stopped. My heart beat violently. Were we there? Were we going to be let out of this inferno?

The bolt was pushed back and the door slid open. Fresh air. Forty pairs of lungs sucked it in. I started to move from the bunk; the objective was the open door. But a soldier hopped on and the door was closed behind him. He carried a pail of water and a ladle. He told us that this water was for drinking and for rinsing our faces. He pointed to a V-shaped opening opposite the door. That was where we were to wash and that opening was our toilet. Our toilet? No wonder my poor mother had resisted suffering this most animallike indignity. The soldier told us that we were to get some food. He opened the door and jumped down on to a muddy platform. We had stopped at a tiny rural station.

Once again the door was closed and bolted.

So we were not to be released. Soon I would give up all expectation of this ever happening.

And so we were on our journey – its route and its destination unknown. In the sinister twilight of that car, time too became an abstraction, but one the grown-ups clung to as if it were all that remained of sanity; they even squabbled over it. "Today must be the Sabbath. Isn't that so?" my grandmother would ask. My mother would disagree, which would upset my grandmother; my father would try to make peace. Everyone would remain uneasy. Was it or wasn't it the Sabbath? No one could tell for sure. Day was grey and night was black, but which day? which night?

The soldiers refused to answer any questions: Where are we? Where are we going? How much longer are we to be kept sealed up? We stopped asking them. But, from the accents of the peasants who sold us their produce, and the place names on the stations. Father was able to give us some notion of our general location. We were travelling though Byelorussia, the Ukraine, central Russia, chugging along about ten or twelve miles an hour, and sometimes staying for hours at a siding, perhaps to let another train go by, sometimes for no apparent reason at all unless it was to prolong our misery.

One day in the third or fourth week of this journey, Father, who had been looking through the hole, called to me to come quickly. I scrambled up beside him and he moved away so I could look out. We were approaching a ridge of mountains. To me, viewing it from a cattle car, the snow-covered peaks, the untouched pine forests were so painfully beautiful I almost wept. Father said with wonder, that these must be the Urals, and that once we passed them we would be in Asia. Asia! I gasped. Asia! Well then, soon I would be seeing women in colourful costumes, bearded men in turbans, and the air would be heavy with the smell of spices. One still dreamed – in vain.

On the other side of the Urals, in Asia, the people at the stations were even shabbier than before, and the soup still smelled of cabbage, not spices. The scenery along the tracks was wilder and more desolate and our stops were less frequent. The daily ration of soup and water was served more irregularly, and it became more difficult and much more expensive to buy bread and milk.

We had been travelling six weeks by my father's count when the train stopped. We were used to long waits and no one thought anything of it. The train would move again; it always had. I heard some commotion and for some reason I thought that perhaps we had developed engine trouble, which would only prolong the journey.

I sat up to look out and, to my amazement, I saw that at this little railway station there was a crowd milling around the train's first cars. Our end was deserted, except for a few soldiers here and there.

Then I saw the doors of the cars being opened, one by one, and people leaping out of them. I still couldn't believe that we, in this car, would be released. I couldn't believe it. But at last our door was opened too.

No soup and water this time. Instead, a soldier read from a document that sounded very much like the one I had heard – was it centuries ago? – in Vilna.

We had reached our destination. We were now in Rubtsovsk in the Altai Territory of the Russian Soviet Federated Socialist Republic of the great and mighty Soviet Union. There were no cheers in that car. Forty people gathered their belongings together, silently, in a near frenzy, as if there were some danger that the door would close again and leave them behind in that car.

The First Day Out
John Foster Fraser, 1901

All through that first hot afternoon the train went grudgingly along, as though it were loath to move Siberia-wards. It was made up of corridor carriages, first class painted blue, second class yellow, third class green.

There must be fifty little towns within fifty miles of Moscow. The train stopped at every one of them, sometimes for only five minutes, more often for twenty, and once for an hour and a half.

Everybody tumbled out on the platform, a motley throng. The men wore the conventional pancake-topped and peaked caps, and without exception top-boots, very soft about the ankle, so the leather clung in creases. The difference in the garb between the better class and poorer class Russian is in the matter of shirt. The better class Russian favours a shirt of soft tone, a puce, a grey, and now and then a white, and he tucks it away like a decorous European. The poorer Russian has a shirt of such glaring redness that, be it as dirty as it might, its flaming hue is never lost. He wears it hanging outside his trousers as though it were an embryo kilt.

As evening closes in and the train bundles over a prairie I see the meagre harvest has been garnered. There are no hedges, hardly a tree. It is possible to see all round, as though to the edge of the world, and that is not more than two miles away. The roads are ribbony tracks across the waste. Far off are awkward V-shaped carts, each making a huge wake of dust. A greyness hangs over the earth. Like the white sails of a ship looming out of a sea haze, a white object pierces the gloom. Nearer you see it is the cupola of the village church, always a massive, imposing building, whitewashed. The village is like a hem of rubbish thrown about.

There is the sadness of the sea on a plain that has no break in the horizon. As night closes a cold wind soughs.

The railway line stretches endlessly behind; it stretches endlessly in front. The train is like a fly trailing across a hemisphere.

Every verst there is a rude cabin made of logs, painted yellow. In each cabin is a peasant, and sometimes a wife and daughter. As the train comes along a little green flag must be shown to prove the line is clear. Each cabin is within sight of the next, a verst ahead, and the one behind. And these little green flags stretch from Moscow to the Pacific coast. It is usually the mother or the daughter who shows the flag. They are stunt women in scant clothing and bare feet. Only occasionally is the little banner unfurled. Generally it is wrapped round the stick and tied, and is held out jusl for form's sake. They are old and worn, many of the banners, and, like some umbrellas look well while folded, but would show a tattered face if unfurled. When darkness comes it is a green lamp that is displayed.

The train creaks and groans and growls. On theengine front are three great lights, as if it would search a path through the wilderness. So we crawl into the night on our way to Siberia.

Eastern Russia
Michael Myers Shoemaker, 1902

All day long northward over these rich plains of Eastern Russia. As night approaches the green-domed churches and green-roofed white villages vanish from sight, and as the stars come out in the heavens the peasants go plodding homeward to their thatched hovels. There is none of the joyousness to be seen which is so apparent with most peoples when the day's work is done. Even the dogs follow their masters with a depressed air, never venturing a solitary bark, much less a wild scurry after a rabbit, or after nothing save their own joyous spirits. With the beggars – and there are few of them – there is none of the wild importunity of Persia. They approach quietly and almost whisper, and at the first sign of refusal retreat as though struck ...

Modern Ufa is a pretty town of fifty thousand people and possesses many schools and churches and two mosques, also some charitable institutions.

Perhaps, as the outer world has rather limited notions as to what Russia does for her people, it would be well to give a list of the institutions of this small city. There are twenty-three churches, two monasteries, one Roman Catholic church, two Mohammedan mosques, twenty-four schools, five with gymnasiums, a geodetic school, a seminary, two clergy schools, a commercial school, a district school, several primary and parish schools, two homes for orphans and waifs, a poorhouse, a free hospital, free lodgings for the poor, an old women's asylum, the Alexander poorhouse for women, an asylum for aged Mohammedans, a free workhouse, a free information bureau for work people, a school for the blind, a division of the Red Cross Society and of the Imperial Humane Society, a society for agriculture, artisans' asylums, a diocesan committee for helping poor clergymen, scientific societies, society of physicians, a committee for public readings, amateur musical and dramatic societies, and a racing society. There are libraries and a museum, – and all these in a town of only fifty thousand people. Can any American city of five times that population show the like? And yet why are these people in the blackness of night? The masses cannot even read. There is more enlightenment, more knowledge, in an American village than in this city of many institutions. Where does the fault lie? What is the reason?

Left Behind
Deborah Manley, 1984

Not long after I had decided to make the journey a friend brought to supper an American adventurer in her mid-seventies. She had made the journey that summer.

On the first day out of Moscow, when the soft-class passengers were only just beginning to get to know each other, the train had stopped at a small station and Lilian and some of the men had climbed down to stretch their legs. Suddenly the train set off, without any apparent warning. The men managed to clamber aboard. Lilian could not, and the train lumbered off out of sight leaving her standing in a white trouser suit, clutching two Kleenexes, out along the tracks far from the station buildings.

She made her way back to the station and appeared as if like a creature from outer space to a quartet of gossiping baboushkas, the only people left on the platform. There was no common language except signs and smiles. They gave her tea, and more tea, and someone must have made a telephone call.

After four hours, many smiles and much tea, a little car came across the vacant Russian landscape. Two men got out and signalled to her to join them. She bade farewell to the *baboushkas* and climbed into the little car with the men. They drove her for miles until they eventually reached an aerodrome. There a little aeroplane stood ready for take off. Lilian was put aboard and the plane flew eastwards. When it landed at another aerodrome, she saw that there was another little car and two more men awaiting her. They drove her to the station and put her back on to the Trans-Siberian train with her party.

Lilian was a committed New York communist. "Of course it was the KGB," she said. "If Russians were lost in the States, the CIA would not help them, of course, " she explained.

Perm: A Russian City
Bryn Thomas

The city of Perm, Pasternak's Yuryatin in *Dr Zhivago*, is the gateway to Siberia. Lying in the foothills of the Ural Mountains it's an industrial city of just over a million people, and the focus of the region. The surrounding area is good for hiking and skiing, and some operators offer white-water rafting trips.

Perm dates back to 1723 and the construction of the Yegoshikhinsky copper foundry, established by VN Tatichev, a close associate of Peter the Great. Its location on two major trading rivers ensured that Perm grew as both an industrial and a trading city. Salt caravans arrived along the Kama River while wheat, honey and metal products from the Urals travelled along the Chusovoy River.

The arrival of the railway in 1878, the discovery of oil in the region and the transfer of factories from European Russia during WWII all boosted the local economy further.

The city's most familiar product is the Kama bicycle which, while rarely seen on the streets of Russian cities, is still widely used in the country. Nearly all of Russia's domestic telephones are made here too, but Perm's most specialized products are the first-stage engines for proton heavy-Lift rockets.

Despite its industrial history Perm has a tradition of culture and scholarship, thanks largely to the revolutionaries, intellectuals and political prisoners exiled here in the 19th century. Perm had the Urals' first university, whose most famous student was Alexander Popov (1859-1905), a local boy (born in nearby Krasnoturinsk) and according to Russian historians, the inventor of the wireless. Popov is said to have demonstrated his invention in 1895, the same year that Marconi proved his concept.

From 1940 to 1957 Perm was called Molotov, after the subsequently disgraced Soviet Foreign Minister who signed the 1939 Ribbentrop-Molotov Pact, dividing up Poland with the Nazis.

Today Perm remains a major centre for culture, administration and business in the region. Its main industries include processing wood from the surrounding forests as well as producing three percent of Russia's oli output. The city is home to several major universities, including Perm State University and the Perm State Technical University. Its sister city is Oxford, England.

First Stages
John Foster Fraser, 1901

The second day out from Moscow it became dull and cold, and a bleak wind scoured the plain. There was little but a sandy wilderness. The gale sounded round the crawling train with eerie moan. It picked up the sand and engulfed us in a brown gritty cloud. Everything in the carriage became thick with dust. It was to be tasted in the mouth and felt achingly in the eyes. To gaze from the windows was to look into a scudding fog that curved thick from the earth and thinned skywards. The train lumbered creakingly.

Suddenly there was a lull. Either we were running out of the sandstorm or it had spent itself. The rain came in great drops, pat, pat, pat, for a long time. Then swish came the deluge, and the carriages rattled with the tattoo of the downpour. When it had passed the air was sweet to breathe. The sun shone clear over the refreshed land. I set about with an old towel to thrash some of the grime from my belongings.

We traversed the Volga in the early afternoon. We went at a crawl over the great square network of a bridge perched high on stone pillars, whilst all devout Russians on the train stood by the windows ardently crossing themselves. It is a wide muddy river, flowing sluggishly, and draining a stretch of country twice as large as Great Britain.

There were two steamers surging a way up, and great islands of rafts were floating down on the tide. When the train halted it was easy to hear the quaint, rhythmic oar-beating songs of the Volga boatmen. They had brought their rafts from the north, beyond Niini Novgorod, the city of the great Fair, and it would be months yet before they reached their journey's end down in the wild country of Astrakan on the Caspian Sea.

Towards sundown we grunted into the bustling town of Samara, and here we had an hour and a-half to wait. The platform was all excitement and uproar. Samara is on the Volga, and a flock of folk from the north and south had come by the waterway to catch the Siberian train.

There were officials to take up posts in the far interior. There were a lot of slothful Tartars, sallow-skinned, slit-eyed, wisp-bearded, who had slouched their way from Mongolia and were now slouching back. There were fine-set Cossacks, carrying themselves proudly, their white sheep-skin hats perched jauntily, a double row of silver cartridge cases across their plum-coloured coats, that fall from the waist like a quilted petticoat, and each wore long riding boots of the softest red morocco. Above all were more peasants, unkempt and ragged, bent beneath bundles, driven hither and thither like sheep, mostly apathetic, crowding into the already overcrowded waggons, and camping on any spare patch of floor.

Again we went snorting across the steppes. Now and then we ran through clumps of darkened pine. Forest fires have been raging during the summer, and hundreds of villages were laid waste. The refugees had hastened to the railway line, expecting there they would receive assistance. For twelve miles at one place there was a string of camps.

It was evening as we passed, and the glow of the camp fires on the lanky peasants, as they stood and shouted while the train puffed by, made a striking scene.

Next morning, as we rolled towards the Urals, the country became undulating and passing pretty. There was plenty of woodland and herbage, and many a time it was easy to imagine a stretch of English scenery on a large scale.

Over the Urals
Michael Myers Shoemaker, 1902

Grey dawn. The train has a rising sensation, and I know that we have reached the Ural Mountains. It is cold, and too early to get up, but a glimpse from my window shows me long lines of low hills splotched with snow. By nine o'clock we are well among the hills, and later on the chain strongly resembles our Adirondacks, but the panorama is dull and sad – there are so many ghostly birch forests.

To the right we have passed Suleya, near which are some of the most extensive iron mines of the Empire – that of Bahal produces four hundred million pounds. Zalatouse, reached at 11 a.m., is another iron centre. The railway zigzags and circles down the mountains. There are no tunnels now in all its vast length. It crosses the tops of all the hills which come in its way. Eighteen versts east of Zalatouse is Urzhumka, the frontier town. There is a pyramid there with Europe on one side and Asia on the other, and there is passed the summit of the Ural Mountains, never more than hills so far as altitude is concerned. Weary of the interminable steppes of Russia, the earth seems to have sighed itself up into long ridges, only to settle again wearily into the far more interminable steppes of Siberia.

But these expressions of weariness continue for some time longer. We are passing a train of the fifth class just now. I asked the conductor if it was not fourth class, but he replied, "No, fifth; fourth would have windows." These are freight cars fitted up with wooden bunks and crammed to overflowing with emigrants for Siberia.

As I looked out in the grey of morning today, we were passing, as I supposed, one of these trains, but I noticed that the windows were barred and the faces crowding to them shadowed with even more than the usual allotment of sadness observable in Russia, – a prison train, with all that that means in the dominions of the Czar.

Over the Urals
George Kennan, 1891

On Thursday, June 11, at half-past nine o'clock in the evening, we left Perm by the Ural Mountain railroad for Ekaterínburg. As we were very tired from two days spent almost wholly in walking about the streets of the former city, we converted two of the extension seats of the railway carriage into a bed, and with the help of our blankets and pillows succeeded in getting a very comfortable night's rest.

When I awoke, about eight o'clock on the following morning, the train was standing at the station of Biser near the summit of the Uráls. The sun was shining brightly in an unclouded sky; the morning air was cool, fresh, and laden with the odor of flowers and the resinous fragrance of mountain pines; a cuckoo was singing in a neighboring grove of birches; and the glory of early summer was over all the earth. Frost made hasty botanical researches beside the railroad track and as far away from the train as he dared to venture, and came back with alpine roses, daisies, wild pansies, trollius, and quantities of other flowers to me unknown.

The scenery of the Urál where the railroad crosses the range resembles in general outline that of West Virginia where the Baltimore and Ohio railroad crosses the Alleghanies; but it differs somewhat from the latter in coloring, owing to the greater preponderance in the Urál of evergreen trees. All the forenoon, after leaving Biser, the train swept around great curves in a serpentine course among the forest-clad hills, sometimes running for an hour at a time through a dense larch wood, where there was not a sign of human life; sometimes dashing past placer mining camps, where hundreds of men and women were at work washing auriferous gravel; and sometimes coming out into beautiful park-like openings diversified with graceful clumps of silver birch, and carpeted with turf almost as smooth and green as that of an English lawn. Flowers were everywhere abundant. Roses, dandelions, violets, wild strawberries, and lilies of the valley were in blossom all along the track, and occasionally we crossed an open glade in the heart of the forest where the grass was almost entirely hidden by a vivid sheet of yellow trollius.

We were greatly surprised to find in this wild mining region of the Urál, and on the very remotest frontier of European Russia, a railroad so well built, perfectly equipped, and luxuriously appointed as the road over which we were travelling from Perm to Ekaterinburg. The stations were the very best we had seen in Russia; the road-bed was solid and well ballasted; the rolling stock would not have suffered in comparison with that of the best lines in the empire; and the whole railroad property seemed to be in the most perfect possible order. Unusual attention had been paid evidently to the ornamentation of the grounds lying adjacent to the stations and the track. Even the *verstposts* were set in neatly fitted mosaics three or four feet in diameter of colored Urál stones. The station of Nizhni Tagil, on the Asiatic slope of the mountains, where we stopped half an hour for dinner, would have been in the highest degree creditable to the best railroad in the United States. The substantial 10 feet wide building extending along the whole front, was tastefully painted in shades of brown and had a red sheet-iron roof. It stood in the middle of a large, artistically planned park or garden, whose smooth, velvety greensward was broken by beds of blossoming flowers and shaded by the feathery foliage of graceful white-stemmed birches; whose winding walks were bordered by neatly trimmed hedges; and whose air was filled with the perfume of wild roses and the murmuring plash of falling water from the slender jet of a sparkling fountain.

The dining-room of the station had a floor of polished oak inlaid in geometrical patterns, a high dado of dark carved wood, walls covered with oak-grain paper, and a stucco cornice in relief. Down the center of the room ran a long dining-table, beautifully set with tasteful china, snowy napkins, high glass epergnes and crystal candelabra, and ornamented with potted plants, little cedar trees in green tubs, bouquets of cut flowers, artistic pyramids of polished wine-bottles, druggists' jars of colored water, and an aquarium full of fish, plants, and artificial rock-work. The chairs around the table were of dark hard wood, elaborately turned and carved; at one end of the room was a costly clock, as large as an American jeweler's "regulator," and at the other end stood a huge bronzed oven, by which the apartment was warmed in winter. The waiters were all in evening dress, with low-cut waistcoats, spotless shirt-fronts, and white ties; and the cooks, who filled the waiters' orders as in an English grill-room, were dressed from head to foot in white linen and wore square white caps. It is not an exaggeration to say that this was one of the neatest, most tastefully furnished, and most attractive public dining-rooms that I ever entered in any part of the world; and as I sat there eating a well-cooked and well-served dinner of four courses, I found it utterly impossible to realize that I was in the unheard-of mining settlement of Nizhni Tagil, on the Asiatic side of the mountains of the Ural.

Early in the evening of Friday, June 12, we arrived at Ekaterinburg.

The traveler who has not studied attentively the geography of this part of the Russian empire is surprised to learn, upon reaching Ekaterinburg, that although he has passed out of Europe into Asia he has not yet entered Siberia. Most readers have the impression that the boundary of European Russia on the east is everywhere coterminous with that of Siberia; but such is by no means the case. The little stone pillar that marks the Asiatic line stands beside the railway track on the crest of the Ural mountan divide; while the pillar that marks the Siberian line is situated on the Ekaterínburg-Tiumen post road, more than a hundred miles east of the mountains. The effect of this arrangement of boundaries is to throw a part of the European province of Perm into Asia, and thus to separate Siberia from Russia proper.

The Trans-Siberian Time Warp
Bryn Thomas, 2007

During his trip on the Trans-Siberian Railway in 1902, Michael Myers Shoemaker wrote: 'There is an odd state of affairs as regards time over here. Though Irkutsk is 2,400 miles from St Petersburg, the trains all run on the time of the latter city, therefore arriving in Irkutsk at 5pm when the sun would make it 9pm. The confusion en route is amusing; one never knows when to go to bed or when to eat. Today I should make it now about 8.30 – these clocks say 10.30 and some of these people are eating their luncheon.'

You will be pleased to know that this at least has not changed. The entire system operates on Moscow Time (same as St Petersburg Time), and all the timetables list Moscow Time. Crossing the border from China after breakfast, the first Russian station clock you see tells you that it's one o'clock in the morning! The restaurant car, however, runs on local time. Passing through as many as seven time-zones, things can get rather confusing. The answer is to ignore Moscow Time and reset your watch as you cross into new time zones. A watch that shows the time in two zones would be handy; otherwise just add or subtract the appropriate number of hours every time you consult the timetable in the train corridor.

Getting enough exercise on so long a journey can be a problem and most people make full use of their brief stops: 'We even managed to persuade our carriage attendant (never seen out of her pink woolen hat) to take part in our efforts to keep fit on the platforms. However, if your attendant indicates that you shouldn't get off at a stop, take her advice. At some stops another train pulls in between the platform and yours, making it almost impossible for you to get back on board. Always carry your passport and valuables with you in case you miss your train.

Europe: Asia
George Kennan, 1891

No other boundary post in the world has witnessed so much human suffering, or been passed by such a multitude of heart-broken people. More than 170,000 exiles have traveled this road since 1878, and more than half a million since the beginning of the present century. In former years, when exiles were compelled to walk from the places of their arrest to the places of their banishment, they reached the Siberian boundary post only after months of toilsome marching along muddy or dusty roads, over forest-clad mountains, through rain-storms or snow-storms, or in bitter cold. As the boundary post is situated about half-way between the last European and the first Siberian *étape*, it has always been customary to allow exile parties to stop here for rest and for a last good-by to home and country. The Russian peasant, even when a criminal, is deeply attached to his native land; and heart-rending scenes have been witnessed around the boundary pillar when such a party, overtaken, perhaps, by frost and snow in the early autumn, stopped here for a last farewell. Some gave way to unrestrained grief; some comforted the weeping; some knelt and pressed their faces to the loved soil of their native country, and collected a little earth to take with them into exile; and a few pressed their lips to the European side of the cold brick pillar, as if kissing good-by forever to all that it symbolized.

At last the stern order 'Stróisa!' [Form ranks!] from the under officer of the convoy put an end to the rest and leave-taking, and at the word "March!" the gray-coated troop of exiles and convicts crossed themselves hastily all together, and, with a confused jingling of chains and leg-fetters, moved slowly away past the boundary post into Siberia.

Until recently the Siberian boundary post was covered with brief inscriptions, good-bys, and the names of exiles scratched or penciled on the hard cement with which the pillar was originally overlaid. At the time of our visit, however, most of this hard plaster had apparently been pounded off, and only a few words, names, and initials remained. Many of the inscriptions, although brief, were significant and touching. In one place, in a man's hand, had been written the words "Prashchái Márya!" [Goodby, Mary!] Who the writer was, who Mary was, there is nothing now left to show; but it may be that to the exile who scratched this last farewell on the boundary pillar "Mary" was all the world, and that in crossing the Siberian line the writer was leaving behind him forever, not only home and country, but love.

After picking a few flowers from the grass at the base of the boundary pillar, we climbed into our carriage, said "Good-by" to Europe, as hundreds of thousands had said good-by before us, and rode away into Siberia.

Life Aboard
Peter Fleming, 1933

Everyone is a romantic, though in some the romanticism is of a perverted and paradoxical kind. And for a romantic it is, after all, something to stand in the sunlight beside the Trans-Siberian Express with the casually proprietorial air of the passenger, and to reflect that that long raking chain of steel and wood and glass is to go swinging and clattering out of the West into the East, carrying you with it. The metals curve glinting into the distance, a slender bridge between two different worlds. In eight days you will be in Manchuria. Eight days of solid travel: none of those spectacular but unrevealing leaps and bounds which the aeroplane, that agent of superficiality to-day makes possible. The arrogance of the hardbitten descends on you. You recall your friends in England, whom only the prospect of shooting grouse can reconcile to eight hours in the train without complaint. Eight *hours* indeed ... you smile contemptuously.

Besides, the dignity, or at least the glamour of trains has lately been enhanced. *Shanghai Express, Rome Express, Stamboul Train* – these and others have successfully exploited its potentialities as a setting for adventure and romance. In fiction, drama, and the films there has been a firmer tone in Wagons Lits than ever since the early days of Oppenheim. Complacently you weigh your chances of a foreign countess, the secret emissary of a Certain Power, her corsage stuffed with documents of the first political importance. Will anyone mistake you for No. 37, whose real name no one knows, and who is practically always in a train, being 'whirled' somewhere? You have an intoxicating vision of drugged liqueurs, rifled dispatch-cases, lights suddenly extinguished, and door-handles turning slowly under the bright eye of an automatic... .

You have this vision, at least, if you have not been that way before. I had. For me there were no thrills of discovery and anticipation. One hears of time standing still; in my case it took two paces smartly to the rear. As I settled down in my compartment, and the train pulled out through shoddy suburbs into a country clothed in birch and fir, the unreal rhythm of train-life was resumed as though it had never been broken. The nondescript smell of the upholstery, the unrelenting rattle of our progress, the tall glass of weak tea in its metal holder, the unshaven jowls and fatuous but friendly smile of the little attendant who brought it – all these unmemorable components of a former routine, suddenly resurrected, blotted out the interim between this journey and the last. The inconsequent comedy of two years, with the drab or coloured places, the cities and the forests, where it had been played, became for a moment as though it had never been. This small, timeless, moving cell I recognized as my home and my doom. I felt as if I had always been on the Trans-Siberian Express.

The dining-car was certainly unchanged. On each table there still ceremoniously stood two opulent black bottles of some unthinkable wine, false pledges of conviviality. They were never opened, and rarely dusted. They may contain ink, they may contain the elixir of life. I do not know. I doubt if anyone does.

Lavish but faded paper frills still clustered coyly round the pots of paper flowers, from whose sad petals the dust of two continents perpetually threatened the specific gravity of the soup. The lengthy and trilingual menu had not been revised; 75 per cent of the dishes were still apocryphal, all the prices were exorbitant. The cruet, as before, was of interest rather to the geologist than to the gourmet. Coal dust from the Donetz Basin, tiny flakes of granite from the Urals, sand whipped by the wind all the way from the Gobi Desert – what a fascinating story that salt-cellar could have told under the microscope. Nor was there anything different about the attendants. They still sat in huddled cabal at the far end of the car, conversing in low and disillusioned tones, while the *chef du train*, a potent gnome-like man, played on his abacus a slow significant tattoo. Their surliness went no deeper than the grime upon their faces; they were always ready to be amused by one's struggles with the language or the cooking. Sign-language they interpreted with more eagerness than apprehension: as when my desire for a hard-boiled egg – no easy request, when you come to think of it, to make in pantomime – was fulfilled, three-quarters of an hour after it had been expressed, by the appearance of a whole roast fowl.

The only change of which I was aware was in my stable-companion. Two years ago it had been a young Australian, a man much preoccupied with the remoter contingencies of travel. 'Supposing', he would muse, 'the train breaks down, will there be danger of attack by wolves?' When he undressed he panted fiercely, as though wrestling with the invisible Fiend; he had a plaintive voice, and on his lips the words 'nasal douche' (the mere sound of Siberia had given him a cold) had the saddest cadence you can imagine. This time it was a young Russian, about whom I remember nothing at all. Nor is this surprising, for I never found out anything about him. He spoke no English, and I spoke hardly any Russian. A phrase-book bought in Moscow failed to bridge the gap between us. An admirable compilation in many ways, it did not, I discovered, equip one for casual conversation with a stranger. There was a certain petulance, a touch of the imperious and exorbitant, about such observations as: 'Show me the manager, the assistant manager, the water closet, Lenin's Tomb', and 'Please to bring me tea, coffee, beer, vodka, cognac, Caucasian red wine, Caucasian white wine'. Besides, a lot of the questions, like 'Can you direct me to the Palace of the Soviets?' and 'Why must I work for a World Revolution?' were not the sort of things I wanted to ask him; and most of the plain statements of fact – such as '1 am an American engineer who loves Russia' and 'I wish to study Architecture, Medicine, Banking under the best teachers, please' – would have been misleading. I did not want to mislead him.

So for two days we grinned and nodded and got out of each other's way and watched each other incuriously, in silence. On the second day he left the train, and after that I had the compartment to myself.

There is a great deal to be said against trains, but it will not be said by me. I like the Trans-Siberian Railway. It is a confession of weakness, I know; but it is sincere.

You wake up in the morning. Your watch says its eight o'clock; but you are travelling east, and you know that it is really nine, though you might be hard put to it to explain why this is so. Your berth is comfortable. There is no need to get up, and no incentive either. You have nothing to look forward to, nothing to avoid. No assets, no liabilities. Most men, though not the best men, are happiest when the question 'What shall I do?" is supererogatory. (Hence the common and usually just contention that 'My schooldays were the happiest days of my life'.) That is why I like the Trans-Siberian Railway. You lie in your berth, justifiably inert. Past the window plains crawl and forests flicker. The sun shines weakly on an empty land. The piles of birch logs by the permanent way – silver on the outside, black where the damp butts show – give the anomalous illusion that there has been a frost. There is always a magpie in sight.

You have nothing to look at, but no reason to stop looking. You are living in a vacuum, and at last you have to invent some absurdly artificial necessity for getting up: 'fifteen magpies from now', or 'next time the engine whistles'. For you are inwardly afraid that without some self-discipline to give it a pattern this long period of suspended animation will permanently affect your character for the worse.

So in the end you get up, washing perfunctorily in the little dark confessional which you share with the next compartment, and in the basin for which the experienced traveller brings his own plug, because the Russians, for some reason connected – strangely enough – with religion, omit to furnish these indispensable adjuncts to a careful toilet.

Then, grasping your private pot of marmalade, you lurch along to the dining-car. It is now eleven o'clock, and the dining-car is empty.

You order tea and bread, and make without appetite a breakfast which is more than sufficient for your needs. The dining-car is almost certainly stuffy, but you have ceased to notice this. The windows are always shut, either because the weather is cold, or because it is warm and dry and therefore dusty. (Not, of course, that the shutting of them excludes the dust. Far from it. But it is at least a gesture; it is the best that can be done.)

After that you wander back to your compartment. The *provodnik* has transformed your bed into a seat, and perhaps you hold with him some foolish conversation, in which the rudiments of three languages are prostituted in an endeavor to compliment each other on their simultaneous mastery. Then you sit down and read. You read and read and read. There are no distractions, no interruptions, no temptations to get up and do something else; there is nothing else to do. You read as you have never read before.

And so the day passes. If you are wise you shun the regulation meal at three o'clock, which consists of five courses not easily to be identified, and during which the car is crowded and the windows blurred with steam. I had brought with me from London biscuits and potted meat and cheese; and he is a fool who does not take at least some victuals of his own. But as a matter of fact, what with the airless atmosphere and the lack of exercise, you don't feel hungry on the Trans-Siberian Railway. A pleasant lassitude, a sense almost of disembodiment, descends on you, and the food in the dining-car which, though seldom really bad, is never appetizing and sometimes scarce, hardly attracts that vigorous criticism which it would on a shorter journey.

At the more westerly stations – there are perhaps three stops of twenty minutes every day – you pace the platforms vigorously, in a conscientious British way. But gradually this practice is abandoned. As you are drawn further into Asia, old fetishes lose their power. It becomes harder and harder to persuade yourself that you feel a craving for exercise, and indeed you almost forget that you ought to feel this craving. At first you are alarmed, for this is the East, the notorious East, where white men go to pieces; you fear that you are losing your grip, that you are going native. But you do nothing about it, and soon your conscience ceases to prick and it seems quite natural to stand limply in the sunlight, owlish, frowsty, and immobile, like everybody else.

At last evening comes. The sun is setting somewhere far back along the road that you have travelled. A slanting light always lends intimacy to a landscape, and this Siberia, flecked darkly by the tapering shadows of trees, seems a place at once more friendly and more mysterious than the naked non-committal flats of noon. Your eyes are tired, and you put down your book. Against the grey and creeping distances outside memory and imagination stage in their turn the struggles of the past and of the future. For the first time loneliness descends, and you sit examining its implications until you find Siberia vanished and the grimy window offering nothing save your own face, foolish, indistinct, and as likely as not unshaved. You adjourn to the dining-car, for eggs.

No Dining Car
Malcolm Burr, 1930

Early in the morning of the Monday we crossed the Urals. They are not an impressive range and there are neither great altitudes nor alpine scenery. They are but grassy uplands covered with forests of pine and birch, but unrivalled in their mineral wealth and for the splendid climate. I succeeded after a vigorous argument in overcoming the natural repugnance of Naum Moiseivich to opening the window and revelled in the pure morning air. No wonder the Urals are one of the most health-giving spots in the world. It was like breathing dry champagne. But we were across all too soon and ran into Ekaterinburg, once famous as the centre of the mining industry of the Urals, to-day infamous under the name of Sverdlovsk, after the organizer of the murder of the imperial family, in "honour" of whom the town has been renamed.

As my companion and I were strolling up and down the platform he eyed the dining-car with the air of a connoisseur.

"That car will not reach Irkutsk," he exclaimed dogmatically.

"Why not?" I asked him.

He pointed out a mechanical defect, and, surely enough, they soon uncoupled it and left it behind, so that we proceeded on our long journey without a restaurant. I was somewhat dismayed at the idea, though really we lost little. The meals had been both dear and dirty, and we should be able to buy food at wayside stations along the road. Catering became in fact the chief amusement of the day, and zest was added by the irregular hours at which we arrived at the stations for meals; when it was not until the evening our appetites were unbridled. The chief disadvantage was that we were caught unprepared and had no plates, forks or spoons; pocket-knives we had and tumblers were available, and of course in a Russian train tea is on tap at any hour of the day or night. The station markets were allotted a substantial area on the platforms, arranged in crescent-shaped buildings open at the front; behind the counter were peasants selling their goods classified in groups; at one end large stacks of bread, black, brown and white, *kolachi* or rolls and great loaves in abundance and variety and all excellent; another group would be selling bottles carefully labelled "boiled milk," but a doctor in the train warned us against the danger of dysentery lurking here, in spite of the perfunctory precaution; at another, honey in homemade jugs of the wood and bark of the birch, a design familiar throughout Siberia under the name of *tuyess*. Another again would have smoked sterlet, perch, pike and ide or burbot, the latter a rich and juicy fish, also *keta*, the dog salmon of the Pacific, which makes such handsome big pink caviar; then there were great cauldrons simmering over wood fires with cutlets, tongues, whole chickens and ducks and game, as hazel hen, hares, blackcock and capercailíe. At others there were eggs at fivepence a dozen, and at others fruit as apples, bilberries and whortleberries and great water-melons, an excellent investment on a railway journey.

All this abundance seemed strange and unexpected in the land of famine. It was but a few years since something like nine million people had died of starvation in South Russia, and in the previous year there had been a failure of crops when two or three million perished – a mere trifle in Russia, hardly worth mention in the European press, even if the news leaked through. But there was no sign of hunger here. The difference is that this was Siberia, and in that land of vast distances and poor communications one quarter may revel in abundance while another starve.

Beyond the Urals
John Foster Fraser, 1901

I saw Chelyabinsk under difficulties. We were all turned out of the train – which was an excellent thing to do, for the cars were in need of a wash and brush up – and there was a wait of five hours before another train was got ready in which we could proceed to Central Siberia.

It was raining in torrents. Everybody had an enormous excess of baggage, and as there is no left-luggage office at Chelyabinsk everything was carried or dragged or thrown into the buffet – all except the belongings of the emigrants, who camped on the platform, sitting on bundles and spreading their evil-odoured sheepskin coats to act as waterproofs.

I have joined in a scramble for food at an English railway station, but that was the decorum of a court reception compared with the fight at Chelyabinsk. Though there was so long to wait, we were all in as much hurry as if the train started within ten minutes.

I would have fared badly had I not made the acquaintance of a pleasant, stout and elderly baroness, who was on her way to visit her married son living at Ekaterinburg, on the eastern slopes of the Urals. I had seen her for half a day standing in the corridor smoking cigarettes. The car corridor has no extra width, and when I tried to pass the lady we jammed. It was awkward, and I grunted.

'Ah, you are an Englishman,' she exclaimed. Then with a wrench we tore ourselves asunder; I raised my hat and she bowed, and we exchanged cards.

We became capital friends. I presented her with some English novels I had in my bag, and she presented me with a tin teapot. It is usual for everyone to make their own tea on Russian trains. She also gave me tea and sugar. Thereupon I proceeded to make the floor of my carriage in a mess with crunched sugar, and my papers became disreputably marked with tea stains. Amateur housekeeping in a railway carriage has its drawbacks.

My thanks were as profuse as I could make them, and I asked the baroness how I could relieve my obligations. "Give me a box of your

English wax matches," she said; and I gave her the only box I had. An hour later she sent me fifty of her cigarettes.

She told me she loved the English. She wore an English cloth cap and carried a stick, and was much like an English country gentlewoman.

When she found the buffet crowded at Chelyabinsk she took it as a personal insult, called the manager, and spoke to him vigorously. So we got a special table, and though we had been informed there wasn't another chair in the place two must have been speedily manufactured, for they were forthcoming instantly. I saw her to her train for Ekaterinburg, and we parted with expressions of mutual esteem.

Then I explored Chelyabinsk.

Conceive a field in which a cattle show has been held for a week, and it has been raining all the week. That will give you some idea of Chelyabinsk. The buildings were sheds, and the roadways mire.

And yet it is a place that has been muttered m tears for centuries. All convicts and exiles for Siberia were marched over the Urals to Chelyabinsk. It was the dividing station, one gang going to the arid north, and another gang going to the mines in the far east; others condemned to labour on the waterways – all expelled from Russia, with the piled-up horrors of Siberia before them.

Comparatively speaking, the emigrants in the autumn are few. I talked to one group. There was an old man and an old woman, a youngish woman, and three children, the eldest not more than four years. They were sitting in the drenching rain, the elders munching black bread and onions, and the two children that could toddle dancing in a muddy puddle as happy as could be. I asked the old man if he hadn't got too far on in life to come to Siberia to face its fierce winters. He said he and his wife were going to live with their son, who had come to Siberia in the spring with a little money. The Government had given him land. Now he had a home ready, and he had sent for his wife and children and his mother and father.

Again it was a fight, like an excursion crowd, climbing into the train bound for the interior of Siberia. There were more folks than there was room for. I believe I was the only first-class passenger, but the wily second-class passengers, who understood the art of travelling, made no haste, allowed all the second-class places to be filled up, and then insisted, as they are entitled to do under Russian railway regulations, on travelling first. They stormed my particular stronghold, but as foreigners are supposed to ooze roubles, a six-foot-four conductor cleared them out and locked me in.

We were all in our places a full hour before the train started. I kicked my toes to keep myself warm. It was a bedraggled leaden day, and my window looked upon the goods yard, where stood rows of waggons. It was like a delay on a branch line in a colliery district.

At last came the clang of the bell, twice: "Get ready," three times: "Off you go," and the engine, with three preparatory shrieks, lumbered off with us across two thousand miles of land so flat that there wasn't a rise the whole distance that would serve as a teeing ground at golf.

The country was featureless. Here and there were clumps of silver-limbed larch which broke the monotony. But we ran for hours at a time with little else taller than grass blades between us and the horizon.

If you have been on a steamer in a dead calm, and seen nothing but a plain to the edge of the world, and heard nothing but the thump-thump of the engines, you will understand exactly how traversing Western Siberia impresses one: nothing but sun-scorched grass and deep grunting of the engine surging through the wilderness. There is one stretch of line without a yard of curve for eighty miles.

The line is raised about a foot above the level of the land, and there is no fence to protect it. I could see from the digging on either side, to obtain this slight bank, that the soil was black and rich. What the British corn-grower will say when Siberia is populated and given up to the production of cheap wheat he himself best knows.

It is a wonderful grazing country. Of that there is no doubt. I saw herds of horses and cows. One young Siberian, whipping up cattle, challenged our train to a race. That he won, amid the plaudits of us all, does not prove so much the swiftness of his horses as the slowness of our train. Fifteen miles an hour was its top speed.

Very seldom was a house to be seen except the guard huts stationed every verst. All the men in charge were good-conduct convicts. The stations were at long intervals, perhaps every twenty miles. There was, of course, the station building, neat and yellow painted. There was the inevitable water tower. In the background were one or two official-looking, yellow-hued, one-storey houses. That was all.

No, not all. For, as it is the proper thing for everybody to carry their own tea and sugar, there was on every platform a great cauldron of a samovar, where rich and poor alike could help themselves to hot water. Also, on one side was a long covered stall, where the local peasantry – where they came from I've no idea – sold cooked fowls, hot or cold, as you liked, for a shilling, very hot dumplings, with hashed meat and seasoning inside, for twopence-halfpenny, huge loaves of new made bread, bottles of beer, pats of excellent butter, pails of milk, apples and grapes, and fifty other things. Passengers loaded themselves with provender at the stall, and ate picnic fashion in the carriages until the next station was reached. There it all began over again.

Wasn't a journey through this great lone land dreary? Of course it was. The eye began to ache with the monotony of the horizon line, and peasants ceased to be picturesque because every group at every station was exactly like the other groups.

Yet, as the days passed and we went rolling on and on across a sea of prairie, with nothing before but two threads of steel stretching over the edge of the world, and nothing behind but two threads of steel stretching back to eternity, a glimmer of consciousness how big Siberia is, and what this thread of railway means to Russia, crept into the mind.

I got tired reading my novels. So I went and sat in the gangway and under the spell of the wide waste – so that the train, while crunching and grunting along, always seemed to be in the very middle of it – my thoughts strayed vagrant through all I had read about the mysterious land of Siberia. And there sprung up the name of Yermak. Yermak was a kind of Alfred the Great, with a difference. In the beginning he, like many other empire-founders, was a freebooter. He was a pirate of the Volga. He seized boats and their contents, and cut the throats of the crews. It was, therefore, hut natural he and his companions were chased by the troops of Ivan the Terrible to the Urals. Yermak, however, was befriended by a great merchant, who knew there were wonderful sables to be got on the far side of the hills. It was on New Year's Day, 1581, that Yermak and his Cossacks set off. For years they fought and raided and traded. All his men were killed in time, and Yermak himself was drowned in the Irtish while trying to escape an old Tartar enemy. But he had captured Siberia for Russia. Ivan, who had despatched soldiers to hang him, sent, before the end came, the Imperial pardon, the title of prince, and a robe that had rested on his own shoulders. There was a dash and daring in Yermak's character that appeals to the imagination. He is the national hero, and his banner hangs in the cathedral of Tomsk.

So, as we rolled across the prairie in corridor cars and caught sight, now and then, of the old foot road – nothing but a rutted track, hardly ever used since the coming of the train – I let my fancy play on the times of long ago, when adventurous traders came here after the precious sable, fought with the tribes, died in the snow, ate one another from brute hunger, and then I thought how many a weary procession of convicts had trudged across the steppes, taking two years to accomplish a journey the Siberian express will now do in a fortnight. I confess the railway, a twin thread of steel spreading over the continent, began to fascinate me as nothing had done for a long time.

Here is a land, one and a-half times as large as Europe – forty times, indeed, as big as the United Kingdom – that has lain dormant through the ages, but is at last being tickled into life, as it were, by the railway, as a giant might be aroused from slumber by a wisp. Until ten years ago, when the building of the line began, there were more people in London alone than in all Siberia. Even now there are only ten millions of inhabitants, one person to every two square miles, and out of every hundred persons ninety-three are men. Half the people to-day are convicts or the descendants of convicts.

Looked at from the rear window of the tail car, the railway does not signify much. And yet never since the Great Wall of China was built has there been such a thing accomplished by the hand of man. It is 5,449 miles long, and cost 85 millions of pounds....

But the solitude of this great lone land laid hold on one. It is an ocean of parched grass land, silent, awesome. And yet surely some day it will flourish, and be bountiful to the earth!

173

Onward from Chelyabinsk
Michael Myers Shoemaker, 1902

As our train moved out of Cheliabinsk the light grows colder and colder, like that over the face of the dead, and then fades away into darkness, and night settles over the steppes. Presently there is a sobbing and sighing as of lost souls as the wind rises, and then the wavering shadows flee away before a full moon moving majestically heavenward and gazing downward upon this sad country. But the wind does not last. Siberia is almost a windless land, otherwise the cold of winter would be past endurance.

There is an odd state of affairs as regards time over here. Though Irkutsk is 3400 miles from St. Petersburg, the trains all run on the time of the latter city, therefore arriving in Irkutsk at 5 p.m., when the sun would make it after 9 p.m. The confusion *en route* is amusing; one never knows when to go to bed or when to eat. In an endeavour to follow my instinct yesterday I arrived in the dining-car before the fires were lit, and promptly went back to bed. To-day I should make it now about 8.30 – these clocks say 10.30, and some of these people are eating their luncheon. One cannot but wonder that this state of affairs is permitted, but so it is.

One man is eating iced cake and cheese and boiled eggs. The two former are served only on Easter Sunday, which comes to-day. The cake is called Kulich. There is also an Easter whipped cream called Pascha.

These Russians are very fond of sweets and perfume. The former you can buy in quantities where you cannot purchase the necessities of life. As for the perfume, they use it constantly and compel you to do the same. As I stood in the door of my compartment just now the porter came along with a large vaporizer and before I knew what he was about had sprayed me all over and I still reek with perfume. This is the first day this has occurred, and perhaps it is an Easter greeting. His amazement was immense when I objected strongly and promptly opened all the windows at my command.

One Day in Ekaterinburg
Eric Newby, 1977

At 3.49 pm, having passed a large lake, and an old church, we came to the nearest thing the driver could manage to a swerving halt in the station at Sverdlovsk, the largest city in the whole region, 'the Pittsburgh of the Urals', with over a million inhabitants. From 1721, when it was founded in the reign of Catherine the Great, until 1924, when it had its name changed to Sverdlovsk (in honour of Jakob Sverdlov, first chairman of the Central Executive Committee, who died of typhus in 1919), it was called Yekaterinburg. I found it difficult to become interested in Sverdlovsk or Yekaterinburg, partly because I wished I was in England, partly because it was three-quarters dark and there was nothing to see, partly because I find it difficult to get worked up about a place that non-Communists are not allowed to visit. So after fifteen minutes, when the *Rossiya* moved out with a TAN 75 diesel engine pulling it along, as the next stretch wasn't electrified, I left with the only two vivid ideas I had had of it still intact. One of them was inspired by an old photograph, taken about a month after a White Russian army took Yekaterinburg from the Bolsheviks, towards the end of July 1918. It shows one end of a smallish room, which could be a cellar, but is, in fact, not a cellar. The walls either have battens running up and down them, which gives the impression that they are covered with striped paper, or else they have had a striped pattern stencilled on to them, as is still done in peasant houses in parts of Italy and eastern Europe, although today it is applied with a roller. The whole of one of the walls of this room, the one to the left of some double doors, is full of gaping holes which penetrate the plaster to the wattle, or whatever it is behind; and the floor is covered with debris.

The other impression is of a girl of about eighteen, sitting in a sentry box in siding 37, on the railway at Yekaterinburg wearing a blood-stained white blouse: a girl who has been trying to escape and has been wounded and taken by Red Army troops in the woods. The date was about 21 September 1918. Perhaps we shall never know if the imperial family actually died in this awful room, or whether the girl in the sentry box was Anastasia, or what then happened to her.

Third Class through Siberia
Bassett Digby and Richardson Wright, 1910

But with desolation outside, we found our third class fellow travelers far more interesting than the little towns we passed. And they, in turn, after the manner of Russians *en route,* gave absolutely no heed to the scenery beyond the windows. Enough for them that their *chainiks* [kettles] were not empty and that the car was kept clean.

The official cleanliness on our train was highly commendable. Every hour or two an assistant conductor, or the man who looked after the steam heating, passed through with a broom or a hand-brush, assiduously sweeping up every cigarette-butt, cedar nut shell – cedar nuts are the peanuts of Russia – or scrap of rubbish tossed on the clean floor. And every two days, during an hour's wait at an important station, an old woman would come through the train to wash the linoleum.

Drawbacks? Well, there were several. The cars were kept too hot, generally at 72° Fahrenheit. On several occasions the thermometer went up to 85° F. and even higher. There were double windows, and three iron doors had to be passed before reaching the open air on the platform at each end of the car. Ventilation was afforded only by little traps in the ceiling that, at night, the Russians insisted on screwing down tight. No amount of argument could convince these simple folk that by morning our coach would rival the Black Hole of Calcutta for atmosphere. It usually did, but the Russians appeared not to mind it.

The mingling of the sexes in sleeping quarters was at first embarrassing. At Tcheliabinsk we had captured two bunks, an upper and a lower. The opposite seats were occupied by an old grandmother and a young girl. By day we sat face to face, hardly an arm's reach separating us. But not until the second night did we grow accustomed to this twenty-year old girl pulling off her boots and generally disrobing, though it was rather annoying when she took a notion to roll a cigarette about midnight and insisted on scattering half the tobacco on the face of the one of us who happened to be asleep on the shelf below.

Nor did the sanitary and washing arrangements in our coach

relieve the embarrassment at all. They were very crude. Men and women shared them alike.

There was still another rather annoying feature to our third class train. Every hour throughout the day and three or four times during the night, the conductor and two assistants raked through the train with a fine-toothed comb, ticket clipping and inspecting. Thirty-one times were our tickets clipped before we reached Omsk. On the twenty-fifth occasion, we begged the conductor to clip them five times and then leave us in peace for a day, but he evidently believed in conserving his simple pleasures for a more leisurely enjoyment.

Thus, passed the time until, a few hours short of five days after leaving the Moscow terminal, our train crept into the station at Omsk.

Ugly Monotony
Peter Fleming, 1933

The Urals were left behind, and we crawled across the Black Soil Belt, where on the hedgeless and forlorn plains man and his beasts were dwarfed to the merest microscopic toys, and each little group of figures seemed a pathetic, unavailing protest against the tyrant solitude. The skies were dark. Rain lashed the streaky windows, and when we stopped at a station the wind made a desolate supplicating sound in the ventilators. In the villages very old, very hairy men, standing in thick black mud, stared up at us, from force of habit, without curiosity. Usually it is difficult to stop looking out of the windows of a train, however monotonous the landscape. You think 'I will read now', but for a long time you cannot take your eyes away from the window, just as for a long time you are reluctant to put back the telephone receiver when your number does not answer. Brrr-brrr ... brrr-brrr ... brrr-brrrr. ... At any moment that aggravating sound may be superseded by a voice. At any moment those dull empty miles may show you something that it would be a pity to have missed. But here it was not like that; here there could be nothing worth waiting for. A grey cold blight had fallen on the world.

Nature when she is frankly hostile, when she is out to do you down, I do not mind. There is stimulus in the challenge of her extremer moods. But when she is drab and indifferent, as though herself despairing, I am oppressed. On the second day of this anomalous November I was driven to seek sanctuary in the communal meal at three o'clock.

Ugly women and uninspiring men; children who squawled, as children have a right to squawl, and sitting on their mothers' laps put their tiny elbows in the tepid soup; Red Army Officers, dour men in blouse-like tunics of a dark khaki and high boots whose corrugated plasticity suggested Wardour Street; one seedy westernized Chinese from Moscow ... .

We were all comrades: all equal: all brother-workers in the Five Year Plan: all actors (I reflected) in the most exciting drama of the modern World ... But none of this could have been deduced from our appearance. We sat and ate, with dull, heavy eyes. If you had been told to name the outstanding characteristic of this cross-section of the New Russia, you would have put it down as constipation. You would not have been far wrong.

I began to eat, without enthusiasm, synthetic caviar.

The Verstmen
Samuel Turner, 1903

A beautiful sunset ripened my thoughts and gave tone to the cold steppes. We passed by long, straggling villages and occasional patches of forest land – the rest was ice and snow, and again ice and snow. The signalmen, armed with green and red flags, and stationed every two-thirds of a mile, seemed a long chain of humanity stretched across this lonely country to relieve it of its cold lifelessness. There are 9000 of these men stationed along the entire route from Moscow to the Eastern Ocean. What a post in the Siberian winter! Standing at the back of the train the signalman will be seen to cross into the middle of the line as soon as the train has passed him, and stand there until it passes the next verstman.* He then returns to this cabin (numbered with the distance from Moscow in versts), where, if he is married, his wife, and perhaps a baby, await him. These men are usually exiles. The lonely verstman was often in my thoughts.

We made our way to the dining-car for dinner and were surprised at the luxurious equipment of this compartment, with its easy chairs and lounges upholstered in Russian leather. A piano at one end and a library containing many books in English and other languages at the other add to the comforts of the journey. The dinner was equal to that provided by a good English commercial hotel and the charges were very moderate.

After dinner everyone became very sociable. Parties were made up at cards and dominoes. Some played chess; one of the passengers possessed a phonograph, and a concert or two helped to pass the evening very pleasantly. On retiring to our compartment we pressed an electric button marked 'attendant' and asked for our beds. The attendant raises the back of the seat, opens it out and presses certain electric buttons; short steel supports spring out of the side upon which the bed rests. Having spread the clean linen he announces that the bed is ready, and with a polite 'Good-night' leaves us to decide who shall take the top bunk. Before retiring to bed I went to the back of the train and stood for some time looking across the silent steppes.

The train threaded its way through the darkness with huge lanterns on the engine, and I noticed that the verstmen had lanterns showing green. The stars were unusually large and brilliant, the pale moonlight bathing the steppes in a light that made them appear almost unreal. I returned to our compartment feeling very well satisfied with my first day on the steppes.

By turning over the little tables in this compartment, the legs of which are made like a step-ladder, it is convenient to climb to the top bunk. The electric lamp can be taken off the table and fixed in a clip just above the top bunk, in a convenient place to enable the occupant, if so inclined, to read before going to sleep.

*One Russian verst is equal to 0.66 mile.

179

Omsk (Zone-Time of the 5th zone: Moscow plus 3 hours)
A.Rado, 1929

District town of Siberia, situated at the mouth of the river Om, falling into the Irtysh. It is an important commercial point of the steppe belt, 161,000 inhabitants. It is the centre of a plain region; it is adjoined by wood-steppe in the North, by steppe in the South.

The city was founded in 1717, under the name of 'Omsky Ostrog' (fortress). Omsk was originally a fortified camp. In 1882, it was made the administrative centre of the Steppe General-Governorship. It began to grow rapidly with the construction of the Railway Mainline. At the inauguration of the Soviet Government in Omsk, it was first necessary to liquidate the uprising of cadets. During the civil war Omsk was Kolchak's capital. The Bolsheviks organized on December 22nd, 1918, an armed uprising against the counter-revolution, which was liquidated by Cossack's detachments, whereby over 1000 revolutionaries were shot and murdered. The second Bolsheviks' uprising took place in Omsk on February 1st, 1919, but it was suppressed at the very beginning. In 1919, with the establishment of the Soviet Government, Omsk became the central Siberian city until the transfer of the Siberian capital to Novo-Nikolaevsk.

Omsk – The Coming City
Bassett Digby and Richardson Wright, 1910

One would be inclined to call Tomsk the capital of Western Siberia – "Why 'Western'?" add the Tomskians, and greatly exaggerate their population – were it not for Omsk, 600 miles to the westward.

Both are big and thriving cities according to Siberian standards; that is to say, great clusters of log buildings, generally one story high and containing two or three rooms; next to no street lighting or paving; no art gallery; a park; three or four murders a week; a scattering of schools; and two or three shabby hotels, each merely a hive of bedrooms and a restaurant among the waiters of which are usually a murderer or two who have served their time in the dread *oblasts* of the frozen north.

Just now the claims of both Omsk and Tomsk are fairly evenly balanced. Omsk is the agricultural center, the hub of 2,000 square miles of fine pasture land: Tomsk is the office of the Altai Mining District, and, with its university and fifty-five other educational institutions, preeminently the educational capital of Siberia. There is a good deal of talk of the huge offices of the Trans-Siberian Railroad, a gem in the crown of Tomsk, being transferred to her rival city. At the best of times there is keen competition existing between the two, and wherever two or three Tomskians and Omskians are gathered together in a Siberian *vodka* shop there is usually trouble.

Omsk
Baedeker, 1914

Omsk (285 ft.), founded in 1717, is the headquarters of the 4th Siberian Army Corps and the capital of the General-Government of the Steppes (comp. p. 523). It is situated on the right bank of the *Irtúish*, just above its confluence with the *Om*. Pop. 128,000. – From the main railway station, adjoining which is a settlement with about 20,000 inhab. and large railway-workshops, we proceed to the N. to the Nikólskaya Square, passing a park with the *Officers' Summer Casino*. In the square is the *Church of St. Nicholas*, containing an alleged banner of Yermák (p. 524), brought hither from Berezov on the lower Ob. Adjacent are the large *Cadet School*, a three-story building, and a *Roman Catholic Church*. We continue to the N. along the Dvortzóvaya and then cross an iron bridge over the Om, with the steamboat-wharf to the left. At the other end of the bridge we reach the Lyúbinski Prospékt. Adjacent, on the bank of the Om, is the Dyetski or *Children's Playground*, with a summer theatre. The Lyúbinski Prospékt ascends to the Bazaar Square, with the *Museum* of the Imperial Russian Geographical Society, which is open in summer (except from June 10th to Aug. 10th) on Thurs. & Sun., in winter Frid. & Sun., 12-3 (adm. 15 cop.; conservator, A. N. Sedelnikov). The contents of the Museum include ethnographic collections from the steppes, specimens of the domestic industries of the district, a collection of birds, and prehistoric relics. Close by are a *Lutheran Church* and a *Municipal*

Theatre. Behind the Museum lay the old fortress, the four gates of which are still standing. The building in which the author F. M. Dostoyévski (d. 1881) was imprisoned from 1849 to 1853, and in which he wrote his 'Recollections of a Dead House' (Engl, translation entitled 'Buried Alive in Siberia'), stood in the N.E. corner of the fortress, but has been removed. – About 2/3 M. to the N. of the town is a Birch Grove, much frequented by the inhabitants of Omsk 50 cop.).

Railway from Omsk to *Yekaterinburg*, see p. 261.

FROM OMSK TO TOBOLSK, 1127 V. (747 M.), steamer down the Irtúish in 4-5 days (fare 8 rb.). The *Irtúish,* the largest tributary of the Ob, rises on the S.W. slopes of the Altai Mts. and is 2500 M. long. The right bank is higher than the left. – 380 V. *Tara,* on the left bank, a district-town with 12,500 inhabitants. Near (770 V.) *Ust-Ishim* the Ishim joins the Irtúish on the left.

1127 V. (747 M.) Tobólsk, *(Loskútiiaya; Kommértche-skaya,* kept by Ackermann, R. 1-1 3/4 rb., bed-linen 30 cop.; izvóshtchik from the landing-stage to the lower town 40, to the upper town 50, per drive 25 cop.; steamer to Tomsk, see p. 530, to Tyumen, see p. 261), the capital of the Government of Tobolsk and seat of the Greek Catholic Bishop of Tobolsk and Siberia, has 21,400 inhabitants. It was founded in 1587 on the steep right bank of the *Irtúish,* opposite the mouth of the *Toból,* and consists of an upper and a lower town, the latter being unhealthy. In the upper town is a *Kremlin* enclosed within walls and containing a 'Swedish Tower", built with the labour of captured Swedes after the battle of Poltava (see p. 390). At the entrance to the *Yerinák Garden* is a *Museum* (open daily except Mon., in summer 12-7, in winter 12-3; adm. 20 cop.; director, V.N.Pignatti), with works on Siberiaj bronzes, and an ethnographical collection (Ostyak and Samoyede curiosities). The Yermák Garden also contains a marble *Obelisk* erected in 1839 to the memory of Yermák. Adjoining the *Bishop's Palace* is a chapel, in which the Bell of Uglitch (see p. 348) hung down to 1892. In the Tulyatzkáya, which leads from the upper to the lower town, is the *Lutheran Church.* Not far off is a *Roman Catholic Church.* On the bank of the Irtúish stands the *Známenski Monàstery,* the oldest in Siberia. – About 13 M. from Tobolsk, on the right bank of the Irtúish, lies *Kutchumovo Goro-dishtehe,* with the ruins of the old town of *Iskér* (p. 524).

FROM TAIGA TO TOMSK, 82 V. (54 M.), branch-railway in 3 hrs.

Tomsk, TOMCKb. – *Railway Restaurant.* – HOTELS. *Yevrópa* (Pl. a; B, 3), cor. of Potchtámskaya and Blagovyéshtchenski Pereúlok, R. 1 ½-8 rb.; *Rossíya* (Pl. b; B, 4), Spásskaya; *Metropol,* Magistrátskaya 11 (Pl. B, 1-3), all three with cafés chantants; *Dresden (Pl.* c; B, 3), Magistrátskaya, quiet, without oafé chantant.–RESTAURANTS. At the two first named hotels; at the *Club*; P*l.* B, 4; introduction by a member necessary), Potchtámskaya; beer at *Krüger's,* Potchtámskaya.

IZVÓSHTOHIK from or to the railway stations 75 cop. (luggage included); to the steamboat wharf, see p. 530; per drive 20-25, at night (12-6) 30 or 35, per hr. 40, at night 60, each additional hr. 30 or 45 cop.

POST & TELEGRAPH OFFICE (P*l.* 18; B, 4), Potchtámskaya. – Bookseller, *I. I. Makúshin,* Blagovyéshtchenski Pereúlok (Pl. B, 3).

The city-office of the railway is in the Magistrátskaya (Pl. B, 1-3).

Tomsk (485 ft,), situated on the high right bank of the *Tom.* (free from ice May 1st to Nov. 1st) and at the mouth of the *Usháika,* in lat. 56°29' N., is the capital of the government of the same name and the seat of a Greek Catholic bishop. Pop. 112,000. It was founded in 1604. – In the S.W. quarter stands the UNIVERSITY, founded in 1888 (Pl. B, 5; 1000 students), the only one in Siberia. It consists of a medical and a legal faculty. Its collections include an *Archaeological and Ethnological Museum* (open free daily 12-3; director, P. Bogayevski); a *Zoological Museum* (closed at present; director, N. F. Káshtchenko); a *Botanical Cabinet* (open on weekdays in winter 10-1; director, V. V. Sap6zhnikov); a *Min-eralogical Museum* (open Sun. and holidays in winter 12-1; closed in June, July, and Aug.; director, P. Pilipenko); and the *Library,* with 250,000 volumes. Near the University is a *Students' Dining Hall* (Pl. B, 5). A *Technological Institute* (Pl. B, 5) was opened in 1900; it is attended by 1200 students. – The Greek Catholic *Cathedral of the Trinity.*; Pl. 3, B 4) was finished in 1900. The recluse Theodore Kuzmítch (d. 1861), widely known on account of his resemblance to the Tzar Alexander I., *is* buried in the *Alexéyecski Monastery*; Pl. B, 4), which was founded in 1605; the cell actually occupied by him is still shown in the Tchistakov House, in the Monastúirskaya. The *Nikólskaya Church* (Church of the Nativity; Pl. B, 3) occupies the site of an old nunnery, where, in 1740, Princess

Catherine Dolgoruki, the bride of Peter II., was forced to take the veil. She was, however, freed from her vows in 1742 by the Empress Elizabeth. Tomsk contains a *Lutheran Church* (Pl. 7; B, 4) and a *Roman Catholic Church* (Pl. 8; B, 3). –The town is the headquarters of a mining district (comp. Pl. B, 5), and possesses gold-smelting works.

The Post Train – Taiga – Tomsk
Annette Meakin, 1900

We had not been long in Siberia before we knew from experience that the only way to enjoy life was to give ourselves over entirely to a state of blissful uncertainty about everything in the future. If people told us when a train would arrive or when a steamer would start, they invariably told us wrong. Any information gleaned in one town about another to which we were going was sure to be flatly contradicted on our arrival. Of course this could be partly accounted for by the great distances. When a town is separated from its nearest neighbour by a railway journey, say, of two nights and three days, it certainly has some excuse on its side. Still, after having made your home for several days in a comfortable railway carriage, or yet more comfortable house boat, it is somewhat trying to arrive without warning at your destination several hours before you expected to get there, or to have to unpack and spend another night in a carriage you had expected to leave at midday.

We left Omsk by the post train which ought to have started at 9.30 p.m., according to the time table. It was only four hours late, a mere nothing in Siberia, where time is *not* money. As we sat waiting at the station the good news was brought us that Mafeking had been relieved. The bearer of these tidings was the Finnish Pastor, who had only an hour before received word by telegram from Finland. The Finns have all along shown great sympathy with the English with regard to the Transvaal war. Pastor Erikson met us with a hearty handshake and a beaming face. A burst of military music close at hand seemed very opportune to our English ears. We looked out and saw a pretty sight. Under the bright electric light on the platform from which we were to start gleamed the white hats and jackets of some thirty bandsmen. Their music was in honour of the colonel of their regiment, who, after a period of twenty-four years' service at Omsk, was leaving with his family for a better appointment at Irkutsk.

The train seemed to carry music with it as it glided into the station, and the crowded platform was a whirl of gaiety and excitement. All this in the middle of the night! We found our *coupé* on the post train not less comfortable than the one we had occupied on the express. The cushions were all covered with neat washing covers, and looked tolerably clean. Under the window was a little folding table which was most useful for reading and writing. I speak of *the* window because there was only a window at one end of the carriage. Like the express, the post is also a corridor train. The door opening into the corridor had a mirror in place of a window; it opened outwards and could be fastened back against the outer wall when we wished to travel with it open. The mirror was useless when the door was shut, as one stood in one's own light when looking into it. We occasionally went out into the corridor to complete our toilette when a glass was indispensable. This however was not so bad as in Canada, where I have seen a gentleman shaving in the public "sleeper." The corridor was so wide that the stoutest traveller could promenade in it with ease. On wet days we could get a walk here of about twenty-five paces; seats could be opened out from the walls between the windows as in the express, and passengers used to congregate here in the evenings when it was too dark to read.

The post train has no dining car, and we were obliged to keep a sharp look out for stations where there was something to eat. The first day after leaving Omsk we passed a buffet station about 11 a.m., but being asleep, did not take advantage of it.

"You must be hungry," said a fellow passenger pityingly about seven in the evening; "but we shall reach Kainsk in about an hour, and there is a good buffet there." Just then the train began to pull up. It soon came to a dead stop. There was no human habitation in sight.

"The engine has smashed up," said a jolly Russian sailor in broken English, (he was bound for Port Arthur). 'She is sixty years old,' he continued. 'She was made in Glasgow. She is no use any more.'

The conductor had got out. He came along the line and confirmed what the sailor had said. The other passengers did not seem to mind; they were soon exploring the neighbourhood. The children from the fourth class began to paddle barefoot in a muddy stream not far from the line. The poor old engine was now "towed to her last berth." I had whipped out my "Kodak" and taken her photograph thinking of Turner's "Fighting Temeraire."

After a delay of two hours a fresh engine arrived from Kainsk and we reached the buffet at last. Never again, we vowed, would we be subject to such pangs of hunger as we suffered that day; in future we took care to have some food always with us, if it was only a loaf of bread. The serving man was willing for a few kopeks to fetch us hot water at the stations, so that with the help of bread and tea there was no need to starve.

At dinner that evening as we pulled out of Taishet where the new railway line to the Lena and beyond crossed ours, two young men who had just boarded the train sat down at our table. They immediately began talking and when they heard I was a foreigner insisted on buying food and drink for me. One was the chief road-engineer of the Taishet district though he was only twenty-two and barely out of his polytechnic. That I was to find was not at all unusual for Siberia. His companion, no older, was head of public transport in the district. Their zest, vitality and open-heartedness was overwhelming. They made me promise I would dine with them in Irkutsk and were plainly disappointed that I would not get drunk with them there and then.

"You know why they are going to Irkutsk?" my friend asked me afterwards. "To renew their driving licences."

"But Irkutsk is more than 300 miles away!" I exclaimed.

"That's the point," he laughed. "We have a saying that in Siberia 100 kilometres is no distance at all, 100 roubles no money and 100 grammes of vodka no drink!"

Tomsk – A City of Orgies and Education
Bassett Digby and Richardson Wright, 1910

Over a day's journey eastward of Omsk lies Tomsk. It is not on the Trans-Siberian. When the engineers who build the road visited the Tomskian city fathers for their contributions they were refused, it is said. Tomsk was the capital of Western Siberia, and the natives could see no reason for the mountain going to Mahomet. The engineers, thus failing to get their graft, pushed the trunk line on, erecting a little junction and calling it Taiga (in the woods!) and condescending to put a sprout forty-eight miles up country for the accommodation of such Tomskians as should care to leave their town.

It is almost worth a special journey across Europe and a substantial section of Siberia, to arrive in Tomsk on the Taiga night train. Far ahead through the darkness flares a group of tall arc lamps at a point on the rim of the great bowl in the bottom of which lies the city. As you approach you see scores of rude sledges, mere rafts of birch poles held together with twine, waiting in long rows along the edge of the birch coppice that skirts the station.

From the train we descended into picturesque pandemonium. Shaggy *moudjiks* flung themselves upon our baggage and hove out of sight. Deep snow lay under foot, and a heavy snowstorm was sweeping down upon the surging, shouting, cursing, shoving mob of fur-coated passengers and *istvostchiks* and plunging horses.

We found items of our baggage loaded on to three different sledges, and a ruffian with a guileful eye endeavoring to persuade our fox-terrier, Jack, to board a fourth. It is an education to get baggage away from a fareless Siberian sledge driver but, rather to our astonishment, we found that the enterprise can be achieved without bloodshed.

The sledge swung round, and off we dashed down the long hill through the birch woods to Tomsk. It is a steepish hill, three miles long, and our pair of horses galloped every yard of the way. Soon we arrived at the portals of the "Hotel Roosia," and, paying off the *istvostchik*, pushed through the treble swing doors into the hall. It was just after Sunday midnight.

Shades of a New England Sunday!

A uniformed band was blaring out a brassy march to the accompaniment of loud bursts of laughter and shouted greetings and the popping of champagne corks. In our fur coats and big felt hip boots we waited in what seemed to be the wings of oldtime Daly's. Around us floated ravishing creatures in high spirits and ultra-abbreviated crimson silk skirts. Sloe-eyed maidens, attired as for the ballet, flitted by to join peroxide blondes in tight pale blue knickerbockers; and be-wigged fairies in fleshings dived hither and thither in the throng. Every now and again came a crash of broken glass or a prodigious stamping of feet from the long restaurant, the stage at the end of which was given up to vaudeville.

We stayed a couple of weeks in Tomsk, and the same sort of thing went on every night. If we entered the restaurant at half-past nine in the evening, we found the lights low and not a person present. The evening begins an hour later – and no one thinks of going home till three or four in the morning.

The Tarakan
Samuel Turner, 1903

The Siberian Hotel at Tomsk, where we stayed, is well built, but as usual the supply of water is scanty. There were no bedclothes. The tarakans, which I found awaiting our arrival in the bedroom, were, on the other hand, sufficiently plentiful. The tarakan is not so common as that other member of the creeping fraternity for which it has sometimes been mis-taken. It is a small and fragile variety of cockroach. It has three legs on each side of the body and two feelers. I was quite impressed with the tickling capacity of the latter. Its legs are long and enable it to run at great speed; two or three hundred will race across the floor together at a terrific rate and vanish under the wall paper or down a chink in the wood. I should think them the swiftest insects alive. I concluded that they were too brusque and abrupt in their manners for it to be worth my while to try to shoot them, but assumed that they might be amenable to reason in the form of insect powder, so I spread a tin of Keating's round the bed to form a frontier and retired to rest with a piece of muslin over my mouth. Perhaps it was just as well that the company were too rest-less to allow me to sleep, for I had to be up early on the morrow for a long day's work. As soon as it was light I complained of the nuisance to the night porter, but he only laughed. They do not think very much of tarakans in Siberia. It sometimes happens, in fact, that a peasant will take a handful of these insects from an old house when removing to a new one, for luck. Englishmen are obviously too particular.

The Taiga
Malcolm Burr, 1930

On the Wednesday our station was Taigá, a poor place of no interest in itself, but marking the boundary between two worlds. Behind us we were leaving the steppe, and before us lay the primeval forest that extends from here to the Pacific and almost to the Arctic Ocean, over three thousand miles in length and nearly a thousand from north to south. And so we entered the *taigá*, from which the settlement takes its name – the huge, dense, impassable jungle where the trees struggle with each other to reach the light and upper air, where giants die and crash down to lay rotting on the ground and make soil for the next generation. It is a strange world. Only three roads cut it, the great rivers Yenisei and Lena, which run away to waste in the Arctic, and this great long ribbon of a railway which has cut its path through it from west to east. The rest is roadless, a mass of bog and rock covered by shrub and the endless forest with here and there an oasis cut by some enterprising settler in the neighbourhood of the line or along the rivers. It consists of larch, the Siberian tree par excellence, pine, fir, spruce in the southern portion, Siberian "cedar" and birch, the latter more silvery than in Europe, its groves looking like ghostly patches against the dark evergreens. There is little sign of life. During the two and a half days that we ran through it we kept our eyes open for game, but all we saw was a single capercailie, flushed by the train, which flew startled to the top of a lofty pine.

As we penetrate deeper into the *taigá* the country becomes poorer and poorer; the few scattered settlements of hardy pioneers are but ramshackle huts built of logs and boards, and one wonders at the enterprise which makes them hew themselves a home out of this virgin land and enables them to eke out some kind of an existence, though perhaps it is better than the one they left. On the Thursday evening we came to Nijni Udinsk, the last township before Irkutsk. Here we took our usual constitutional up and down the platform, when my companion suddenly smote the back of his neck. A moment later something stung my face, and then we saw that we were attacked by a swarm of flies, small but numerous and aggressive; we put up no defence but bolted back to our carriage, where we sought protection behind closed windows. It was *Simulium,* a little black devil that comes in swarms and drives man and beast into a frenzy.

Krasnoyarsk: A Siberian Commercial Town
Morgan Phillips Price, 1910

In general appearance it was not unlike the outskirts of a mining town in North-East Canada that I remembered visiting some years before.

The hotels are like great two-storeyed barns, one of which we selected after a verbal conflict with the owner about the value of his rooms. One can generally obtain a room for a couple of roubles a night in a tolerable state of cleanliness, even in these wilder parts of Russia, but in this case we soon discovered that as far as back premises and so-called lavatories were concerned, the less we saw of them the better. For my part I decided, on inspection, to perform my morning and evening toilets in the Yenisei River, about half-a-mile away on the outskirts of the town.

One can generally get a fair idea of certain aspects of human life in a town like Krasnoyarsk by spending a few hours a day in one of the most frequented restaurants. As a boy I had always thought of Siberia as a country inhabited by fur-clad hunters, dwelling for months in snowed-up log-houses, or by exiles chained to barrows in the galleries of the gold mines till they fell dead of cold and exhaustion. These impressions received a rude shock when I beheld the type of humanity in the restaurant under our hotel, which styled itself "The Pride of Old Russia." Here were commercial travellers from old Russia, selling anything from peppermint lozenges to pianos, sitting chattering in groups over glasses of cognac and vodka; mining prospectors who had returned from up country, and gold washers fresh from the lower reaches of the Yenisei, Jewish fur traders and salt-fish dealers. Those who had been making money at gold dredging or such occupations were testifying to their success by the size of the dinners they were eating, and the volume of the alcohol they were consuming, while sallow-faced students from the middle schools were already in the singing stage, prior to their final resting-places beneath the table. There was, moreover, a considerable contingent of persons of doubtful virtue.

The decorations in the restaurants and other public places of recreation and pastime were of a most primitive character. Walls covered with loud yellow paint, vermilion curtains, sky-blue sofas, seemed to be the highest efforts of local art, and to contribute no little to the enjoyment of the visitors. Some of the restaurants had stages for impromptu theatricals, but, judging from the quality of the audience, I fear that the art would not have proved inspiring or entertaining if I had witnessed it. Under such circumstances as the above I heard a gramophone bawl forth a Russian comic song, followed immediately by the strains of the "Songe d'Automne" and other beautiful waltz airs from Western Europe. What irony! The air which I had last heard in an English ballroom I now heard in a low coffee-house of a Siberian mining town.

Next day I strolled down to the quay on the banks of the Yenisei and found a rough wooden platform laid on piles against which some grimy paddle-steamers were moored. On the banks lay stacks of merchandise waiting to go up country by the first steamer as soon as the ice broke. There were sacks of flour from Tomsk, reaping machines from America, ploughs from European Russia, cream separators from Sweden and Germany, and bales of cotton manufactures from Moscow. Incidentally I may note that I saw nothing from England, whose businessmen at present have been timid in this land, where no one speaks English, to cultivate a land which Germans, Americans and Swedes are capturing wholesale.

8

IRKUTSK

During the winter of 1903 Iosif Vissarionovich Dzhugashvili spent a period of exile in Irkutsk. As Stalin, he later became its ruler. It is a good place to stop over, though he may not have agreed. There is much to be seen despite the modern Soviet dreariness. Baedeker provided a detailed description of the city in 1914. Lindon Bates Jr had trouble at the station in 1908, Archibald Colquhoun was very critical in 1898, but Sir Henry Norman in 1901 was impressed.

Digby and Wright, of course, discovered the rougher side of the city. Eric Newby found it full of contrasts in 1977.

Continuation of the Railway Journey to Irkutsk
Baedeker, 1914

CONTINUATION OF THE RAILWAY JOURNEY TO IRKUTSK. The train runs at first on through the 'Taiga' (p. 524). – 1583 V. *Súdzhenka* (810 ft.), with coal-pits. Just before reaching (1617 V.) *Izhmor-skáya* (790 ft.) we cross the auriferous *Yaya.* – 1685 V. *Martirksk* (450 ft.; Rail. Restaurant), a district-town with 18,700 inhab., on the left bank of the *Kiya.* About 2 V. farther on the train crosses the Kiya by a bridge 232 yds. long, and then ascends to the watershed between this stream and the *Tyazhin.*– 1810 V. *Bogotól* (975 ft.: Rail. Restaurant). Beyond (1841 V.) *Kritovo* the line passes from the Tomsk Government into that of Yeniseisk, and crosses the *Tchulúim* by a bridge 302 yds. long. –1875 V. *Atchinsk* (700 ft.; Rail. Restaurant). About 2 V. from the railway station is the district town of that name, situated on the high right bank of the Tchulúim, with a population of 11,000. It is the northernmost town (lat. 56° 16'N.) on the Trans-Siberian Railway. A highroad runs hence to the S. to (333 V. or 221 M.) Minusinsk (p. 531).

The country now becomes hilly. 1910 V. *Tchernaryétchenskaya* (885 ft.; Rail. Restaurant). The train now ascends the watershed of the *Great*

Kemtchug and the *Katcha,* crosses the Katcha just short of (1995 V.) *Katcha* (1545 ft.), and then descends to –
2040 V. (1352 M.) Krasnoyársk, (520 ft.; *Railway Restaurant; Métropole,* Voskresénskaya, without cafe chantant, R. from 1¼ rb., D. from 50 cop.; *Stáraya Rossiya,* Blagovyéshtchenskaya; izvoshtchik to the town 50 cop.; British vice-consul), the finely situated capital of the Government of Yeniséi, with 80,000 inhabitants. It was founded in 1628, and lies on the left bank of the *Yeniséi,* here 2/3 M. broad, at the mouth of the Katcha. Near the railway station, on the W. side of the town, are the *Railway Technical School* and the *Town Park* (restaurant at the club). A fine view is obtained from the promenade above the steam boat-wharfs. The Municipal Museum is open free in winter on Sun. and holidays 11-3 (closed from May 15th to Aug. 15th). Besides 18 Greek Catholic churches, there are a Lutheran and a Roman Catholic church.

We may proceed by the pretty highroad (330 V. or 219 M.), or by steamboat down the Yeniséi, to *Yeniséisk,* a district-town of 12,000 inhab., pleasantly situated on the left bank of the Yeniséi. It has a Municipal Museum.

A very enjoyable steamboat trip (4-5 days; magnificent scenery at first) may be taken up the Yeniséi, which is here generally flanked by lofty rocky banks, to *Minusinsk* (Rossiya), a district-capital in the government of Yeniséi, with 15,600 inhabitants. The Municipal Museum, founded by N. M. Martyanov in 1877, and containing 70,000 objects, is worth visiting (open free, Sat. 11-3, Sun. 11-2). Highroad to Atchinsk, see p: 530.

Just beyond Krasnoyarsk the train crosses the *Yeniséi* by a bridge of six spans, having a total length of 1010 yds. 2044 V. *Yeniséi.* About 4 M. beyond (2163 V.) *Klyúkvennaya* (1205 ft.; Rail. Restaurant) we cross the *Rúibnaya.* Beyond (2211 V.) *Ka-mala* (1085 ft.) the train crosses the watershed of the *Tuirbúil* and the *Little Urya* and traverses the *Kan* valley. 2267 V. *Kansk Yeniséiski* (680 ft.; Rail. Restaurant), a district-town on the left bank of the Kan, with 17,500 inhabitants. About 2 M. farther on we cross the Kan by a bridge 278 yds. long. 2293 V. *Ilánskaya* (885 ft.; Rail. Restaurant); 2374 V. *Klyutchi* (1280 ft.). After crossing the auriferous *Biryusá,* the line enters the Government of Irkutsk. Beyond (2425 V.) *Taishét* (1040 ft.; Rail.

Restaurant) we traverse hilly country via (2531 V.) *Kamuishét* (1175 ft.), with cement-works, and (2547 V.) *Uk* (1635 ft.) as far as (2573 V.) *Nizhne-Udinsk* (1360 ft.; Rail. Restaurant), a mountain-girt district-town on the *Udé,* with 6500 inhabitants.

We now proceed through a cultivated district, crossing the Udá, to (2618 V.) *Khudoelánskaya* (1915 ft.), the highest-lying station between Tchetyabinsk and Irkutsk. 2683 V. *Tulún* (1635 ft.; Rail. Restaurant). About 2 M. beyond (2813 V.) *Zimá* (1510 ft.; Rail. Restaurant) we cross the *Oká* by a bridge 510 yds. long. – 2952 V. *Polovina* (1790 ft.; Rail. Restaurant). We cross the *Byélaya* 11 M. farther on. About 10 M. to the N.E. of (2994 V.) *Telma* (1425 ft.) is the village of *Alexándrovskoye* (p'. 532). We cross the *Kitói* 5 M. beyond Telma.–3042 V. *Innokéntyevskaya* (1455 ft.; Rail. Restaurant), 2 M. from which is the *Voznesenski Monastery,* founded in 1672, and containing the bones of St. Innocent (d. 1713) in its principal church (to the right).–Just before reaching Irkutsk we cross the *Irkút.*

3049 V. (2021 M.) Irkútsk, – The RAILWAY STATION *(Restaurant)* is on the left bank of the Angará, in the suburb of Gláz-kovskoye, which is connected with the town in summer by a pontoon bridge. *Offices of the State Railways* in the Náberezhnaya Angari, cor. of the Kharlampiyevskaya (Pl. B, 0, 3), open on week-days 8-12 & 1-6 (winter 1-4), Sun. & holidays 8-12; the sale of tickets ceases 2 days before the departure of the train; English, French, and German spoken.

HOTELS. *Central* (Pl. b; C, 3), Bolshaya, R. 1½-8½ rb; *Grand-Hôtel* (Pl. c; D, 3), Bolshaya; *Kommértcheskoye Podvorye* (Pl. d; C, 2), cor. of the Tikhvinskaya and Basninskaya, R. 1½-4 rb., bed-linen 40, D. (1-5 p.m.) 60-75 cop.; *Centrálnoye Deko,* Bolshaya; *Métropole* (Pl. a; C, 3), Lugováya, R. 1½-6½, D – (2-6 p.m.) ½ -1¼ rb. – *Restaurant Modern,* in the Central Hotel (see above).

IZVÓSHTCHIK from the rail, station to the town 90 cop., at night (10-7) 1 rb. 20 cop., incl. bridge-toll; per drive 25 (at night 50) cop.

POST OFFICE (Pl. C, 2), Potchtámskaya. –BATHS at *Kurbatov's,* cor. of the Náberezhnaya Angari and Savinski Pereúlok; bath from 1 rb. – BANKS. *Commercial Bank of Siberia* (Pl. D, 3), Bolshaya; *Russo–Asiatic Bank* (Pl C, 8), Bolshaya. – *Makushin Library,* Bolshaya.

Irkútsk (1455, ft.) is situated in 52° 17'N. lat, and 104° 16'E. long.,

on the right bank of the clear and swift-flowing *Angará* (hero 660 yds.
wide), 44 M. from Lake Baikál, and opposite the mouth of the *Irkút*.
It was founded in 1652, and is the see of a Greek Catholic bishopric,
the capital of the General Government and of the Government of
Irkutsk, and the headquarters of the 3rd Siberian Army Corps. Pop.
113,000.– On the N. side of the town, in the centre of a large open
space, is the *Cathedral of the Virgin of Kazan* (PL C, 1), a modern building, with five domes and a detached belfry. Opposite the Cathedral is
a *Roman Catholic Church*. In the Bolshaya, the main street of the town,
which it traverses from S.W. to N.E., are the *Lutheran Church* (Pl C,
3), the *Theatre* (Pl C, 4), completed in 1897 from the plans of Schröter,
and the *Residence of the Governor-General* (Pl B, 4). facing the Angara.
Opposite the last is the interesting *Museum* of the Imperial Russian
Geographical Society (Pl C, 4), which is open on week-days (except
Sat.) 1-3, on Sun. 11-3; adm. 10 cop. (at other times adm. 50 cop.;
conservator, N. N. Bogorodski). It contains archaeological collections
from E. Siberia, Buddhistic objects of worship, mammoth remains,
and Chinese birds. The Observatory is open from dusk to 10 or 11
p.m.; adm. 30-50 cop. On the Angará is a bronze *Statue of Alexander
III.* (Pl. B, 4), by Bach (1908).

About 70 V. (40 M.) to the N.W. of Irkutsk (post-horse 3 cop. per
verst) is the village of *Alexándrovskoye* (comp. p. 531), containing a
large and well-equipped prison on the radiating system. Visitors are
generally admitted on application to the director, but it is as well to
have an introduction from the Governor of Irkutsk.

Arriving at Irkutsk
Lindon Bates Jr, 1908

The train pulls slowly to the white station-house at Irkutsk. A swarm
of porters, *nasilchiks*, white-aproned, with peaked hats, and big, numbered arm-tags, invade the carriage. They seize each piece of luggage
and run with it somewhere into the crowd outside. You, encumbered
with your heavy coat, laboriously follow. Irkutsk station, more than
any previous one, is crowded with passengers and Cossack guards.
Train officials are shouting instructions, and every few paces a sentry

is standing his silent watch. This is the transfer entrepôt for all through traffic, as well as the depôt for the largest and most important city of Siberia.

Threading the press on the platform, you struggle with the outgoing human current, and in time reach the big waiting-room of the first class. It likewise is crowded with a mass of people, and its floor is cumbered with heaping mounds of baggage. One of these hillocks is constructed from your impedimenta, which are being guarded now by a porter, apparently the residuary legatee of the half-dozen original competitors within the car. The man takes the long document that witnesses your claim to two trunks, and departs. Upon you in turn devolves sentry duty for the interminable time during which those trunks are being culled out from the baggage-car.

It is an exasperating wait, but the fundamental rule for Russian traveling is, "never separate from the baggage." The parcel-room here at Irkutsk held for six months a suit-case left by a friend to be sent to this traveler. The officials would not give it up to its owner or to any person save the forwarder, though he, oblivious to sequels, had gone on to San Francisco.

Like the rest, now, you camp, with the baggage in front of you, on the waiting-room floor. It is a very country fair, this station. At the far end is a big stand crowded with dishes, on which are cold meats, potato salad, heaps of fruit and cakes, sections of fish from which one may cut his own slices, boxes of chocolates, and cigarettes. All are piled up in heaping profusion. One can get a glass of vodka and eat of the *zakuska* dishes free, or while waiting he may buy a meal of surprisingly ample quantity and good quality at the long tables that run down the centre of the room. Most of the Russians order a glass of tea, and with it in hand sit down till such indefinite future time as the luggage situation shall unroll itself.

We move our baggage and join the tea caravan. Across the table is a slight, brown-faced man, with an enormous black astrakan cape falling to his ankles, and wearing a jauntily perched astrakan cap on his head. "One of the Cossack settlers," a friend from the train remarks. Beyond are half a dozen tired-looking women, with dark-gray shawls over their heads. Near them are men with close-fitting *shubas,* or snugly-belted sheepskin coats, fur inside, and rough-tanned black leather outside. Beside the lunch-stand are a couple of young men with huge bearskin caps, short coats, and high leather boots tucked into fleece-lined overshoes.

A general at one of the little side tables is talking volubly to a plump dame with furs, which are attracting envy from many sides. The lady merely nods between puffs of her cigarette, and sips her tea. A large fat merchant waddles past, wrapped in a paletot made of the glistening silvery skin of the Baikal seal. The room is stifling, full of smoke, and crowded with people. Yet no one seems to feel the discomfort, even to the extent of taking off the heavy outer coats, which, with the thermometer at twenty degrees below zero, they have worn on the sleigh-ride in, from across the river.

Hardly What One Would Expect
Archibald Colquhoun, 1898

Even here, however, the streets and squares – many of them built of stone – are badly kept and out of repair. The lack of completeness and harmony is noticeable in all Siberian towns – for instance, at Irkutsk a really fine opera-house is spoiled by miserable corridors and foyer. In this large city, whose population is already over fifty thousand, there is only one indifferent public library, and the booksellers' shops contain merely a second-class collection of books, such as French novels, *Le Nu au Salon* picture-books, and equally edifying publications. It does not speak well for the civilizing missions of Russia to the "savage tribes" among whom she has planted her flag that such a state of things should exist in her great outpost cities, which ought to be centres of light and learning. The inhabitants of these cities have not yet acquired, even in the smallest degree, "the gentle art of beauty." Their clothes, bought ready-made (there are only four tailors in all Irkutsk), are ugly and unbecoming, a fact much to be regretted, especially in the case of the fair sex, who are no better in this respect than their male-folk, for the Siberian woman is not sufficiently endowed by nature to be able to dispense with artificial aids to comeliness.

It is, however, doubtful whether any efforts of an eclectic nature would have much influence at present, in raising the standard of life, for from highest to lowest the ruling passions are still gambling and drinking, while lying and all sorts of official corruption are still notoriously the rule and not the exception. Academical education is not enough. What is essential is the infusion of a new spirit from outside, consequent upon the opening up of the country to the world; new objectives and ideals, competition and rivalries, which will leave no room for the existing slothful debaucheries; new standards of morality, or, at the least, of commercial expediency, which will discredit as stupid and clumsy such a semi-civilized weapon as promiscuous lying.

Sights of Irkutsk
Sir Henry Norman, 1901

At first sight, as it nestles within the embrace of the broad Angara, [Irkutsk] is charming, and one is astonished at the proportion of imposing buildings rising from the flat brown mass of wooden houses. A second surprise is that the suburb where the station is situated is called Glascow. But when you drive away through mud a couple of feet deep, in which the droschky rolls about so alarmingly that people invariably ride with their arms about each others' waists, you fear that first appearances were deceptive. The streets, in fact, are awful, and the local paper of the morning after my arrival told how two little boys returning from school fell in the middle of the street and were only just rescued from drowning by some passing carters. Your first impression, however, returns and remains when you have seen more of this remote Siberian capital. It is an astonishing place.

Here are a few plain facts to begin with. Irkutsk has 51,464 inhabitants. It spends ten per cent, of its municipal income on primary education. It has five hospitals and thirty doctors. There is an astronomical and meteorological observatory, of which the magnetic observations possess peculiar importance. Its theatre, a handsome building of brick and stone, cost over £30,000. There is a museum, an offshoot of the Russian Geographical Society, with an extremely interesting ethnological collection, as well as almost complete collections of the birds and animals of the district. From its telegraph-office messages can be sent to any part of the world in any language, but I must add that a telegram sent to me from London on Monday was only delivered at midday on Friday. There is a perfectly organised telephone service, and the outlying manufactories, one of them as much as sixty miles away, are all connected with the city by telephone. A fire-extinguishing service is excellently equipped with an English steam fire-engine among other apparatus, and I saw some smart drill. Finally, besides an imposing cathedral, Irkutsk boasts no fewer than twenty Orthodox churches, one Roman Catholic and one Lutheran chapel, two synagogues, and two monasteries, for in Siberia a greater religious tolerance exists than in Russia. That is not a bad list for a town which, until a few months ago, could only be reached by an exhausting journey of several weeks, driving at full speed day and night...

Irkutsk, however, is not saved by its churches from an amount of crime, actual and potential, that would be considered excessive in a new mining-camp. The night before I arrived a church was ransacked of its plate; the night of my arrival the principal jeweller's shop was robbed; a few days later a flourishing manufactory of false passports – a peculiarly heinous crime in Russia – was raided by the police; the day I visited the prison a man clubbed nearly to death, who never recovered consciousness, was picked up in the street; a short time previously the mail, carrying gold-dust, had been ambushed and three of its armed guards shot; and no respectable citizen would dream of passing along through its suburbs after dark. Indeed, people often fire a revolver-shot out of the window before going to bed, to remind whom it may concern that a strong man armed keepeth his goods.

Irkutsk, the Unregenerate
Bassett Digby and Richardson Wright, 1910

What San Francisco was in '49 when it flourished as the gilded Gomorrah of the West, Irkutsk, the largest town of Siberia and metropolis of the Asiatic goldfields, is today – with additional trimmings.

Residence in Irkutsk is not altogether a rest cure for the nerves. With a population of close on to 113,000, crammed into a couple of square miles on a picturesque bend of the river Angarar, it produces some hundreds of murders and murderous assaults in the course of a year, with a few dozen arrests and fewer convictions, with sentences of a short residence in jail. That was the situation a couple of years ago, and with a throb of civic pride, the natives told us 1910 was quite an off year.

"In the spring, a young man's fancy (in Irkutsk) fondly turns to thoughts of blood." One fine day in May, a year or two back, there were twenty-two assorted murders and attempted murders within a short distance of the city. These included a disastrous picnic on an island in the lower Angarar, to which an enterprising Irkutskian invited a dozen persons he disliked. He saw that they were all busy unpacking lunch and then put off in the boat and managed to shoot down half a dozen before one of the guests hit him.

Then the street cleaners and insurance agents voiced a protest, and there was talk of reviving the old Vigilance Committee that citizens used to frame up among themselves after the manner of 'Frisco once on a day.

The Vigilance Committee that held sway in Irkutsk was not altogether a success. The scheme, projected by a handful of law-abiding citizens, was enthusiastically received – by ex-convicts and delegates of professional murderers. They rolled up in their dozens and scores and volunteered for service. The governor granted them exceptional powers, and they made the best of them. While such police as there were bribed into passivity, wealthy merchants were shot down in broad daylight as "suspects"; and under the cover of "house-raiding" and "punitory confiscation," burglary put out blossoms and flourished like a green bay tree. That is why the Vigilance Committee idea is no longer as popular in Irkutsk as it might be. Still, though Vigilance Committees are banished to the limbo of the past, the police and Cossacks keep life lively.

***

The city's policing is done partly by municipal, partly by private patrolmen, the latter subsidized by property owners. The private constables deserve an honored niche in the gallery of Twentieth Century philosophers. The Irkutsk night patrolman, with the high-souled purpose of warning prospective burglars of his approach and causing them to abstain from sinning, makes the night hideous by perpetually clattering a powerful wooden rattle. He parades the streets, whirring it round and round at every few paces.

The method of assault practiced by the Siberian outlaw is "garroting." He approaches his victim from behind and throws over his head a loop attached to a stick. One quick jerk, and the unfortunate wayfarer is hurled backward, gasping for breath, or dead – his neck broken. There are few holdups in Siberia without murder; murder gives a nice touch of finality to the deed. One is disposed to ask if the natives do not protest against their streets being littered up in this manner; what a house-holder does when he goes out to sweep the pavement of mornings and finds a stray corpse lying on his doorstep. Innately religious, the Siberian gives Christian burial to those he finds garroted to death. He even erects a cross over the grave, a cross inscribed with the petition asking whosoever passes by that spot to pray for the soul of him who died. Siberia is filled with these crosses. One encounters them everywhere, in the fields, along country roads, and on the mountainsides.

The fun at Irkutsk starts at midnight. An hour before, the city is as dead as a New England Sunday. Then the theaters and the moving picture shows close down, and everyone crowds into the restaurants.

You enter a pair of swing doors, kick off your felt snow boots, hand your furs to an attendant and pass on into a long room thronged with diners, gay with the uniforms of the garrison and women in smart Parisian costumes. At the far end is a small stage on which a score of maidens in a minimum of skirt and a maximum of smile go through fatuous double-shuffles and fancy dances executed with a degree of incompetency that would leave a Bowery "amateur night" audience dumb with scorn.

An act over, the dancers skip down to mingle with the crowd, scattering around the tables and ordering the costliest fruits and the rarest wines that the management can provide. There are songs, curious yelping conceits by untrained feminine voices; and sleek, swarthy Poles sing their national comic songs, with snatches of patter and pathetic attempts at a "cellar flap" which help to capture the guests' straying attention for a few moments. Till dawn there are gay music and crude vaudeville, crude, but going with a genuine verve and spirit of unforced fun that is lacked by many a better show – fine fare for the groups of self-condemned exiles, the mining agents and engineers, officers of the garrison, fur traders, merchants, concessionaires and miners, snatching a brief holiday in town from the desolation of the Siberian wilds.

Off the Big Red Train,
Eric Newby, 1977

I liked Irkutsk best in the early morning. I used to go out around five-thirty when the air was still so cold that my breath smoked like a steam engine. At this hour the city was deserted, and it would remain so for another hour and a half, except for the lady sweepers wielding their brooms and chewing gum, a few athletes jogging along the embankment of the Angara, one or two rude looking little dogs and swarms of small birds which chattered away to one another among the branches of the poplar and maple trees which gave a sylvan air to the streets. And when the sun came up behind the spire of the Roman Catholic church, whose only support now that it was closed was a scaffolding of timber, and shone down on to the domes of the Spasskaya, the Church of the Saviour, the Cathedral of the Epiphany in what had formerly been Gorodsk Square, and the Znamensky Convent, they looked like golden fungi growing in the springtime of the world. Next to the cathedral was what had been, until the Revolution, the Nicholas 1 High School for Young Ladies. If Baedeker had got its location right it was now a bakery.

I discovered that behind the brick and stone buildings put up before and after the great fire, which embraced an astonishing variety of architectural styles from the cool, neoclassical splendour of the White House – the residence of the tsarist governors of eastern Siberia – to the dignified dottiness of what had been the premises of the Russo-

Asiatic Bank, there were whole networks of streets of chocolate-coloured single- and two-storey wooden houses, a few with their original raised sidewalks of wooden planks. Some of the two-storey houses with their carriage gates and courtyards were like little palaces, and had been built with such delicacy that all that seemed to be needed was one good gust of wind to carry them away. Others, with walls built with what appeared to be whole trunks of trees, resembled the *izbas* of the Siberian countryside and were so heavy that one end or the other had sunk into the earth giving them the appearance of sinking ships. Nearly all of them, large and small, had beautifully carved baroque window frames. Most fantastic of all were the houses built with shingles. On these, the eaves, the barge-boards, the porches and every other imaginable appendage that could be decorated, all of which were of Siberian cedar, had been so extravagantly fretworked that some of them were more air than timber.

The demolishers were everywhere at work and in some places entire streets of houses were in process of destruction, either by being knocked down and the timbers burnt or by being set on fire while still standing, which could be done quite easily if they were sufficiently isolated from all houses that were not yet scheduled for destruction. Soon they would be replaced, as they had been in many other parts of the city, by apartment blocks.

I asked the chief of The Agency at Irkutsk why the authorities were destroying these beautiful and apparently sound buildings. 'Because', he said, 'they are full of bed-bugs; because they cannot be adapted for steam central heating and because they are not appropriate for modern, Soviet citizens.' And he went on to try to distract my attention from this subject, about which he knew that I felt strongly, by uttering some of his ventriloquial calls. 'Listen Ivan,' I said, 'when I was a sailor before the war I fed more bed-bugs than you will ever see in your life; but that was nearly forty years ago. There's been a lot of progress in the anti-bed-bug field. If you Russians are too busy fooling about in outer space to order up some bug killer why don't you ask the World Health Organization to do posterity a favour by presenting you with a few

hundred thousand tons of the stuff. Don't you ever think of your patrimony?' 'We think of our patrimony,' Ivan said, 'but we don't think of
it in the same way that you do.'

'Well, you'd better start thinking in the same way,' I said, 'or we'll
have bed-bugs on the moon.'

9

CROSSING LAKE BAIKAL

Nowadays the train passes along the southern shore of Lake Baikal. Until 1904 the lake had to be crossed on the ice or by ferry. The official *Guide to the Trans-Siberian Railway* describes the lake; Shoemaker tells of the crossing on the great ice-breaker *Baikal.* John Foster Fraser enjoyed the trip; Bassett Digby, as ever, discovered drama. Maurice Baring's crossing was outstandingly beautiful.

In 1918 members of the Czech Legion, resisting with the White Russians the advance of the Reds, set fire to the train ferry *Baikal,* but the smaller ferry *Angara* still survives and was reportedly used for a short time to ferry passengers across the lake when the southern loop was flooded in the 1970s.

Lake Baikal
Guide to the Trans-Siberian Railway, 1900

The Baikál, one of the largest alpine lakes in the world, is called the Holy Sea by the local Russian population. It is the largest freshwater lake in the old world, and lies between 50°28' and 55°50' N. lat. and 73°25' and 80° E. long. The Chinese call it Pe-Khoi, which means Northern Sea, the Mongols, Dalai-Nor, Holy Sea or Bai-kul, Rich Sea. The north American Lakes, Superior, Michigan, Huron and the African Nyanza alone surpass it in size. The extent of its clear surface and its configuration recall Lake Tanganyika situated in Central Africa in proximity to the Nyanza.

The superficial area of the Baikal is 30,034 square versts (34,179 square kilom.), its length, 600 versts. It bends slightly from southwest to north-east; its breadth is not so considerable and varies from 27 to 85 versts. The depth of the lake in its southern part, sounded by Engineer Bogoslovsky, is 791 sea sazhens or 3,185 feet. Situated 1,561 feet above the level of the sea, the bottom of the lake at its deepest parts is much lower than the level of the ocean. According to the

soundings, which give but a slight idea of the relief of the bottom, it may be said that the bottom of the lake presents an immense basin, with deep cavities which, at some places, begin at the shore and run almost through its whole extent.

The World's Deepest Lake
Bryn Thomas

Lake Baikal, 64 km (40 miles) south-east of Irkutsk, is 1637m (5371 ft) deep and estimated to contain more than 20,000 cubic kilometers of water, roughly 20% of the world's freshwater supplies. If all the rest of the world's drinking water ran out tomorrow, Lake Baikal could supply the netire population of the planet for the next 40 years.

Known as the 'Blue Eye of Siberia', it is also the world's oldest lake, formed almost 50 million years ago. It is also among the planet's largest lakes; about 400 miles long and between 20 and 40 miles wide. The water is incredibly clear and, except around Baikalsk and the Selenga delta, completely safe to drink owing to the filtering action of numerous types of sponge which live in its depths, along with hundreds of other species found nowhere else.

Russian colonists called Baikal the 'Holy Sea' since there were so many local myths and legends surrounding it. The Buryats believed that the evil spirit Begdozi lived on Olkhon island in the middle of the lake, though Evenski shamans held that this was the home of the sea god Dianda. It is hardly surprising that these primitive tribes were impressed by the strange power of the lake for at times sudden violent storms spring up, lashing the coast with waves two metres high or more. It freezes to a depth of three metres for four months of the year, from late December. The Angara is the only river that flows out of the lake. Since a dam and hydroelectric power station were built on the Angara in 1959 the level of the lake has been slowly rising.

Crossing The Holy Sea Westwards
Francis E. Clark, 1900

We found [Lake Baikal] in a peaceful mood, but it is not always so by any means. "No man has ever said his prayers until he has ventured on Lake Baikal," is a common saying of the peasants on the shore. Lying, as it does, in a comparatively narrow valley, between the mountain ranges, the terrible gales which have their homes between the mountain peaks are often let loose with but scant warning. Then woe betide the little fisherman's craft that is caught far from shore, and even the passengers on the stout steamer may well tremble.

To unite the two shores with a strong, substantial ferry-boat which can run throughout the winter months, the railway has had constructed in England and brought out piecemeal the huge "icebreaker," so called. Several of the parts of this great craft were lost, strayed, or stolen on the way, and infinite difficulty was experienced in putting it together again when it reached the lake. Even now some tell me that it is no great success as an ice-breaker.

On a fine day, with a smooth sea, nothing could be more delightful than a little journey on the great ships. Into the hold of the steamer runs the whole train without unloading; or, rather, that is to be the way when the railway is in running order. Three parallel tracks throughout the entire length of the boat afford ample room for the longest trains. Above are elegant accommodations for first-class passengers, while the steerage people dispose of themselves in the hold as best they can.

Four great stacks belch out smoke and cinders, and the engines are of the most powerful pattern. A half acre of deck room over all gives the passenger unrivalled opportunities of viewing the magnificent lake, whose southern end he is about to traverse.

A fine breakwater of wooden piles, nearly half a mile long, provides a safe little harbor on the eastern side of the lake, while another, not quite so large, affords a refuge from the winds on the other side. Between these harbors the ice-breaker plies back and forth, making the distance of about fifty miles in four hours.

As we approach the western shore, the scenery grows more lovely than on the eastern side. The crystal lake, fifty feet deep at the shore, dashes in places against precipitous cliffs; the banks are clad in freshest grass, dotted with poppies and lilies and blue honeysuckles, while a little village nestles in a cove beneath a frowning cliff. Rarely have I seen in all my travels a scene more lovely than is presented as the ice-breaker makes her way cautiously into the little artificial harbor of Listvinitschnoie, at the southwestern end of the Holy Sea.

In the early morning we could see, as we thought, the seals disporting themselves in the icy waters, for it is a singular fact that in Lake Baikal alone, of all the freshwater lakes in the world, are seals found. It is thought by some that in prehistoric times they made their way up the River Yenisei, that flows from the lake into the Arctic Ocean, two thousand miles away. At any rate, they made themselves very much at home in the Baikal, and have increased and multiplied and replenished the lake.

The determination of the Russian government to have through steam communication between the oceans is shown by the fact that while such sums have been spent for an ice-breaker and for harbors to make the link across the Baikal possible, the railway is also being pushed around the southern end of the lake, only a short distance away. Both of these routes will be needed, I understand, to facilitate the mobilization of her armies.

The Winter Passage
Michael Myers Shoemaker, 1902

The day is clear and cold and brilliant as we get out of our train in the early morning on the shores of this famous lake. A long pier extends quite out into the water and our steamer lies at its extreme end, affording us a brisk, fresh, and very welcome walk after the confined air in the car.

A descent into the cabin and several glasses of hot tea place us in better condition to enjoy the day. Bundled in fur we are seated on the top deck with the great lake all before us. The air is clear and so transparent that far-off capes and mountains seem but a short distance away. The water for some hundred square yards around us is free of ice and lies silent and darkly blue under the brilliant sun. Off and away north and east spreads the surface of the lake, a vast field of glittering white until it meets the mountains rising some four thousand feet above the eastern shore, blue at the base, snow-capped on all the long line of their jagged summits. To the northward the ice-bound surface of the lake meets the bending arch of a deep-blue sky; the dry air glitters and quivers and is very cold, yet with a coldness that seems full of life and health. Here as elsewhere there is no wind, hence all Siberia seems a land of deathly stillness, with no dampness to render it insupportable.

We are not on the great ice breaker *Baikal*. She is off up the lake clearing a pass for us, but this ship is of like construction, though smaller, and of course of less power.

We meet on this ship an English engineer, Mr. Handy, whose explanations are most interesting and who gives us some interesting photos of hereabouts. As we start I ask where we are to find passage, and he waves his hand directly towards the apparently perfect field of ice. The little ship takes on full headway quickly, and as we near the ice I notice what appears to be a broad belt of jagged ice apparently frozen solid once more. Into this our ship rushes at full speed and we hold on fast in anticipation of the coming jar, and a jar it is, but the boat is equal to the occasion and the ice parts before her. It is a wonderful sight, and most thrilling. The ship moves steadily onward, turning up great blocks of deep blue ice fifty feet long and three feet thick, which pile up on either side as high as her deck, and then fall back with a sobbing sound into the densely blue waters in our wake. One never tires of watching the churning and tearing up the vast blocks of ice. This ice is sometimes forty-eight inches thick, and then it is too much even for the great breaker, but she has cleared this pathway, breaking through some thirty-six inches and more. Even while I look the channel behind seems again to be a solid surface.

Across the Great Lake
John Foster Fraser, 1901

Presently there came steaming down the lake a huge four-funnelled vessel, white painted, by no means pretty, and rather like a barn that had slipped afloat. That was the *Baikal*, one of the most wonderful vessels in the world, coming back from Misovaya, and carrying two goods trains fully laden. If necessary she could carry three trains and eight hundred passengers, but at present the *Baikal* is used for merchandise and the *Angara* for passengers.

The *Baikal* passed sufficiently near for me to appreciate her great size, and as the fore gates were open I caught a glimpse of red-painted goods waggons. The ship is of over 4,000 tons, close on 300 feet long, and has nearly 60 feet beam. She has three triple expansion engines of 1,250 horse-power, two amidships and one in the bow. This power is required in the ice-breaking. She will break through ice 36 inches thick, and her bow is made with a curve, so that when the ice is thicker she can be backed and then go full steam at the ice, partly climb on it with her impetus, and then crush it with her weight. This means that the *Baikal* sometimes takes a week to cross the lake.

The Baikal is sometimes frozen from December till April. But although the ice puts a hindrance in the way of ships, the lake is busier than in the summer. I have before mentioned that winter is the great time for cheap transit in Siberia, because sledge travelling is easy and quick. So a road is made across the lake; the track is marked by pine trees stuck in the ice; a man holds a contract for keeping the way in repair for the post, and if there is a nasty crack he must board it until it heals by freezing; and all day long there is a constant procession of sledges coming from Trans-Baikalia, Mongolia, and Manchuria, and making for Irkutsk.

Baikal's Past
Bassett Digby, 1928

The big icebreaker had a chapel on board, and at one time there was quite a vogue among romantically-minded young couples of Irkutsk and the Trans-Baikal for having their wedding in it. In stormy weather (and you could get very rough crossings) a number of passengers always came in to pray – the more, the stormier. This used to annoy the wedding parties and led sometimes to unseemly brawls and even free fights. Irkutsk people cherish a story, which they declare to be true, of one of these rough-weather weddings in the dark and crowded chapel saloon with every one, including the officiating priest, very dizzy, and a clamour of disputes going on, that resulted in the wrong young man being married because the bride felt so seasick that she did not open her eyes, and the groom was in a state of collapse, longing for a swift death rather than matrimony.

Before the construction of the Trans-Siberian railroad, one crossed the ice by sledge. There were specially trained horses for this traffic, accustomed to wearing shoes with long spikes in them. The camels of the tea caravans from China, too, used to wear such shoes for the crossing of the frozen lake.

Though, in one instance, a contingent of one hundred and fifty infantry fell through the ice and were drowned, almost to a man, through crossing the lake too soon after the freeze-up, it was usually trains that met with this contretemps. Though parties were sent ahead to make frequent borings in the ice before a new set of rails was laid, the engineers had no means of foreseeing when a current of warm water from one of the numerous volcanic springs at the bottom would invisibly reduce the thickness beyond the safety point. In most cases there was just a violent crack, a great sag in the ice that filled at once with water, a lurch of the string of heavy cars, a snapping of rail bolts, a plunge – and the train and its locomotive had disappeared for ever.

But at least one little locomotive had the luck to go through before she came to the great depths. After a while the grapple hooks got busy. She was located and raised – and she is still on the job.

Baikal in Winter
Maurice Baring, 1905

It was here [Baikal Station] that the real interest of the journey began. The lake was at that time crossed daily by two large icebreakers, the *Baikal* and the *Angora*, which cleft through three feet of half-melted ice, the passage lasting four hours. Baikal Station is only a few hours' journey from Irkutsk. I arrived about one o'clock in the afternoon, and the steamer started at five.

As we left, the scene was one of the most strange and beautiful I have ever witnessed. It had been a glorious day, and the sun in the cold, clear atmosphere – an atmosphere that has a radiant purity which is quite indescribable – was gradually assuming the appearance of a red, fiery, arctic ball. In front of us was a silent sheet of ice, powdered with snow, white and spotless except for one long brown mark which had been made by the sledges. On the horizon westward of us a range of mountains was visible, whose summits seemed to disappear into a veil of snow made by the low-hanging clouds. It was impossible to discern where the mountains left off and where the clouds began; in fact, this low range had not the appearance of mountains at all; it seemed as if we were making for some mysterious island, some miraculous reef of sapphires, so intense was the blue of these hills, so gem-like the way they glinted in the cold air. Towards the east was another still lower and more distant range; the intense deep blue faded here into a deli-cate and transparent sea-green – the colour of the transparent seas in the Greek islands – and these hills seemed like the phantom contin-uation of the other range – unearthly and filmy as a mirage.

As we moved the steamer ploughed the ice into flakes, which leapt and scattered themselves in innumerable spiral shapes, fantastic flowers of ice and snow. As the sun sank lower the strangeness and beauty in-creased, for a faint pink halo pervaded the sky round the sun, which grew more and more fiery and metallic. I knew that I had never seen anything like this before, and yet I felt at the same time that I was looking on something which I had already seen. I racked my brains, and suddenly I became aware of what was teasing my mind. It was the recollection of Coleridge's *Ancient Mariner.* The following lines came into my head:

And now there came both mist and snow,
And it grew wondrous cold:
And ice, mast-high, came floating by
As green as emerald.

It was "wondrous cold," and here in the distance seemed to be the

215

ice as "green as emerald." Above us was the sun "no bigger than the moon," and as we ploughed through the ice which "crackled and growled" like "noises in a swound," I felt we might have been the first that ever burst into that "silent sea."

As the sun sank the whole sky was suffused with a pink glow, and the distant mountains seemed like ghostly caverns of ice.

It was too cold to stay on deck and enjoy the beauty with any comfort, and one took refuge in the comfortable cabin, where an excellent dinner was ready. We arrived at eight o'clock; it was dark, and the other ice-breaker was starting on its return journey to the strains of military music.

I resumed my train journey about eleven o'clock at night. The train was so full that it was impossible not only to get a seat in the first or second class, but at first it seemed doubtful whether one would obtain a place of any kind in the train. On realising the situation I had jumped into a third class carriage, which was at once invaded by a crowd of peasant women and children. An official screamed ineffectually that the carriage was reserved for the military, upon which an irate *muzhik* waving a huge long loaf of bread (like an enormous truncheon) cried out, pointing to the seething and heterogeneous crowd: "Are we not military, also, one and all of us reservists?" – and they refused to move. This was the first example I had of what was borne upon me over and over again during my sojourn among the Russians – namely, that if you ask leave to do anything you will probably be told that it is quite impossible owing to Article 146 of Section IV. of such and such a regulation, or that you must get a paper signed by such and such an official – but if you do the thing it is probable that nobody will interfere with you; there is a Teutonic mass of rules and regulations, but the Slav temperament is not equal to the task of insisting on their literal execution. It is as if an elaborate bureaucratic system were introduced into the internal administration of Ireland. One can imagine the result. Sometimes one blesses Heaven for this fact; at other times it seems to have its disadvantages, and one regrets the rigour of the game.

The confusion was incredible, and one man, by the vehement way in which he flung himself and his property on his wooden seat, broke it and fell with a crash to the ground. The third class carriages are formed in this way: the carriage is not divided into separate compartments, but is like a corridor carriage, with no partition and no doors between the carriage proper and the passage; it is divided into three sections, each section consisting of six plank beds: three on each side of the window, and one placed above the other, forming three storeys. There is, besides this, a tier of seats against the windows in the passage at right angles to the regular seats. The occupant of a place has a right to the whole plank, so that he can lie down and sleep on it. I gave up my place in the first carriage as I had lost sight of luggage and servant, and went in search of them and of the guard.

I found the guard, who stated that the train was full to overflowing, and that no further carriages would be added. I said I wanted four places, and that I did not mind if they were in the luggage van, or anywhere else. He took me to a carriage which was occupied mostly by soldiers. It must be borne in mind that the train by which I was travelling was not a military one, and that these soldiers were stray offshoots going to join their respective regiments.

The guard told the soldiers to make room for me, my servant, and two travelling companions. It seemed to me an impossible task; but it was done. I was presently encamped on a plank near the ceiling in the passage, at right angles to the regular seats. I soon fell into a deep sleep. The next thing I remember was being wakened at sunrise by a furious scuffle. A party of Chinese coolies – for all I knew then they may have been high-class mandarins – had invaded the train. They were drunk, and spat and slobbered, and the soldiers with one voice cried, "Get out, Chinese." They were bundled backwards and forwards, rolled up and down the passage like a football, and were eventually allowed to settle on the platform outside the train. I did not go to sleep again. It was too interesting to sleep, and from my suspended plank I enjoyed myself more than I have ever done in any theatre. The soldiers began to get up. One of them, dressed in a scarlet shirt, stood against the window and reverently said his prayers towards the rising sun, with many signs of the Cross. A little later a stowaway arrived; stowaways who travel in trains in Russia without tickets are called "hares." He was detected by the under guard, who advised him to get under the seat during the visit of the ticket collector. This he did; he remained under the seat about an hour and a half, until the ticket collector paid his visit. Then he crept from his hiding-place and squeezed in among the crowd in the carriage; the ticket collector frequently returned, but on every occasion he managed to escape notice by letting himself be crushed almost to a jelly by the other passengers.

10

TO VLADIVOSTOK

It is only after leaving Irkutsk that the train goes through the first tunnel on the journey from Moscow. Some 100 kilometres after Chita, the Trans-Manchurian line branches off at Karymskoye and follows the route of the old Chinese Eastern Railway to Harbin before turning southwards to Beijing. The Trans-Siberian line continues onwards into the homelands where in 1162 Genghis Khan ("ruler of the world") was born. The railway crosses the Soviet Far East, travelling close to the Chinese border formed by the Amur River, and to Khabarovsk, 8351 kilometres from Moscow, and the boat train to Japan. The journey on to Nakhodka was once made at night, to ensure that prying foreign eyes see nothing of this strategically sensitive area, but the boat train is palatial. Nakhodka, 9297 kilometres from Moscow, was the end of the line for tourists, when Vladivostok was strictly out of bounds. Then in 1986 Gorbachev announced that Vladivostock was to become "a wide open window to the East", and foreigners could go there once more.

Baedeker describes the journey in 1914. Annette Meakin and her mother's journey in 1900 was rough, though they as usual were joyful. The Official Guide, as usual, describes the town of Chita in great detail. This surely is where the equivalent of Intourist guides of that day must have obtained their endless information.

The journey through Manchuria was hazardous for Shoemaker in 1902. Digby and Wright watched the mail being loaded in 1910. Peter Fleming crashed. The journey tailed off for Christopher Portway, and Eric Newby was undoubtedly relieved when it was over.

b. From Irkutsk to Vladivostok
Baedeker, 1914

3029 V. (2008 M.). EXPRESS TRAIN (1st & 2nd class; sleeping and dining cars) four times weekly in $3^{1/3}$ days (fares 167 rb. 45, 108 rh. 10 cop.; to Kharbin 119 rb. 5, 77 rb. 16 cop.; comp. p. 528). The railway-

ticket is good for 11 days (comp. p. 523). The allowance of free luggage is 60 Russian lbs. (54 lbs.) for through-passengers, and 40 lbs. for others; each 10 lbs. (9 lbs.) additional costs 1 rb. 39 cop. -MAIL TRAIN once daily in 5¼ days (fares 142 rb. 20, 55 rb. 95 cop.; to Kharbin 99 rb. 65, 38 rb. 95 cop.); half-a-day is saved by taking the 'Passenger Train' as far as Mandshuriya. Carriages are changed at Mandshuriya (Manchuri).

The so-called zonal tariff of the (Russian) Chinese Eastern Railway is much higher than that of the Russian State Railways, as the following selected fares show: 176 V., 8 rb. 40 cop. & 5 rb.; 625 V., 25 rb. & 15 rb. 66 cop.; 876 V., 36 & 22½ rb.; 1100 V., 44 & 27½rb.; 1400 V., 56 & 35 rb. – Custom-house examination, see p. 523. – The railway-clocks show Irkutsk time (4 hrs. 56 min. ahead of St. Petersburg time) between Lake Baikal and Maudshuriya, and Kharbin time (6 hrs. 25 min ahead of St. Petersburg time) between Mandshuriya and Vladivostok.

From Irkutsk to Muisovaya the train passes through superb scenery. At first we skirt the Angará to Lake Baikál (see below), girt with huge grey cliffs stretching away to the horizon; then, from Baikal to Muisovaya (see below), the line runs on a ledge cut in the rocky bank of the lake, whence, as we emerge from each tunnel, we obtain fresh views of the lake and its girdle of mountains. From Muisovaya to Tchita (p. 534) the country is wooded and hilly, and at times picturesque. [From Tchita (Karuimskaya) to Sryetensk (p. 535) we follow the wild and precipitous bank of the Ingodá.] From Tchita to the Manchurian frontier and thence to Yakeshi (p. 636) the train passes through steppes; from Yakeshi to Barim (p. 536) we traverse a succession of picturesque valleys; between Barim and Pogranitchnaya (p. 587) the steppes begin again, becoming more hilly as we near Pogranitchnaya; thence to Vladivostok (p. 538) we traverse mountains, descending to the sea through a wild and wooded country. Manchuria is an endless steppe, well cultivated in places, bounded on the S. by bare hills, and intersected by four great rivers.

Irkútsk, see p. 531. The railway follows the right bank of the *Angará* (splendid views). 23 V. *Mikhalévo* (1450 ft.). – 61 V. *Baikal (1520* ft.; Rail. Restaurant), where the Angará issues from the lake.

Lake Baikal (1560 ft.), called by the Mongolians the *Bai-Kul*

('Rich Lake'), is surrounded with rocky mountains about 4600 ft. high, many of them covered with forest. It is 13,185 so. M. in area, 400 M. in length, and from 18 to 56 M. in width. Lake Baikál is the deepest lake in the world (over 6500 ft. in places); moreover, next to the Great Lakes of America and the Victoria Nyanza and Lake Tanganyika in Africa it is the largest fresh-water lake in the world. Its water is extraordinarily clear and very cold. It freezes over about the end of December (O. S.). Storms are very frequent and violent, but least so in June and July. The mountains on the E. side are already snow-covered by October. Lake Baikal is rich in fish. The coregonus omul Lepech. (a kind of whitefish) and the Baikal seal (*phoca baicalensis*) are peculiar to its waters.

From Baikal the train rounds the S. end of Lake Baikal, threading forty tunnels and passing through numerous cuttings and over numerous bridges. 105 V. *Maritui* (Rail. Restaurant). From (140 V.) *Kultuk* a highroad leads to Kyakhta (p. 534). The train now turns to the E. 150 V. *Slyudyánka* (Rail. Restaurant); 201 V. *Múrino* (Rail. Restaurant); 251 V. *Tankhói* (Rail. Restaurant; customs examination for passengers from the Trans-Baikal district).

305 V. *Muisováya* (1540 ft.; Rail. Restaurant), on the S.E. shore of Lake Baikal. The line now runs near the lake as far as (349 V.) *Posólskaya* (1570 ft.), but it then enters the broad valley of the *Selengá* and follows the left bank of that stream. 384 V. *Selengá* (1580 ft.; Rail. Restaurant), near the village of *Ilyinskoye,* with the Svyáto-Tróitzki Monastery founded in the 16th century. About 7 M. beyond (423 V.) *Tataúrovo* (1620 ft.), where the valley contracts, the train crosses the Selenga by a bridge 595 yds. long.

459 V. *Verkhne-Udinsk* (1785 ft.: Rail. Restaurant; Sibir, R. 1-3 rb., bed-linen 35 cop., I). ¾-1¼ rb. ; izvóshtchik from the rail. station to the town ½, at night 1 rb.), a prettily situated district town at the junction of the *Udá* and Selengá, is the headquarters of the Western Trans-Baikál Mining Administration. Pop. 15,000.

A highroad, shorter but less interesting than that from Kultuk (see above), runs from Verkhne-Udinsk to the S. to *Selenginsk* (the scene, in 1818-41, of the missionary labours of Wm. Stallybrass and Edw. Swan, who translated the Bible into the Mongolian tongue), *Troitzkosavsk,* and (219 V.) *Kyakhta-Maimátchin,* two towns (the former Russian, the latter Chinese) on the frontier between Russia and Mongolia, formerly the centre of the overland tea trade from China to Russia (now unimportant). At Kyakhta is an agency of the Russo-Asiatic Bank.

About 5 M. beyond Verkhne-Udinsk the train crosses the *Udá.* 492 V. *Onokhói* (1770 ft.), a village occupied by Buryats and Mongols. – 512 V. *Zaïgráyevo* (1880 ft.), with cement-works. We cross the *Bryan.* – The train next ascends viâ (561 V.) *Gorkhón* (2325 ft.) to (593 V.) *Petrovski Zavód* (2635 ft.; Rail. Restaurant), near which is the Petrovski Foundry established in 1790. Farther on we follow the right bank of the *Khilók.* 642 V. *Tolbaga* (2420 ft.). Beyond (685 V.) *Badó* (2535 ft.; Rail. Restaurant) is a short tunnel. 733 V. *Khilók* (2640 ft.; Rail. Restaurant); 846 V. *Mogzón* (2975 ft.; Rail. Restaurant). –About 10 V. beyond (885 V.) *Sokhondó* (3095 ft.) the train leaves the valley of the Khilók. crosses the *Yáblonovi Range,* and penetrates a tunnel 93 yds. long, inscribed at its W. entrance 'To the Great Ocean' and at its E. entrance 'To the Atlantic Ocean'. We then descend rapidly to (907 V.) *Yáblono-vaya* (2775 ft.; Rail. Restaurant), beyond which we follow the winding and picturesque valley of the *Ingodá.* 941 V. *Ingodá* (2265 ft.; Rail. Restaurant).

978 V. (648 M.) Tchitá (2150 ft.; *Railway Restaurant)*; 980 V. *Tchká Town Station.* The prettily situated town (Daúrskoye Podvórye; izvóshtchik to the town 50, at night 80 cop.), situated on the left bank of the Tchitá, near its confluence with the Ingodá, is the capital of the Trans-Baikál Territory and the headquarters of the 2nd Siberian Army Corps. Pop. 73,000. The *Museum* of the Imperial Russian Geographical Society has an interesting collection of objects relating to the mining and smuggling of gold (open free in winter on Sun., 10-1; at other times on application to the conservator, P.M. Tolmatchev; closed from June to Aug.). Many of the Decabrists (the St. Petersburg revolutionaries of Dec. 14th, 1825) were banished to Tchita.

We cross the Tchita and then traverse hilly country as far as Kitaiski Razyezd. 1033 V. *Makkavyéyevo* (2035 ft.). –1071 V. *Karúimskaya* (1985 ft.; Rail. Restaurant).

CONTINUATION OF RAILWAY JOURNEY TO KHARBIN. The railway runs for the most part through a steppe-like district inhabited by Cossacks and Buddhistic Buryats. The winter here is very cold. – At (1084 V.) *Kitáiski Razyézd* (1930 ft.) the line to Sryetensk diverges to the E. (p. 534), while our line runs towards the S. About 1 V. beyond the station we cross the I*ngodá.* Beyond (1091 V.) *Adriánovka* (2075 ft.; Rail. Restaurant) we ascend to the watershed (2885 ft.) between the Ingodá and the Agá, and then descend to (1120 V.) *Buryátskaya* (2580 ft.). 1144 V. *Mogotni* (Rail. Restaurant). A little short of (1165 V.) *Agá* (2060ft.) we cross the river of that name. Hard by is the Aginski Datzán, a Buryat convent. Beyond (1211 V.) *Olovyánnaya* (Rail. Restaurant) we cross the *Onón,* and near (1245 V.) *Buirka* we cross the *Turgá.* 1273 V. *Khadabulak* (Rail. Restaurant). About 7 M. to the W. of (1304 V.) *Borzyá* (Rail. Restaurant) is the *Tchindátskaya Cossack Stanitza.* 1342 V. *Kharanór* (Rail. Restaurant). About 2 V. beyond (1404 V.) *Matziyévskaya* the railway enters Manchuria.

1424 V. (944 M.) Mandshúriya *(Manchuria,* 2135 ft.; *Rail. Restaurant),* with 10,000 inhab., founded since 1900, is the frontier-station between Russia and Manchuria, and the starting-point of the Chinese Eastern Railway. Passengers' luggage is examined here.

As far as the Great Khingán Mountains the train runs through a flat steppe-district. Among the prominent features of interest are the fortified station-buildings (sometimes adorned with apes, dragons, and other Chinese ornaments), the lofty loopholed water-towers, the rude Chinese carts with their two high wheels, and the camels at pasture. – At (28 V. from Mandshuriya) *Tchalainor* (1825 ft.) we cross the outlets of *Lake Kulun* (Dalai-nor), flowing in the direction of the *Argún.* In this vicinity are several coal-pits. Farther on, we traverse the valley of the *Khailár.*

176 V. *Khailár,* (2030 ft.; Rail. Restaurant). Near the station (izvóshtchik, 25 cop.) is the modern town (Popóv Hotel). with 4000 inhab. and a branch of the Russo-Asiatic Bank. The interesting old town, surrounded by a mud wall, lies 2 M. off. An important trade is carried on in the pelts of the bobak or marmot (Russ.). – We cross the *Emin.* 228 V. *Tcharomte,* (2095 ft), in a good arable district.

253 V. *Yakeshi,* (2200 ft.), at the foot of the *Great Khingán Mts.,* the E. slopes of which are richly wooded. Farther on we ascend, viâ (283

V.) *Myandukhe* (Rail. Restaurant) and (340 V.) *Irekte* (2870 ft.; Rail.
Restaurant), to (349 V.) *Khingán* and to the top of the pass, threading
a tunnel (3155 ft.) 2 M. long just beyond the station. We then descend
in windings, including the so-called 'Hingan Loop', to (372 *V.)Bukhedu*
(2210 ft.; Rail. Restaurant), in the *Valley of the Yal.*
At (429 V.) *Barim* (1460 ft.) we obtain a fine view of the mountains. Farther on the steppes begin again, but on this side of the
Khingán they are more fertile than to the W. of it. 487 V. *Tcha-lantun,*
(1055 ft.; Rail. Restaurant), a straggling village; 517 V. *Tchingis-Khan,*
(865 ft.), named after Jenghiz Khan, the Mongolian conqueror (d.
1227), whose home is said to have been a little to the N.
Beyond (603 V.) *Khurkhura* (Хурхура; 525 ft.) we cross the *Nonni*
and reach (623 V.) *Tzitzikar,* (Rail. Restaurant).
A light railway, with a station of its own, runs hence (fares 80 & 60
cop.) to (25 V.) Tzitzikar or *Tsitsikar* (Chinese inns only; Russo-Asiatic
Bank), the capital of the Manchurian province of Heilungchiang,
founded in 1692 and situated near the left bank of the *Nonni.* It is surrounded by a wall and carries on a trade in grain. Pop. 70,000.
From this point to Kharbin the train traverses a treeless and almost
uninhabited plateau. 758 V. *Anda* (495 ft.; Rail. Restaurant). At (847
V.) *Duitzinshan,* (405 ft.), the train leaves the plateau and approaches
the Súngari, which it crosses by au eight-arched bridge 1035 yds. in
length (view).
876 V. (581 M.) Kharbin, _ *Railway Restaurant.* —HOTELS (all in
the New Town). *Grand-Hôtel,* near the station, R. 2½-7 rb., B. 55 cop.,
déj. (12 to 3.30 p.m.) 90 cop. to 1½ rb., D. (7-9 p.m.) 1-1½ rb.; *Méropole,
Oriant,* R. from 2 rb. – IZVÓSHTCHIK from the New Town to the
Harbour Suburb 40, to the Old Town 80 cop.; from the Harbour
Suburb to the Old Town 1 rb. 20; per drive within any one quarter of
the town 25, per hr. 80 cop. Double fares at night. – BANKS. Branches
of the *Russo-Asiatic, Hongkong & Shanghai,* and *Yokohama Specie Banks.*
Branch Office of Kunst & Albers (comp. p. 588). – International
Sleeping Car Co. at the Grand-Hôtel (p. 536). – CONSULS. British,
H. E. Sly: American, *S. P. Warner.* – LLOYD'S AGENTS, *Kunst & Albers.*
– ENGLISH CHURCH SERVICES are held about once a month.
Kharbin or *Harbin* (500 ft.), in a marshy district on the navi-gable
Súngari, is a town of 80,000 inhab., including 30,000 Russians but not

counting the strong garrison. Except for the old town it was founded about 1900, and it owes its importance to the Russo-Japanese war. It consists of four parts: the *New Town* (with the Railway Station, the Headquarters of the Chinese Maritime Customs for Manchuria, the Russian Post Office, the Head Office of the Chinese Eastern Railway, and the residences of the railway and other officials; the *Harbour Suburb*, on the Súngari, $2\frac{1}{2}$ M. to the N., with the larger business houses, most of Which are in the Kitáiskaya; the Chinese Town of *Fud-zyadyan*, to the E. of the Harbour Suburb; and the *Old Town*, to the S. of the New Town, and now without any importance. The former Chinese Citadel, 5 M. to the E. of the Súngari, was razed by the Russians in 1900.

To *Mukden* and *Port Arthur*, see R. 78; to *Mukden* and *Peking*, see RR. 78, 79.

The railway to Vladivostok runs to the E. through a mountainous region. 915 V. *Ashikhe*, (445 ft.), with 40,000 inhab. and a Mission Station of the United Free Church of Scotland. At (934 V.) *Ertzendyantzi*, or, is a hill consisting of white marble (quarries). Beyond (1028 V.) *Imyanpo* (700 ft.; Rail. Restaurant), a Manchurian town with a Russian colony, we ascend through verdant valleys to (1109 V.) *Gaolintzi*, (2075 ft.). 1131 V. *Khandaokhetzi*, (1410 ft.; Rail. Restaurant), with 3000 inhabitants. – Just short of (1230 V.) *Modaoshi*, (1045 ft.), a prettily situated settlement, we cross the *Mudan-kiang*. About 13 M. to the S., in a fertile plain on the left bank of the Mudan-kiang, is the fur-trading town of *Ninguta*. – We ascend through three tunnels to (1254 V.) *Dai-magou*, (2065 ft.), and then descend to (1278 V.) *Mulin* (1080 ft.; Rail. Restaurant). 1309 V. *Matzyaokhe*, (1065 ft.), in a fertile plain; 1345 V. *Silinkhe*, (1265 ft.).

1388 V. *Pogranitchnaya* (1505 ft.; Rail. Restaurant; Russian custom-house, comp.p.535), the frontier-station between Manchuria and the Russian coast-district. It is also the N.E. terminus of the Chinese Eastern Railway. – The Ussuri Railway, which begins here, descends through six tunnels to (1413 V.) *Grodekovo* (585 ft.). 1471 V. *Golenki* (395 ft.), in a grassy plain.

1504 V. *Nikólsk Ussuriski* (75 ft.; Rail. Restaurant; Grand-Hôtel, Nikoláyevskaya 7, with good cuisine; izvóshtchik from the station to the town 50 cop., at night 1 rb.), a district-town in a fertile neighbourhood, was founded in 1866 and contains 52,000 inhabitants. It is the headquarters of the 1st Siberian Army Corps. The sportsman will find good shooting in the neighbourhood (musk-deer, roe-deer, and wild-boar). – About 20 V. beyond Nikolsk Ussu-riski the railway traverses a romantic rocky district on the steep bank of the *Zuifun*. 1539 V. *Razdólnoye* (25 ft.). Beyond (1563 V.) *Nadézhdinskaya* (70 ft.; Rail. Restaurant) are some coal-pits. The train now skirts the *Gulf of Amúr*, passing the villa-colonies of *Okeanskaya* and *Sedanka*, and finally reaching the station of *Vladivostók*, on the W. side of the Golden Horn. 1605 V. (1064 M.) Vladivostók, – *Railway Restaurant*. – HOTELS. *Hotel-Restaurant d' Allemagne* (P1. a, B 2), cor. of Kitáiskaya and Pekinskaya, R. 2-6, bed-linen ½. B. ¾ rb., déj. (12.30 to 2) 80 cop. to 1¼ rb., D. (7.30 to 9 p.m.) l½ rb.; *Versailles* (P1. b; A, 2), Svyetlánskaya 10, cor. of Koréiskaya, these two well spoken of; *Grand-Hotel* (P1. c; A, 3), Aleútskaya, opposite the rail, station; *Centrálnaya* (P1. d; A, 2), cor. of Svyetlánskaya and Aleútskaya, R. 1¼-4, D. (12-4 p.m.) ¾-l rb.

RESTAURANTS. *Zolotói Rog* or *Golden Horn*, Svyetlánskaya 15, with view over the bay, déj. (11-1) ¾-l, D. (12-5) ½-1¼ rb.; *Shuin*, Svyetlánskaya 36; *Unterberger*, Svyetlánskaya 35.

From the station to the town 25 cop. (luggage 20 cop.), per hr. 1 rb.; at night (12-7 a.m.) double fares. – ELECTRIC TRAMWAY (8-20 cop.) from the railway station (P1. A, B, 3) along the Svyetlanskaya.

POST & TELEGRAPH OFFICE (PI. 5; B, 2), Svyetlánskaya. – CONSULS. British, *R. Macleod Hodgson;* American, *J. F. Jewell.* – Head Office of the great commercial and banking house of *Kunst & Albers* (P1. K & A; B, 2), Svyetlánskaya; agents for the Hongkong & Shanghai Banking Corporation, the Hamburg-American Line, the North German Lloyd, the Pacific Mail Steamship Company, and the Occidental & Oriental Steamship Company. – *Imperial Bank* (P1. 1; B, 2), Svyetlánskaya; *Russo-Asiatic Bank* (P1. 7; A, 2), Aleútskaya (open 9.30 to 2). – *International Sleeping Car Co.*, Aleút-skaya 4 (P1. A, 2, 3).

Local time is 6¾ hrs. ahead of St. Petersburg time.

Vladivostók ('Mistress of the East'; 10 ft.) is the prettily situated capital of the Maritime Province, the headquarters of the 4th Siberian Army Corps, and a fortified naval and commercial harbour. It lies in 43°7' K. lat. and 131°54' E. long., on the slopes of the Coast Range, at the S.W. extremity of a peninsula between the *Amúr Gulf* on the W.

and the *Ussuri Gulf* on the E. The harbour is formed by the bay of the *Golden Horn*, 4 M. long and $^2/_3$ M. wide, on the W. and N. sides of which the town lies. The town, founded in 1860, was a free port from 1865 to 1909. It has about 120,000 inhab., including many soldiers and some Chinese, Koreans, and Japanese. Living is extremely dear. The mean annual temperature is about 40° F. (comp. p. 522), and the climate is unattractive, Sept. being the most agreeable month. The bay is ice-bound from the middle of Dec. to the beginning of March, but sea-communication is rendered possible by ice-breakers.

The main street of the town, the Svyetlánskaya (P1. A-D, 2, 3), runs from E. to W. not far from the Golden Horn and is crossed by the railway. On the S. side of it lie the *Municipal Garden* (P1. A, B, 2) and the *Museum* of the Amúr Exploration Society (PL 3, B 3; open free on Tues., Frid., & Sun. 10-4; at other times, on application to the Director; entr. at Ulitza Petra Velikago 7), containing costumes and weapons of the Russian Far East; on the N. side is a monument to *Admiral Zavoiko*, erected in 1908. Farther to the E. are the Greek Catholic *Uspenski Cathedral* (P1 B, 2) and a memorial (1897) to *Admiral G. I. Nevélski* (d. 1876), who in 1848 discovered the Amúr estuary. On it are inscribed the words of Nicholas I.: – ('Where once the Russian flag has been unfurled, it must never be Lowered'). Here also are a *Lutheran Church* (P1 2; B, 2) and the docks and barracks. A fine view is obtained from the heights above the *Observatory*. Also worthy of mention are the *Roman Catholic Church* (P16; C, 2) and (in the Púshkinskaya) the *Oriental Institute* (PL 4, B 2), for the study of E. Asiatic languages, opened in 1899.

About 30 M. to the S.E. of Vladivostok is the island of *Askold*, on which the Manchurian sika deer ('spot deer') is preserved.

STEAMERS of the Russian Volunteer Fleet run viá *Nagasaki* to *Odessa* in 40-45 days (fare 500 rb., including food); to *Tsuruga* (branch-line to Yokohama & Tokio), twice weekly in 40 hrs. (fare 37 rb., in-cluding food); to *Shanghai*, once weekly (fare 81 rb., in-cluding food). – Japanese steamers (Nippon Yusen Kaisha) ply to *Kobe, Nagasaki, Shanghai, Hong Kong*, and other ports.

† The station-names are taken from the official Russian time-tables.

Transbaikalia
Annette Meakin, 1900

A train composed of fourth-class carriages stood waiting for the passengers as they came off the ice-breaker. We got into a compartment and tried to keep it to ourselves, but there was no sign of starting, and more and more people kept coming in. Those who got there first took the lower places, and the rest clambered up on to the shelves above, which were three deep. At last those above us became an object of desire to two men of so dirty and unkempt an appearance that we became desperate. I put up my hands to ward them off, and cried "Conductor" in the most threatening tones I could muster. It was no use; they had gone into the next division, but only to climb quietly over into our shelves when they thought we were not looking. The sight of a wretched pair of feet hanging out over my head was too much for me. I rushed on to the platform, and addressed the first man in uniform I came across. This happened to be an engineer who had charge of that part of the line. As he spoke French I was able to explain what was the matter. He came with me at once to our compartment. The two men seeing him approach slid stealthily back the way they had come.

"This is not a fit place for ladies," said our new friend, looking round at our grimy companions – "and *English* ladies too! Oh, this will never do. I will arrange something better for you." Then he hurried off. In a few minutes he came back to say that he had ordered an engineer's private carriage to be put on the train for us. "You will have sleeping berths and a little room with a samovar, where you can make tea," he added; "but it will not be ready for two hours. I fear you must wait here till then."

The two hours seemed as though they would never pass, and the dirty men had climbed above us once more. At last, when it was getting quite dark, the engineer came again.

"I am very sorry," he said, "but a telegram has come ordering us to keep the carriage I promised you for an official from St. Petersburg, who is expected shortly. His Excellency, M. Iswolsky and his family, who passed through last week, took all the other carriages. What I can do for you I will. A captain and six soldiers have got a luggage van to themselves. If you don't mind sharing it with them as far as Stretinsk, I will have part of it curtained off for you."

"Anything, anything but this," we cried.

Once more he left us and we waited on. The night was getting chilly and rain began to come down in torrents. At length two men appeared with a lantern. They were the engineer and the conductor. The engineer gave my mother his arm, and they escorted us out into the rain and along the line to the last carriage on the train. The step was very high, but we clambered in.

How we blessed that kind engineer! With curtains from his own house he had partitioned off one corner of the luggage van for our use. The deal boards that had been put there for the soldiers were all we had to sleep on by night, or to sit on by day. But that was nothing so long as we had it all to ourselves. The size of our *coupé* was ten feet by eight. In the centre of the van was a stove with a chimney going through the roof.

"The captain thought you might be cold, so he made the soldiers light a fire," said the engineer, and we were most grateful for the genial warmth, for we had got wet as well as cold in coming across.

With heartfelt thanks we bade our deliverer good night, and the train started. It was just midnight.

Of course there was no going to bed for us that night, or for the three that followed. We lay down just as we were on our rugs, which we had folded as thickly as possible to take off the hardness of the eighteen inch boards. Oh, how our bones ached after ten minutes in one position!

My mother had the side nearest the curtain; a soldier slept on a similar board to ours on the other side of it, and she occasionally felt his elbow. We had a tiny window in the corner, so high up that to look out we had to stand on the seat. *Still, we had it all to ourselves.*

Three days and four nights we spent in that luggage van. The soldiers and their captain were kindness itself. They fetched us hot water and milk at the stations, and when we came short of bread gave us some of their own, which was brown, with sour lumps of uncooked dough here and there.

As the line was not yet open to the general public there were no buffets ready. We lived on bread, milk and tea. We washed our faces every morning with some of the water brought for tea. Happily we had neither dust nor extreme heat to contend with; for there was a gentle and continuous rain nearly all the time.

The next two vans to ours were prison vans. The windows were strongly barred, and instead of ordinary doors they had a sliding one in the side with a special lock.

Four of our soldiers sprang out the moment the train stopped, no matter whether there was a station or not, and stood with shouldered bayonets one on either side of each of the prison vans. Whenever I looked up at the prison bars I saw a cluster of children's faces peering out – hardly ever a man's face. The prisoners must have spent their time in sleep. There certainly did not seem much danger of their escaping. Once one of the soldiers picked some flowers and handed them in to the children. They stretched out their hands eagerly, and looked so pleased to get them.

Chita
Guide to the Great Siberian Railway, 1900

Chita is the chief town of the Transbaikál territory. It is the residence of a military governor, and the centre of the local administration (51° 1' N. lat. and 83° 10' E. long.). The town is situated on the left bank of the river Chita, near its junction with the Ingoda. The small river Kaidalóvka, a tributary of the Chitá, flows through the town. The Chitá is not navigable; rafts are floated on the Ingodá. In the middle of the XVIII century, a Cossack stockaded post stood on the site of the present town. This unknown place, which formerly was a poor village consisting of 26 peasants huts with 300 inhabitants, became in 1827 from administrative considerations the place of banishment for those who were condemned for participation in the conspiracy of the 14 December, 1825. Buildings, narrow, low and dark, surrounded by a high wall of pointed stakes, were allotted for the accommodation of the exiles, and received then the name of the Casemates, each being marked with its No. The unsatisfactory conditions of the building required the construction of a new prison, which was begun in the spring

231

of the year 1827. All the prisoners of the casemates were obliged to take part in the work, and thus the new building was ready by the autumn of the same year. Most of those condemned for the conspiracy of the 14 December lived three years and seven months in this prison built by their own hands.

During this period, the poor village of Chitá, which formerly, on account of its situation on the low bank at the junction of the rivers Chitá and Ingodá, was used as a suitable spot for the construction of rafts floated along the rivers Ingodá and Shilka, became a considerable settlement. It owed its outwardly prosperous appearance to the Dekabrists, who drained the place, filled up ditches etc., while the actual prosperity of the inhabitants was due to the money expended by the prisoners in the satisfaction of their daily requirements. One of the streets of the town up to this day is called the Dámskaya or Ladies street in memory of the ladies Trubetskói, Volkónsky, Muravióv, Annenkov, Naryshkin and Davydov, wives of the Dekabrists, who accompanied their banished husbands and had their own houses in it. Having developed into a commercial centre under the influence of the exiles. Chitá very soon acquired the foremost position in the country. On the organisation of the Transbaikal territory in 1851, it became the centre of the local administration. From that time, the newly founded town has developed rapidly.

The last census showed a population of 11,480 (6,877 males, 4,603 females). The town is very well laid out, but the streets are unpaved and very badly lighted. On the 1 July, 1899, the town was supplied with a telephone at Government cost for the use of the public. The total number of the mostly wooden houses is 1,412. There are 9 churches and a nunnery of the Holy Virgin; a vast stone cathedral, founded on the 12 August, 1899, in commemoration of His Imperial Majesty's visit to Chitá in 1891, and of the Sacred Coronation in Moscow in 1896; a Roman catholic chapel and a Jewish synagogue. There are 13 schools: gymnasium for boys and girls, diocesan school for girls, central missionary school attached to the Archbishop's house, artisans' school, urban three-class school, and two parish schools; one of them was founded in memory of His Imperial Majesty, the Emperor Nicholas II's visit to Chitá on the 17 – 18 June in 1891; the other was established in commemoration of the marriage of Their

Imperial Majesties, the Emperor Nicholas II and the Empress Alexándra Feódorovna; a Sunday-school and three parish schools attached to the convict children's home, to the central missionary school, and to the nunnery; a military school for surgeons' assistants and a school for midwives. The children's home is under the management of the Transbaikál Relief Society.

Charitable and sciéntific societies:
The Chitá Brotherhood of the Apostolic Saints Cyril and Methodius and St. Innocent the Miracle-worker of Irkútsk. The Transbaikál branch of the Relief Society for the families of exile convicts, under the patronage of Her Majesty the Empress Mary Feódorovna. The Transbaikál Committee for the assistance of emigrants. The Chitá branch of the Imperial Russian Geographical Society of the Amúr region, with museum and library. The Doctors' Society in Chitá. The Transbaikál branch of the Imperial Society for the Preservation of Animals and for Legitimate Sport. Local committee of the Red Cross Society. An amateur society for singing, music, literature and dramatic art. A pupils' aid society.

There is an official daily paper "The Transbaikál district Gazette" published in Chitá. In 1897, a newspaper entitled: "Life in the Eastern Borderland" was published in Siberia without censorship, in Russian and Mongolian, edited and published by Mr. Badmáev.

The town contains the following military institutions: headquarters of the Transbaikál territory; department of the Transbaikál military commander; local commissariat administration, artillery stores; artillery park; military medical department; military economic department of the Transbaikál Cossack troops; the reserve battalion of Chitá; 1 Transbaikál Cossack regiment of Chitá; 1 Transbaikál Cossack regiment of Nérchinsk; 2 Transbaikál battery: local brigade.

Medical establishments: military hospital of Chitá; military hospital for the Transbaikál Cossacks; branch lunatic asylum; and town hospital. A station for experimental medicine, for the study of the plague and inoculation of anti-plague serum was established in 1899.

The hotels are "Tokio" and Bianchinsky with rooms at R. 2 a day. The rooms are very bad.

Through Chita to Manchuria
Michael Myers Shoemaker, 1902

I notice that our car and the first-class cars are constantly guarded. Remembering the reports of Irkutsk, I am not surprised, and do not object in the least.

It is absolutely necessary to bring provisions with one after leaving Irkutsk, though I believe there is one train each week to Stretensk on the Amur with a dining car; go therein by all means if you can.

Otherwise, bring baskets of provender. Today, for instance, we had no opportunity for food until 3 p.m., and then it was vile. There was one wretched little eating-room filled with Russians, all of whom had long since finished their meal, but to the Russians the long smoke after dinner is an absolute necessity, and they do not leave their seats until that is finished to their satisfaction. You may stand around and starve for all they care. So it was today. We had to fairly shove our way between them. However, it is over and past, and we shall not return to Chita. But don't forget my warning when you come this way.

We are now in the Amur district and all the rivers flow into that great stream. A traveller in these far eastern lands gradually loses his impatience and finally ceases to care whether his train or taran-tass goes fast or slowly, or does not go at all. Certainly we have been two hours at this station for no apparent reason.

We branch off here towards Manchuria. The point is called Karyinskaya, where not even a barking dog breaks the silence of the night – the luminous Siberian night. There is no moon but the stars are very bright and the northern lights cast a pale glow off towards the polar sea.

It seemed for a time that we had been dropped and lost, as apparently the train had vanished into the night. But why worry? If so, it cannot be helped. My man and my luggage have gone, but again, – why worry? An hour later I go out to the little buffet, and there sits the man, while the luggage van has come back from somewhere.

So good-bye to Siberia! I shall always remember it as two vast stretches of sadly silent country, – limitless steppes, silent forests, dreary mountains, all leading up to that one great point of interest, that sea of ice, – frozen Baikal. Somewhat of the fascination which possesses Arctic explorers is understood by the winter passage of that lake, with its stretching snow fields, its black waters and fields of floating, plunging ice, and its grand air.

If inclined to suicide, I should avoid that passage of Baikal as I would Niagara, for like that cataract, the death cold waters of that awful channel fascinate and are intolerable.

Mail to Transbaikalia
Bassett Digby and Richardson Wright, 1910

On the platform at Chita we passed the panting locomotive and came suddenly upon that awe-inspiring melodrama of daily Siberian life, taking the mails aboard a train.

The post-office coach, with its crossed post-horns painted on its sides and dainty blinds of flounced Holland in the windows, was up forward near the baggage coach. It was the town policeman girt about with a sword and a heavy revolver who blocked our path and excitedly waved us to go away, far away. It was the two big station policemen, also armed to the teeth, who blocked the platform in the other direction. Between them circulated three post-office clerks, two of them wearing revolvers, and the other with a gleaming butt poking out of his greatcoat pocket.

The mails, in long, shabby black leather sacks laced down one side with a bright steel chain, had been driven to the station in the dirty, ramshackle farm cart that was backed up near by. All the parcels and registered mail packets were dumped loose on the gravel underfoot. They had been brought to the station, loose then, on the floor of the cart, a floor that held at least one crack big enough for you to put your foot through. Probably sacks are more costly than the services of a handful of perambulating arsenals; besides, there is the gratuitous dignity of the scene.

A mailing slot is let into the side of the Siberian mail coach. An old woman had hurried down from the town that morning, to take advantage of this opportunity for late mailing, but the police made her stand aside for twenty minutes till the leisurely loading had been accomplished and the massive steel doors of the coach swung back, bolted, barred and padlocked, before they would let her step forward and pop her letter in the slot.

A few moments later, a train came in from the east, out Mongolia way, and there descended upon us the hordes of Tartary. Quite 200 Booriats, men, women and children, any one of a score of whose costumes would need a page of detailed description, surged out to the hack stand and eagerly sifted transportation bids. The tribe in its curious hats and richly colored garments, the women wearing in their hair and dangling on cords handfuls of strange metal trinkets that would have been the envy of a museum curator, bargained fiercely for many minutes with the *istvostchiks* before resigning itself to a minimum rate of forty *kopecks* for as many as could crowd into each little chaise. Then with yellings and howls and crackings of whips, off galloped the entire station hack-rank of the city of Chita. One wondered whither.

At midday we came to Karimskaia, the little station where the track of the Trans-Siberian bifurcates, one line – the original Trans-Siberian – running northeast to Sretensk, the other passing over the bridge, on to Manchuria and the Pacific.

The seven hour run to Sretensk was the most picturesque stage of the train journey. The line followed the Shilka bank, now half a mile of flat pasture or dense willow swamp separating it from the river, now creeping round a narrow ledge blasted out of the living rock, with the swirling ice débris grinding the face of the cliff below.

You do not see anything in the home newspapers about small accidents – derailings and the like – on the Trans-Siberian Railroad, but they are frequent.

Crash!
Peter Fleming, 1933

And now the journey was almost over. Tomorrow we should reach Manchuli. The train pulled out of Irkutsk and ran along the river Angara until it debouched into Lake Baikal. At the mouth of the river men were fishing, each in a little coracle moored to a stake at which the current tugged. It was a clear and lovely evening.

Lake Baikal is said to be the deepest lake in the world. It is also said to be the size of Belgium. Its waters are cold and uncannily pellucid. The Russians call it "The White-Haired", because of the mist which always hangs about it. To-night the mist was limited to narrow decorative scarves which floated with a fantastic appearance of solidity far out above the unruffled waters. Out of the mist stood up the heads of distant mountains, dappled with snow. It was a peaceful, majestic place.

Contrary to general belief, the railway round the southern end of Lake Baikal is double-tracked, as indeed is the whole Trans-Siberian line from Chita westward to Omsk, and doubtless by now further. This is however a very vulnerable section. The train crawls tortuously along the shore, at the foot of great cliffs. The old line passes through about forty short tunnels, each lackadaisically guarded by a sentry. The new line skirts round the outside of the tunnels, between the water and the rock. This is the weakest link in that long, tenuous, and somewhat rusty chain by which hangs the life of Russia's armies in the Far East. In 1933 her military establishments on the Amur Frontier totalled about a quarter of a million men, including reservists.

There is no more luxurious sensation than what may be described as the End of Term Feeling. The traditional scurrilities of

'This time to-morrow where shall I be?
Not in this academee"

?? have accompanied delights as keen and unqualified as any that most of us will ever know. As we left Baikal behind and went lurching through the operatic passes of Buriat Mongolia, I felt very content. To-morrow we should reach the frontier. After to-morrow there would be no more of that black bread, in consistency and flavour suggesting rancid peat: no more of that equally alluvial tea: no more of a Trappist's existence, no more days entirely blank of action. It was true that I did not know what I was going to do, that I had nothing very specific to look forward to. But I knew what I was going to stop doing, and that, for the moment, was enough.

I undressed and got into bed. As I did so, I noticed for the first time that the number of my berth was thirteen.

For a long time I could not go to sleep. I counted sheep, I counted weasels (I find them much more efficacious, as a rule. I don't know why). I recited in a loud, angry voice soporific passages from Shakespeare. I intoned the names of stations we had passed through since leaving Moscow: Bui, Perm, Omsk, Tomsk, Kansk, Krasnoyarsk. (At one a low-hung rookery in birch trees, at another the chattering of swifts against a pale evening sky, had made me home-sick for a moment.) I thought of all the most boring people I knew, imagining that they were in the compartment with me, and had brought their favourite subjects with them. It was no good. My mind became more and more active. Obviously I was never going to sleep ...

It was the Trooping of the Colour, and I was going to be late for it. There, outside, in the street below my window, was my horse; *but it was covered with thick yellow fur!* This was awful! Why hadn't it been clipped! What would they think of me, coming on parade like that? Inadequately dressed though I was, I dashed out of my room and down the moving staircase. And then (horror of horrors!) the moving staircase broke. It lurched, twisted, flung me off my feet. There was a frightful jarring, followed by a crash ...

I sat up in my berth. From the rack high above me my heaviest suitcase, metal-bound, was cannonaded down, catching me with fearful force on either knee-cap. I was somehow not particularly surprised. This is the end of the world, I thought, and in addition they have broken both my legs. I had a vague sense of injustice.

My little world was tilted drunkenly. The window showed me nothing except a few square yards of goodish grazing, of which it offered an oblique bird's eye view. Larks were singing somewhere. It was six o'clock. I began to dress. I now felt very much annoyed.

But I climbed out of the carriage into a refreshingly spectacular world, and the annoyance passed. The Trans-Siberian Express sprawled foolishly down the embankment. The mail van and the dining-car, which had been in front, lay on their sides at the bottom. Behind them the five sleeping-cars, headed by my own, were disposed in attitudes which became less and less grotesque until you got to the last, which had remained, primly, on the rails. Fifty yards down the line the engine, which had parted company with the train, was dug in, snorting, on top of the embankment. It had a truculent and naughty look; it was defiantly conscious of indiscretion.

It would be difficult to imagine a nicer sort of railway accident. The weather was ideal. No one was badly hurt. And the whole thing was done in just the right Drury Lane manner, with lots of twisted steel and splintered woodwork and turf scarred deeply with demoniac force. For once the Russians had carried something off.

The air was full of agonizing groans and the sound of breaking glass, the first supplied by two attendants who had been winded, the second by passengers escaping from a coach in which both the doors had jammed. The sun shone brightly. I began to take photographs as fast as I could. This is strictly forbidden on Soviet territory, but the officials had their hands full and were too upset to notice.

The staff of the train were scattered about the wreckage, writing contradictory reports with trembling hands. A charming German consul and his family – the only other foreigners on the train – had been in the last coach and were unscathed. Their small daughter, aged six, was delighted with the whole affair, which she regarded as having been arranged specially for her entertainment; I am afraid she will grow up to expect too much from trains.

Gradually I discovered what had happened, or at least what was thought to have happened. As a rule the Trans-Siberian Expresses have no great turn of speed, but ours, at the time when disaster overtook her, had been on top of her form. She had a long, steep hill behind her, and also a following wind; she was giving of her best. But, alas, at the bottom of that long, steep hill the signals were against her, a fact which the driver noticed in the course of time. He put on his brakes. Nothing happened. He put on his emergency brakes. Still nothing happened. Slightly less rapidly than before, but still at a very creditable speed, the train went charging down the long, steep hill.

The line at this point is single track, but at the foot of the hill there is a little halt, where a train may stand and let another pass. Our train, however, was in no mood for stopping: it looked as if she was going to ignore the signals and try conclusions with a westbound train, head on. In this she was thwarted by a pointsman at the little halt, who summed up the situation and switched the runaway neatly into a siding. It was a long, curved siding, and to my layman's eye appeared to have been designed for the sole purpose of receiving trains which got out of control on the hill above it. But for whatever purpose it was designed, it was designed a very long time ago. Its permanent way had a more precarious claim to that epithet than is usual even in Russia. We were altogether too much for the siding. We made matchwood of its rotten sleepers and flung ourselves dramatically down the embankment.

But it had been great fun: a comical and violent climax to an interlude in which comedy and violence had been altogether too lacking for my tastes. It was good to lie back in the long grass on a little knoll and meditate upon that sprawling scrap-heap, that study in perdition. There she lay, in the middle of a wide green plain; the crack train, the Trans-Siberian Luxury Express. For more than a week she had bullied us. She had knocked us about when we tried to clean our teeth, she had jogged our elbows when we wrote, and when we read she had made the print dance tiresomely before our eyes. Her whistle had arbitrarily curtailed our frenzied excursions on the wayside platforms. Her windows we might not open on account of the dust, and when closed they had proved a perpetual attraction to small, sabotaging boys with stones. She had annoyed us in a hundred little ways: by spilling tea in our laps, by running out of butter, by regulating her life in accordance with Moscow time, now six hours behind the sun. She had been our prison, our Little Ease. We had not liked her.

Now she was down and out. We left her lying there, a broken, buckled toy, a thick black worm without a head, awkwardly twisted: a thing of no use, above which larks sang in an empty plain.

If I know Russia, she is lying there still.

On to Stretensk
Bassett Digby and Richardson Wright, 1910

After the fifty hour train journey from Irkutsk, we all bustled joyfully out on the platform with hotels and nice warm beds looming large in our thoughts – only to be told laconically that, as the ice was just beginning to run out of the Shilka and its feeders, the boatmen did not care to take any risks after dark, and that everyone would have to squat on their baggage in the buffet room, like good philosophers, till eight o'clock in the morning.

You may imagine what a scene that announcement would have made had it been sprung upon a trainload of tired Americans. Think of the incredulous exclamations, the angry protests, the sheaves of threatened letters to the newspapers; the fiery and over-adjectival conversation that would vibrate the rafters of the waiting-room!

Russia can be excited on occasion, but never, never, on being confronted by delays. Everyone took the matter with the utmost nonchalance. *Neitchevo!* with a shrug, was the correct attitude. And while the bachelor element among us made itself cosy at the tables with flasks of *vodka* and nips of alleged cognac, the staider men gathered up their wives and families and encamped in nooks and crannies among the softer constituents of the mountainous piles of baggage.

From a purely personal point of view, it was a ghastly night. Every now and then, until dawn, someone would wade over our sleeping selves and snatch away what happened to be officiating as our pillow, mattress or leg-rest. Three successive pillows and two of the most sensuously comfortable back-rests in or out of Christendom were thus torn away from us in less than an hour. And all night long, at intervals of a few seconds, someone would dash into or out of the buffet, through the door that grated loudly on its hinges and lapsed into a long-drawn, protestant squeak.

We roused up at six. Bright sunshine was streaming through the windows. The tables were still thronged with an eating and drinking crowd. No one showed any alacrity to get out and about.

"Monsieur, ce n'est pas possible, je vous assure. A huit heures. A huit heures!" replied the young lieutenant with whom we had been chatting last evening, when we asked why in the name of common sanity it should be necessary to wait till eight o'clock for a safe crossing, when the sun was already blazing in the heavens.

Nevertheless, we gathered up our baggage and went out to the river bank. Already, as we had fully expected, ferries were plying – two big, flat-bottomed barges. From what one could see through the slight haze that dimmed the far side of the river, there seemed to be some hitch in embarking at that terminal. A large crowd thronged the bank there, watching operations.

In a few minutes, however, a barge got away, and, crammed with standing passengers, came swiftly down in a drift of broken ice. On account of the inshore water having frozen hard during the night, she had some trouble getting in; and the passengers had to be landed in carts.

By this time our bank was crowded with three times the capacity of the barge, everyone eager to avoid a long wait for the next. Only by a moving picture film and a number of talking machines could justice be done to the way that barge took aboard her complement of passengers.

While the drivers lashed their horses down the stony beach and through yards of shallow ice mush to the craft, fat men and screaming women, officers tripping over their swords, three men with dogs on leads that caught around one's legs, and white-aproned porters with the set features of men going into battle against heavy odds, flung their baggage-encumbered persons upon the four small carts, and, being fortunate enough to clamber on, clung together – sitting, standing, kneeling.

The End in Sight
Christopher Portway, 1970

I slept well for the last full night before Khabarovsk. The landscape was as flat as a pancake again, with just a hint of strained-out mountains in the far distance. Around mid-day we crossed another mammoth river, which might have been the Bureya, a tributary of the great Amur which formed the border with Manchuria only a cannon's shot away. I noticed that each and every bridge was guarded by soldiers. Somewhere in the night we had passed out of Siberia to enter a region called the Soviet Far East.

Lack of proper exercise was affecting my appetite. Pilgrimages to the restaurant car became rare, and meals turned to snacks. A furtive little man came in to offer me a string of anti-Soviet jokes of the 'What Lenin said to the bishop' variety. I couldn't understand any of them but laughed politely. It came to me that these 'new Siberians' tended to take the State less seriously and tragically than other Russians. With Moscow thousands of miles away they were 'off the leash', more suspect of authority and able to rely on their own judgement and assessment of a situation. In a way they are like the Americans; convinced that their forests, rivers, lakes and towns have no equal in the world.

The joke merchant was my last caller. Though the train was not due at Khabarovsk until midnight I was left severely alone as if by intention. Not since Irkutsk had I a resident in the compartment, yet the other compartments were reasonably full. I began to view the coach attendants with deep distrust. It could only have been they who diverted potential occupants. Yet Intourist it was that made the reservations and surely even their deviousness could not ensure my segregation when such reservations were being made over the whole length of the line?

An early sunset coincided with a return of the hills, and the beautiful autumnal gold of the trees tempted me to the rear of the coach to take some last photographs. Hardly had I focused on a scene I wanted when the camera was knocked sideways and I received a severe castigation from a blue-uniformed policeman who had appeared from nowhere. And then I understood the reason for the shunning I was receiving. The line ran very close indeed to the Chinese border and, being in a restricted zone, police patrols were on the train. And with authority came fear, or at least prudence. I stalked back to my empty compartment.

The final halts were fun no longer. The sculptures of Lenin and the absurd slogans became oppressive. There was little food left in the restaurant car and the station stalls could produce only potato mash and pumpkins. I began to long for a sight of something luxurious. Only the train itself maintained a splendour and a dignity in the face of an atmosphere gone sour.

It was after one in the morning when we crawled into the city of Khabarovsk. The fact that we were an hour late was obviously an exception and the tannoy was making a meal of it explaining the reasons. For the first time since I started the journey I was glad to leave a Russian train.

4140 km. Vladivostock
A. Rado, 1929

... a district town, the main port of the USSR on the Pacific coast, situated at the south-western extremity of the Muraviev Amursky peninsula, on the northern and western shores of the bay 'Zolotoy Rog (Golden Horn). Vladivostock lies from Greenwich under 131" 54' eastern longitude and 43" 7' northern latitude, i.e. is the southernmost town of the RSFSR; 102,000 inhabitants.

Vladivostock is the best arranged city of the Fareast and Siberia, a military and commercial port. The main objects of export are the Manchurian beans and products therefrom: oil, oil-cakes, ; cereals are alos exported in grain, especially wheat, as well as coal and linseed. Powerful ice-breakers service makes the Vladivostock port a practically non-freezing port at the present time.

Journey's End
Eric Newby, 1977

Then, just after seven o'clock, the train began to descend a wide, mist-filled valley, the steep sides of which were densely wooded with tall, deciduous trees, and in which the villages of white-painted houses had more geese than human beings visible in them, down to the Suchan River which rises in the same massif as the Ussuri.

At nine o'clock the *Vostok* was running down the right bank of the Suchan River on a ledge cut out of the sheer cliffs that rose above it. Beyond the river there was a low range of mountains covered with smoking cloud, and in the meadows down by the water big herds of cattle were huddled together, steaming. It was damnably cold for June.

Now the *Vostok*, uttering wild, bellowing noises as it went, ran past a big isolated bluff which rose out of the valley floor. Then, quite suddenly, there was the Pacific, lots of it, greyer than the grey sky above, and with a Chinese-style sugar loaf hill rising above the coastline away to the north. As the *Vostok* curved away to the right from the river a mass of merchant ships, anchored in the outer roads, came into view. Then it ran in behind the port warehouses with dozens of cranes rising beyond them and there were fleeting gnmpses or ships moored alongside, piles of what looked like silver ingots, and behind a disused bus in an open lot a momentary view of some small boys puffing away at cigarettes. Finally, at *9.25* am local time (2.25 am Moscow time) on 15 June, the *Vostok* rolled into Tikhookeanskaya Station at Nakhodka, *569* miles from Khabarovsk, 5900 miles from Moscow. We had made it. The journey was over.

11

DIFFERENT PERSPECTIVES:
EAST TO WEST

To travel westwards on the Trans-Siberian Railway can be a series of anti-climaxes, as one moves from the unknown and exciting, from the wide open spaces and freedom of Siberia, into the enclosing grip of European Russia and the western world. But, of course, if you are Asian, Australian or American on your way to Europe for the first time, the adventure must be as great as for the European going eastwards. Either way one is travelling half around the world.

Express Trains from Vladivostok
Marcus Taft, 1907

As late as 1880 Russia had no railways in Asia, although Great Britain had nearly 10,000 miles of iron road in India.

Today trains run daily between the Pacific and the Urals. Each week three express trains go each way between Vladivostok and the old and new Russian capitals, while a fourth runs between Irkutsk and Moscow. These three expresses include one of the International Wagons Lits and two of the Imperial Siberian Express. So far as our observation went, the Wagons Lits trains had the advantage of a conductor who could speak some English, German, and French, besides Russian; the fares were higher, the cars were usually more crowded, and their condition in regard to cleanliness would have given a New England housewife a conniption fit. Doubtless, as soon as the attention of the company is called to this untidy state of affairs, it will be promptly remedied. We well remember in the early days of the Canadian Pacific Steamship Company, how hash, disguised as "Pepper Pot," "Bubble and Squeak," and other mystic, euphonious names, were frequent dishes on the menu. But after complaints reached the London office, a director was dispatched personally to investigate, with

the result that to-day probably no better table is to be found anywhere.

On the other hand, the Imperial State Express had the advantage of the same speed, lower rates, a conductor who could speak German, French, and Russian, while the cars were both cleaner and less crowded. Passengers, first and second-class, in both expresses, had the right to the same dining car. Generally, the same car was provided with coupes, partly first and partly second-class. A corridor or passageway extended along one side of the car. Overhead in this corridor were racks for baggage, while near the windows were adjustable seats and tables.

We tried a second-class compartment on the Imperial State Express and found it so comfortable and satisfactory that we had no desire to change to the first.

Off from Vladivostok
Francis E. Clark, 1899

But the time has come for the start, of which we have been made fully aware by numerous bells and gongs and whistles. There is no excuse for any one to get left at a Siberian railway station. Five minutes before the train starts a large station bell is rung. Four minutes more the passengers stroll up and down the platform or visit the buffet. Then the bell is rung once more, the conductor blows his whistle, the engine shrieks a warning blast, and at last we are off, with St. Petersburg 9877 versts (more than 6250 miles) away.

The scenery for a few miles out of Vladivostock is superb. The railway skirts one of the great bays between which the city lies, high up above the water, while off in the distance, beyond the blue ripples, lie the blue mountains, only partially obscured by the morning haze. Chinese junks, loaded with firewood for the locomotives, are dancing on the waves, or unloading their cargo by throwing the pieces into the sea for the waves to wash ashore, since the shallow water prevents the junks from coming close to the bank. Occasionally the railway diverges from the shore and runs through a copse of birch or beech, fresh and bright in their new spring livery, and then returns once more to give us a glimpse of the bright blue sea. The day was charming. Our most delicious spring weather in America is no more delightful than this first day of June in frozen Siberia.

The meadows were lush and rank in their growth, and the cattle waded knee-deep in their delicious fodder, and were, of course, as sleek and fat as cattle could be. The trees were nearly in full leaf, though some of the later varieties had not as yet donned their full suit of green. Great dandelions, almost as large as peonies, starred the fields with yellow, and bluebells and tiger-lilies made the roadway gay.

At the stations little girls with bare feet offered great bunches of lilies of the valley for sale, and I noticed that they were not unlike the rest of the world in taking advantage of the unsophisticated traveller, for, while I paid fifteen kopeks for a bunch, a Russian by my side, who knew how to dicker and bargain in the vernacular, paid but three kopeks for his lilies. But every traveller in a strange land must pay dear for his experience as well as for his lilies.

The one scarce article is fresh, cold water. Beer, wine, vodka, tea, especially tea, flows freely, but to order a glass of water to drink, or a basin of water, much more a tub of water for a bath, creates a commotion, and the water desired is often unattainable, except after strenuous effort. A Siberian writer remarks, naïvely, that "Englishman have the bad habit of washing themselves all over every day. *As a consequence of this habit,* their bodies emit an unpleasant odor." It must be said in all fairness, however, that hotels, cars, and steamers in Siberia are, outside of the wash-rooms, clean and wholesome for the most part. To one who has just come from China or Corea, and who has tasted the rare discomforts of travel in those countries, they seem to be beyond criticism.

Besides the cars already mentioned, a baggage-car and a dining-car completed our train equipment. The latter, at least three times a day, is a place of much interest, and deserves a few words of description.

Pullman would scarcely own the diner as an offspring of his invention. A long table down the middle, at which perhaps twenty people can sit at one time, and a bar at the end, at which all kinds of light and strong drinks are served, and toothsome delicacies dear to the

Russian heart, like caviare, sardines, and other little fishes "biled in ile," are eaten. At the long table *d'hôte* meals are served, consisting of three or four courses, and one can also order what he chooses, at a fixed price. The meals are usually one rouble each, and though not luxurious, from the American dining-car point of view, they are quite sufficient for the average traveller, and worth the price asked for them. To be sure, one must get used to the greasy Siberian soup and to the chunks of tough stewed meat, which may be beef, mutton, or pork, one is never certain which. But travellers who choose to go across Siberia should not be squeamish, and to think of eating in a dining-car, however primitive, while whirling across the plains a little south of Kamchatka, is enough to kill the spirit of criticism in the most confirmed growler who ever went around the world.

Gateway to the USSR
Noel Barber, 1939

So on to Manchouli, which seemed little better than the mud villages we had passed on the way. It had stone houses, true, and a station with a waiting-room and a restaurant, but it was a poor enough place. Manchouli is the last frontier outpost of the Japanese, and it is twenty minutes away from Otpor, the last frontier outpost of Soviet Russia on the western borders of Manchukuo. Who owns that twenty minutes of land I am not quite sure, though the Trans-Siberian, which had started a couple of days or so before at Vladivostok, steams right into Manchouli station.

We got there at about midday and had a couple of hours to wait for the Soviet train, though we were not allowed to leave the station, guards being posted at all exits to watch the foreigners. As well as Kissling and ourselves, there were three nuns, close and diminutive, whom we had not seen before. So we spent the time tramping up and down the snowy platform, wandering in and out of the waiting-room (which was not heated), and at last went into the restaurant, where we had a surprisingly good meal for less than a couple of shillings. At the restaurant all sorts of things were for sale – including whisky, with a perfect replica of Johnny Walker's well-known label on the bottle –

just a plain, deliberate swindle. There were phoney Player's cigarettes, and *ersatz* Fry's chocolate. We bought quite a lot of last-minute provisions, not because they were particularly good, but because we were not allowed to take any of our last remaining yen out of the country.

Half an hour before the train came in the Customs people got to work on us pretty thoroughly, unwrapping our boxes of sugar, sorting out and examining our provisions; they even made Helen unpack a box of powder, and one of them felt inside the powder with a yellow finger.

When we walked out of the Customs shed the Trans-Siberian was already drawn up in the station. Men with axes were chunking away at pieces of ice on the springs and the buffers ... last-minute preparations for a trip through a wilderness. There were icicles all over it, icicles and snow. Soviet guards hopped off each coach, passengers tumbled out and stretched themselves, breathing great clouds of steam into the cold air. Most of them were Soviet soldiers, our first chance to inspect them, to see them at close quarters, to see the clothes they wore, the food they ate, the cigarettes they smoked.

Inside the train was beautifully warm, and as it curved along the track I could see through the double windows Manchouli fading away in the background. It was only twenty minutes to Otpor, where we had to go through the Customs all over again, neither the Japanese nor the Russians (quite rightly) trusting the other.

Pulling the sliding door of our compartment back, I peeped out into the corridor. There were not many people about; one or two Russian soldiers lolling against the windows, looking idly at the snow fleeting past, a woman standing all by herself, a child crying somewhere.

From the Edge of the World
Paul Theroux, 1974

At its eastern limit the Trans-Siberian Express is a stale-smelling Russian ship that sails two or three times a month out of the dust-storm smog of Yokohama, through the windy Tsugaru Straits and the Sea of Japan – in whose bucking currents whole blizzards vanish – to Nakhodka, in freezing Primorsk, a stone's throw from Vladivostok. It is the only way west to Nakhodka, the pneumonia route through gales to the rail head.

The Siberian port of Nakhodka in December gives the impression of being on the very edge of the world, in an atmosphere that does not quite support life. The slender trees are leafless; the ground is packed hard, and no grass grows on it; the streets have no traffic, the sidewalks no people. There are lights burning, but they are like lighthouse beacons positioned to warn people who stray near Nakhodka that it is a place of danger and there is only emptiness beyond it. The subzero weather makes it odorless and not a single sound wrinkles its silence. It is the sort of place that gives rise to the notion that the earth is flat.

At the station ("Proper name is Tikhookeanskaya Station" – Intourist brochure), a building with the stucco and proportions of the Kabul madhouse, I paid six rubles to change from Hard Class to Soft. The clerk said this was highly irregular, but I insisted. There were two berths in the Soft-Class compartments, four in Hard, and I had found the cabin in the *Khabarovsk* a salutary lesson in overcrowding. Russian travel had already made me class-conscious; I demanded luxury. And the demand, which would have got me nowhere in Japan, where not even the prime minister has his own railway compartment (though the emperor has eleven carriages), got me a plush berth in Car Five of the Vostok.

"Yes, you have question please?" said a lady in a fur hat. The platform was freezing, crisscrossed with the molds of footprints in ice. The woman breathed clouds of vapor.

"I'm looking for Car Number Five."

"Car Number Five is now Car Number Four. Please go to Car Number Four and show voucher. Thank you." She strode away.

I found my compartment and thought, How strange. But I was relieved, and almost delirious with the purest joy a traveler can know: the sight of the plushest, most comfortable room I had seen in thirty trains. Here, on the Vostok, parked on a platform in what seemed the most godforsaken town in the Soviet Far East, was a compartment that could only be described as high Victorian. It was certainly prerevolution. The car itself had the look of a narrow lounge in a posh London pub. The passage floor was carpeted; there were mirrors everywhere; the polished brass fittings were reflected in varnished wood; poppies were etched on the glass globes of the pairs of lamps beside the mirrors, lighting the tasseled curtains of red velvet and the roman numerals on the compartment doors. Mine was VII. I had an easy chair on which crocheted antimacassars had been neatly pinned, a thick rug on the floor, and another one in the toilet, where a gleaming shower hose lay coiled next to the sink. I punched my pillow: it was full of warm goose feathers. And I was alone. I walked up and down the room, rubbing my hands, then set out pipes and tobacco, slippers, Gissing, my new Japanese bathrobe, and poured myself a large vodka. I threw myself on the bed, congratulating myself that 6000 miles lay between Nakhodka and Moscow, the longest train journey in the world.

To get to the dining car that evening I had to pass through four carriages, and between them in the rubber booth over the coupling was a yard of arctic. An icy wind blew through the rips in the rubber, there was snow on the floor, a thickness of heavy crystals on the car wall, and the door handles were coated with frost. I lost the skin from my fingertips on the door handles, and thereafter, whenever I moved between the cars of the Trans-Siberian Express, I wore my gloves. Two *babushkas* acknowledged me. In white smocks and turbans they stood with their red arms in a sink. More old ladies were sweeping the passage with brushwood brooms – a nation of stooping, laboring grannies.

Khabarovsk
Paul Theroux, 1974

The city of Khabarovsk appeared in the snow at noon, and over the next week I grew accustomed to this deadly sight of a Soviet city approaching on the Trans-Siberian line, buried at the bottom of a heavy sky: first the acres of wooden bungalows on the outskirts; then, where the tracks divided, the work-gangs of women chipping ice from the switches; the huffing steam locomotives and the snow gradually blackening with fallen soot, and the buildings piling up, until the city itself surrounded the train with its dwellings, log cabins and cell blocks. But in the history of the Trans-Siberian Railway, Khabarovsk is an important place. The great railway, proposed in 1857 by the American Perry McDonough Collins and finally begun in 1891 under Tsarevich Nicholas, was completed here in 1916. The last link was the Khabarovsk Bridge over the Amur River; then the way was open by rail from Calais to Vladivostok (now off-limits to foreigners for military reasons).

Everyone got off the Vostok Express, most of them to catch a plane for a nine-hour flight to Moscow, some – including myself – to spend the night in Khabarovsk before taking the Rossiya Express. I jumped onto the platform, was seared by the cold, and ran back into the Vostok to put on another sweater.

"No," said the Intourist lady. "You will stay here on platform please."

I said it seemed a little nippy out there.

"It is thairty-five below tzero," she said. "Ha, ha! But not Celsius!"

At one bend outside Skovorodino I saw we were being pulled by a giant steam locomotive. I diverted myself by trying (although Vladimir

[Theroux's fellow passenger] sucked his teeth in disapproval) to snap a picture of it as it rounded curves, shooting plumes of smoke out its side. The smoke rolled beside the train and rose slowly through the forests of birch and the Siberian cedars, where there were footprints on the ground and signs of dead fires, but not a soul to be seen. The countryside then was so changeless it might have been a picture pasted against the window. It put me to sleep. I dreamed of a particular cellar in Medford High School, then woke and saw Siberia and almost cried. Vladimir had stopped reading. He sat against the wall sketching on a pad with colored pencils, a picture of telephone poles. I crept into the corridor. One of the Canadians had his face turned to the miles of snow.

The mornings now were darker, another trick of time on the railroad that seemed to be speeding me further into paranoia .After eight hours' sleep I woke up in pitch blackness. In the dim light of the December moon, a silver sickle, the landscape was bare – no trees, no snow. And there was no wind. It was weird, as dawn approached (at nine-thirty by my watch), to see the villages on the banks of the Shilka and the Ingoda rivers, the small collections of wooden huts aged a deep brown, with the smoke rising straight up, a puffing from each chimney that made me think of an early form of wood-burning vehicle stranded on these deserted steppes. After hours of this desolation we came to Chita, a satanic city of belching chimneys and great heaps of smoking ashes dumped beside the tracks. Outside Chita there was a frozen lake on which ice-fishermen crouched like the fat black crows with fluffed-out feathers that roosted in the larches at the verge of the lake.

Stretensk to Irkutsk
Francis E. Clark, 1900

We had supposed, as has already been remarked, that if we had tears to shed, we should need to indulge them on the last part of our river journey [along the Amur River]. But we soon found that we should have saved them all for the journey on the Trans-Baikal Railway between Stretinsk and Irkutsk, as the sequel will show.

Stretinsk is a raw, shabby, straggling frontier town, whose only excuse for being so uninteresting is that it is very new and never thought of being a place of any importance until it suddenly found itself, on the 28th of December, 1899, the terminus of the Trans-Baikal Railway, and an important forwarding point for freight and passengers between the Atlantic and Pacific. The large railway shops and engine-houses are situated across the river from the town, which is connected with them by a ferry, ingeniously worked by the swift current of the Shilka, like the picturesque ferry at Bonn, on the Rhine. The hotels of Stretinsk are wretched inns, and there are absolutely no attractions within the town to persuade the traveller to remain. But, in justice even to the squalid raggedness of Stretinsk, it must be admitted that fine hills encircle and a noble river washes its feet, for the Shilka, in spite of shoals and shallows, is still a mighty stream, and runs even here with a large, impetuous flow.

We were glad enough to find that we must remain in Stretinsk only thirty-six hours, and that the train which was to carry us to Lake Baikal was to start the following night.

We had not been travelling a half-dozen hours when we learned that a bridge had burned down twenty miles ahead, owing to the careless-ness of a fireman who drew the fire on the wooden sleepers, and there we were stranded as fast as though on a sand-bar on the Shilka.

For thirty-six mortal hours we waited at that wretched railway town, which consisted principally of a round-house and a water-tower, then were pulled to the burned bridge, twenty miles away, and, with much difficulty and long delay, were transferred to the train on the other side. Here our good fortune deserted us. Our comparatively fine car could not, of course, cross the bridge, the governor could do nothing more for us, and in the general scramble we found ourselves in one of those dreadful fourth-class cars I have already described, with the Moujiks, the filth, and the vermin destined to be our companions for four weary days and nights.

After passing the burned bridge our train met with no serious delay, though our rate of progress was exceedingly moderate. The whole distance to Irkutsk is about seven hundred miles, and we managed to consume three days and a half of actual travel in covering it. It would seem impossible to the uninitiated in Siberian travel that a railway train that could go at all could go so slowly...

After traversing about half the distance, the streams, which had been flowing east into the Pacific, give way to others that flow west to Lake Baikal. The roof of the world, or, at least, of this part of the world, has been reached, and now we will follow the raindrops towards the distant Atlantic.

The Selenga, which we reach on the last day of this journey, is a great and strong flowing river, as large as the St. Lawrence above the Ottawa. It is crossed by a splendid iron bridge, resting on magnificent piers of cut stone, a bridge which would be an honor to any railway in the world.

It is the custom of the few travellers who have crossed this line, or any part of it, to poke fun at the Trans-Baikal Railway. And, indeed, it is not hard to do so. With its crawling trains, its inordinately long stops, its primitive rolling-stock, it does not inspire much respect.

Out of Asia and into Europe
Francis E. Clark, 1900

Samara is a city nobly situated on the banks of the Volga, and has really a regal appearance on her crown of hills, with her great cathedral and noble churches dominating all.

The railway crosses the Volga, a few miles after leaving Samara, by a splendid iron bridge, nearly a mile long. Even here, so far from its source, this greatest river of Europe is a majestic, swift-flowing stream, bearing upon its ample bosom great rafts from the pine forests near its source, and many great steamers, which carry passengers to the famous fair at Nijni-Novgorod, and other towns along its banks. Most, if not all of these steamers, use petroleum for fuel, brought from the great wells of Batoum, and huge tanks for the storage of oil begin to form conspicuous features of the landscape near every large town.

Indeed, our own locomotive, instead of gorging itself with birch-wood, as its predecessors which drew the *train de luxe* had done, took long deep draughts of crude kerosene oil, which, it must be said, did not improve its breath. Some of the engines I noticed at this end of the line were Baldwin locomotives, a make which I had not seen since we had left Khabaroffsk, on the further side of far Siberia.

On the eighth and last day of our journey on the "Siberian Special," as our train was called in railroad nomenclature, we passed through the large and commanding town of Toula, a great railroad centre, and also famous for the splendor of its churches. The stations we passed on this day were finer than any we had yet seen, and were often embow-ered in trees until they looked like châteaus in lovely green parks. Peasant women stood on every platform with heaps of little wild strawberries, which they sold at a ridiculously cheap price, about two cents a quart. Others had the first red cherries of the season, and others yellow apples that had been kept in water for nearly a year, and that tasted as if baked. Other venders of delicious, sparkling koumyss, milk, Russian kvass, and other more harmful beverages, also appeared upon the scene at many stations.

The devout character of the Russians was shown by the fact that every third-class waiting-room had its shrine, with beautifully framed pictures of Christ and the Madonna and some of the Eastern saints. Before these icons often burned ceremonial candles, and smaller candles were to be had by devotees for two or three kopeks apiece. Rapt travellers, with uplifted eyes, were often to be seen crossing them-selves before these icons.

We still passed frequent trains of Siberian settlers, and others of brawny soldiers, "bearded like the pard," and packed into their fifth and sixth-class cars like the proverbial sardines in their boxes. Occasionally a train of prisoners looked out through their iron grat-ings at us, seeming to cast a murky shadow on the pleasant landscape, as we thought of the dreary years of exile before them. We saw no po-litical prisoners, however, and even the criminals are allowed to take their wives and children with them. These latter often clung to the iron bars with their faces close against them, like so many infant Charlotte Cordays. It must be said that these prisoners, like others whom we had seen, fared a good deal better in their railway accommodations than the emigrants of the soldiers.

More and more cultivated and attractive the beautiful country appeared as we approached Moscow, giving evidence in every smooth and fertile field of five hundred years of tillage, until at last, promptly on schedule time, 197 hours after leaving Irkutsk, the Siberian Special rolled into the beautiful station of sacred Moscow, and our long journey across all the Russias was practically finished. It is a matter of thirteen hours further to St. Petersburg, and two days more by the fastest train to London. Thence six or seven days more by one of the Atlantic liners to New York, and our journey by this new way around an old world was completed.

Growing Siberia
Noel Barber, 1939

On the wall of our compartment I stuck up a small sheet which the travel bureau in Shanghai had presented to us, showing the chief towns through which we were to pass – Chita, Irkutsk, Krasnoyarsk, Omsk, Sverdlovsk and so on – these and fifty or so others. Each time we stopped I tried (sometimes in vain) to find out where we were, so that I could cross the name off the list.

Actually, of course, the Trans-Siberian, as you can see on a map, passes through the most fascinating belt of modern Soviet Russia – the part of the great continent where the Five Year Plans of the Soviet Government have been given more opportunity than anywhere else. We passed through great cities which fifteen years ago simply did not exist; and I am talking about cities of quarter of a million people. And it is on these cities, in this belt, that Soviet Russia today depends mainly for her armaments, for the very stuff of war.

Along the route of the Trans-Siberian there are six big industrial districts. They lie far apart from each other and some of the districts are bigger than the whole of England. They are like separate countries, linked together by the great double-track railway that spans a continent.

Near Vladivostok there is one great region producing coal, iron, and similar raw materials: this, of course, we did not see. We came first to the Irkutsk region, near Lake Baikal. From there on to the Krasnoyarsk district, and so into the great Kuzbas basin, with probably the greatest factories in the world. Then we crossed a thousand miles of villages in the snow to reach the great Urals. Then the Volga, then Moscow. And remember – all but the Volga region are completely isolated from the enemy. Hitler can no more bomb the Kuzbas basin than Japan can bomb London, or America can bomb the South Pole.

Of course, the most amazing thing about this Middle Belt of industrial Russia (and Siberia) is that in 1928 it just did not exist. At that time practically the entire Russian industrial system was grouped in three regions: the Ukraine, Leningrad, and Moscow. What I wonder, would have happened had an enemy attacked then? If they had made as much headway as the Germans did in 1941 then Russia today would have been prostrate.

But in 1928 the great experiment started. The stonemasons, the builders, the engineers, the factory hands, the women, the men, the children – they all obeyed the order of the Soviet Government: "Go east, young man."

And from the wilderness, from the bare Steppe, there sprang up the most astonishing cities the world has ever known – because, of course, every city, every town, is a planned unit. They are not sprinkled haphazardly on the map. They follow the raw materials, the mines, the wealth, with the Trans-Siberian as the nerve of the modern state, and the grouping of the cities reveals more clearly than anything else the plans the Russians have put into operation.

In Siberia I saw time after time large smelting furnaces – but I rarely saw one unless the mine was close at hand. I saw great plants making steel – but never far away from an armaments works. And always, always near at hand, a ring of smaller factories, waiting eagerly to lap up the by-products and turn them to effective uses.

Naturally, it hasn't always worked out quite so idealistically. There have been many snags, and you can see cities that have not sprung up according to plan. But the general idea has been to plan a city according to the raw materials in the neighbourhood. Generally, that is what has been done – and the saving in transport has been enormous, which of course means saving in labour, fuel, power. And time.

Along the Way
Noel Barber, 1939

So the days went on, the train rumbling along the lines, clacking across the points, passing through villages, through towns, through snow plains, past factory, river, lake, or wood. And the extraordinary thing was the speed with which the time flew. The first two days had been long enough – breakfast to bed-time had seemed a long time. But once we were settled down, and once the routine of the train was established, the time sped on golden wings. There always seemed to be so much to do and so little time to do it. In Shanghai I had bought one or two cheap copies of books I had always felt I should read – I forget their titles now, though I remember I got a dog-eared second-hand copy of Samuel Butler's *The Way of All Flesh*.

But had I time to read this improving literature? Not on your life. I can understand a man having no spare time on board a ship, with all its various delights and pursuits, but on a train I did think there would be time to spare. I was completely wrong. Our cabin became a centre for vital chess matches that sometimes kept us up until one or even two in the morning. Discussions kept us up just as late.

Most of the long waits of the train seemed, fortunately, to be in the day-time, but when we did stop for a couple of hours at about eleven o'clock one night, Kissling, Helen, and I got out to stretch our legs. It was very cold, and we hadn't the faintest idea where the station was, but we wrapped ourselves up to the eyes and went outside on to the platform.

A radio was playing on the brightly lit station. It was packed with people hurrying and scurrying. We stumbled over a bundle of rags in one corner ... some wretched beggar. And then Kissling espied a small wicket gate leading away from the platform. He pointed to it, and as casually as we could we walked across to it.

We got through that wicket gate like a streak of triple lightning, scrambled down a little alley, and found ourselves in a broad street outside the station.

"I hope they don't want platform tickets to get back," said Helen doubtfully.

For twenty minutes or half an hour we wandered through the town. It wasn't a very important adventure as adventures go, but it was very exciting all the same. The shops were all closed, but the lights were on, and the pavements were crowded with muffled people going home, doubtless, from their Soviet clubs. Where the place was I don't know, but the streets were broad and clean, the buildings quite modern, and there were electric tram-cars. The next day I asked Alexandrov where we had stopped, but he had been asleep and did not know.

After half an hour or so we made our way back, crept through the wicket gate, and strolled up and down the platform, under the noses of the Soviet sentries who stood with fixed bayonets on most of the stations along the line. It was much better than a schoolboy raid on an orchard.

These stops at stations were always exciting. The first thing to be done was to get busy with pickaxes, and clean the train of ice and shovel away the snow. It was amazing how solidly the ice could form on the chains between two stations. It was as thick as my arm, hard, tough ice, and sometimes every step of the train would be a foot deep in snow – very dangerous, because there were no raised platforms in this part of the world: the platform was on a level with the line itself and if you missed your foot on the step, you went head over heels.

Sometimes, too, they de-frosted the windows. At one station a whole gang of women with long brushes and pails attacked the windows of the train. In quarter of an hour – there were so many of them! – every window had been cleaned, and we could see through them clearly. At each station too, the links between each coach were inspected, usually by women engineers or porters. They even had women wheel-tappers.

Fuel had to be put aboard as well: fuel not only for the engine, but for each central heating stove in each compartment. Sometimes it was coal, sometimes it was wood – it depended on the district through which we were passing. The wood came in huge logs – birches, roughly sawn off without much time wasted on the trimmings. The poor coach attendants – they were all called guards – had a very uneven life. They had always to be keeping an eye on their stove, and had to watch for fuel reserves at each station. The result was that their sleep was very disjointed; they never got a full night's sleep, and the one in our coach was content for most of the trip, to curl up on a seat without getting out of his brown smock. Once I saw him fast asleep in his astrakhan pill-box hat. His was not a pleasant job. He was responsible for the heating and the water and any individual complaints (few: Soviets don't complain much), and though the interior heating varied from tropic temperatures to Arctic freezes, that wasn't really the fault of the guard. He had room for only a certain quantity of fuel, and if the train stopped for some unknown reason and was delayed two or three hours then the fuel ran out. That was all there was to it.

End of the Journey
Paul Theroux, 1974

In the dark corridor early the next morning the Australian librarians and the Canadian couple sat on their suitcases. Irkutsk was two hours away, but they said that they were afraid of oversleeping and missing the place. I thought then, and I think now, that missing Irkutsk cannot be everyone's idea of a tragedy. It was still dark as Irkutsk's flaming chimneys appeared above a plain of shuttered bungalows with tarpaper roofs. It is not the steel fences or even the tall cell blocks where the workers live that gives these Russian cities the look of concentration camps; it is the harsh light – searchlights and glaring lamps fixed to poles – that does it, diminishing the mittened figures and making them look like prisoners in an exercise yard. Vladimir shook my hand and said a sentimental farewell. I was moved and thought charitably about the poor fellow, stuck in Irkustsk for life, until I went back to the compartment and discovered that he had stolen my box of cigars.

The *provodnik* entered the compartment, gathered up Vladimir's blankets, and threw a new set of blankets on the berth. He was followed by a tall pale man who, although it was midmorning, put on a pair of pajamas and a bathrobe and sat down to solve complicated equations on a clipboard pad. The man did not speak until, at a small station, he said, "Here – salt!"

That was the extent of his conversation, the news of a salt mine. But he had made his point: we were truly in Siberia. Until then we had been traveling in the Soviet Far East, two thousand miles of all but nameless territory on the borders of China and Mongolia. From now on, the Siberian forest, the *taiga*, thickened, blurring the distant hills with smudges of trees and hiding the settlements that had swallowed so many banished Russians. In places this dense forest disappeared for twenty miles; then there was tundra, a plain of flawless snow on which rows of light-poles trailed into the distance, getting smaller and smaller, like those diagramatic pictures that illustrate perspective, the last light-pole a dot. The hugeness of Russia overwhelmed me. I had been traveling for five days over these landscapes and still more than half the country remained to be crossed. I scanned the window for some new detail that would intimate we were getting closer to Moscow. But the differences from day to day were slight; the snow was endless, the stops were brief, and the sun, which shone so brightly on the *taiga*, was always eclipsed by the towns we passed through: an impenetrable cloud of smoky fog hung over every town, shutting out the sun, The small villages were different; they lay in sunlight, precariously, between the *taiga* and the tracks, their silence so great it was nearly visible.

I was now the only Westerner on the train. I felt like the last Mohican. Deprived of friendly conversation, denied rest by my bad dreams, irritated by the mute man in pajamas and his pages of equations, doubled up with cramps from the greasy stews of the dining car – and, guiltily remembering my four months' absence, missing my family – I bribed Vassily for a bottle of vodka (he said they'd run out, but for two rubles discovered some) and spent an entire day emptying it.

The next morning, Christmas, I woke and looked over at the zombie sleeping with his arms folded on his chest like a mummy's. The *provodnik* told me it was six o'clock Moscow time. My watch said eight. I put it back two hours and waited for dawn, surprised that so many people in the car had decided to do the same thing. In darkness we stood at the windows, watching our reflections. Shortly afterwards I saw why they were there. We entered the outskirts of Yaroslavl and I heard the others whispering to themselves. The old lady in the frilly nightgown, the Goldi man and his wife and child, the domino-playing drunks, even the zombie who had been monkeying with my radio: they pressed their faces against the windows as we began rattling across a long bridge. Beneath us, half-frozen, very black, and in places reflecting the flames of Yaroslavl's chimneys, was the Volga.

> ... Royal David's city,
> Stood a lowly cattle shed ...

What was that? Sweet voices, as clear as organ tones, drifted from my compartment. I froze and listened. The Russians, awestruck by the sight of the Volga, had fallen silent; they were hunched, staring down at the water. But the holy music, fragrant and slight, moved through the air, warming it like an aroma.

> Where a mother laid her baby
> In a manger, for his bed ...

The hymn wavered, but the silent reverence of the Russians and the slowness of the train allowed the soft children's voices to perfume the corridor. My listening became a meditation of almost unbearable sadness, as if joy's highest refinement was borne on a needlepoint of pain.

> Mary was that mother mild,
> Jesus Christ, her little child ...

I went into the compartment and held the radio to my ear until the broadcast ended, a program of Christmas music from the BBC. Dawn never came that day. We traveled in thick fog and through whorls of brown blowing mist, which made the woods ghostly. It was not cold outside: some snow had melted, and the roads – more frequent now – were rutted and muddy. All morning the tree trunks, black with dampness, were silhouettes in the fog, and the pine groves at the very limit of visibility in the mist took on the appearance of cathedrals with dark spires. In places the trees were so dim, they were like an afterimage on the eye. I had never felt close to the country, but the fog distanced me even more, and I felt, after 6000 miles and all those days in the train, only a great remoteness; every reminder of Russia – the women in orange canvas jackets working on the line with shovels, the sight of a Lenin statue, the station signboards stuck in yellow ice, and the startled magpies croaking in Russian at the gliding train – all this annoyed me. I resented Russia's size, I wanted to be home.

That was the end of my trip, but it was not the end of my journey. I still had a ticket to London, and, hoping to catch the next train west, I canceled my hotel reservation and spent the afternoon arranging for a de luxe berth on the train to the Hook of Holland, via Warsaw and Berlin. I was packed and ready, and I arrived at the station on Christmas night with an hour to spare. The Intourist guide brought me to the barrier and said good-by. I stood for forty-five minutes on the platform, waiting to be shown to my compartment.

It was not a porter who inquired about my destination, but an immigration official. He leafed through my passport, rattling the pages. He shook his head.

"Polish visa?"

"I'm not stopping in Poland," I said. "I'm just passing through."

"*Transit* visa," he said.

"What do you mean?" I said. "Hey, this train's going to leave!"

"You must have Polish transit visa."

"I'll get it at the border."

"Impossible. They will send you back."

"Look" – the whistle blew – "I've got to get on this train. *Please* – it's going to leave without me!" I picked up my suitcase. The man held me by the arm. A signalman passed by, motioning with his green flag. The train began to move.

"I can't stay here!" But I let the man hold on to my sleeve and watched the Holland-bound express tooting its way out of the station: *frseeeeeeeeefronnng.* There were travelers' faces at the windows. They were happy, safely leaving. *It's Christmas, darling,* they were saying, *and we're off.* It was the end, I thought, as I saw the train receding, taking my heart with it. It's the end: duffilled!

267

Two days later I was able to leave Moscow, but the trip to London was not outwardly remarkable. I tried to collect my wits for the arrival; I slept through Warsaw, glared at Berlin, and entered Holland with a stone in my stomach. I felt frayed by the four months of train travel: it was as if I had undergone some harrowing cure, sickening myself on my addiction in order to be free of it. To invert the cliché, I had had a bellyful of traveling hopefully – I wanted to arrive.

THE TRAVELLERS

BIOGRAPHIES

Noel Barber (1909-1988)

Noel Barber, after travelling the world by tramp steamer, became the editor of the *Malaya Tribune* in 1937. He returned to Britain on the Trans-Siberian Railway in the spring of 1939, approaching the journey by way of Shanghai and Harbin. His travelling companions included a German businessman, a Russian officer, three Swedish nuns and Natasha, a red-hot Communist whose ambition was to go to London to organize a Soviet there.

His writings include *Trans-Siberian* (1942), *Prisoner of War* (1944), *Distant Places* (1956), *The Black Hole of Calcutta* (1965), *The Natives were Friendly*, an autobiography (1977), two children's books and five novels.

Maurice Baring (1874-1945)

The Hon. Maurice Baring, journalist and author, entered the Diplomatic Service in 1898, but resigned in 1904 and from 1905 to 1908, during the Russo-Japanese War, was war correspondent in Russia to the *Morning Post*. He travelled from west to east and east to west along the Trans-Siberian Railway at a time when the railway had really come into its own, enabling Russia to defend the most far-flung points of her great empire. The Baikal link's weakness was highlighted by this experience and the railway was soon completed around the southern shore. The Russia Baring described was, by the time he wrote, "a thing of the past", but, as he says in his introduction to *What I Saw in Russia* (1927) "it may not be less interesting on that account, for, as someone said, it is only out of the past that the future is made".

Lindon Bates Jr (1883-1915)

Born in Portland, Oregon, Bates was a construction engineer who worked on the New York Barge Canal and for an oil company in Trinidad. He travelled through Russia in 1896, amongst the islands of Hudson's Bay in 1900, went on a winter sledging journey through

Siberia and Mongolia along the line of the present railway in 1908 and up the Orinoco in 1911.

His writings include *The Russian Road to China* (1900).

Lesley Blanch (1907-2006)

Journey into the Mind's Eye is one of the first books that came into my hands before I set off on the journey myself and was an inspiration for this anthology. It may start others on the dream.

Lesley Blanch began her journey towards the Trans-Siberian Railway when she was about four. Her book is the story of her obsession with and eventual fulfilment of her dreams about that journey. She was a writer and traveller who, educated by "reading and listening to the conversation of her elders and betters", lived and kept house in eight different countries.

Her writings include *The Sabres of Paradise* (1960) about Imam Shamyl, hero of the Caucasian wars of independence, *The Nine Tiger Man*, an irreverent novel about the Indian Mutiny, and *Around the World in Eighty Dishes* (1956).

Malcolm Burr (1878-1954)

Describing himself as a writer and translator, Malcolm Burr was Professor of English at the School of Economics in Istanbul. He had a background in geology and was geological adviser to the Kent coal-fields from 1908 to 1914. He served as a captain in Salonica from 1915 to 1919 and, apart from a period with the Foreign Office and Ministry of Information in Yugoslavia, spent most of his life in Turkey.

His writings include *In Bolshevik Siberia: The Land of Ice and Exile* (1931), *A Fossicker in Angola* (1933), numerous articles and translations and a *Tourist's Guide to Istanbul.*

Siberia, the land of ice and exile, had always fascinated Burr. He had heard much about it on visits to Russia "in the happy old days" and always longed to go there. One morning (in 1931) the call came, unexpectedly, on the telephone, and at short notice he set off. He travelled to Irkutsk by railway and then set off northward to spend the autumn and winter in Siberia.

Rev. Francis E. Clark (c 1852-1927)

Born in the province of Quebec, Clark graduated in both theology and law. He was a pastor and preacher, and founded the Christian Endeavour Society, becoming President of the World Christian Endeavour Union from 1895. With this work he went "five times round the world etc", but he does not explain the "et cetera". He made the Trans-Siberian journey in 1899 with his wife and twelve-year-old son, Harold, only a few days after it had been inaugurated.

His writings include *A New Way around an Old World* (a description of his Trans-Siberian journey published in 1901 and reissued in 1904 as *The Great Siberian Railway: What I Saw on my Journey*).

Archibald R. Colquhoun (1848-1914)

Colquhoun was a travel writer and gold medallist of the Royal Geographical Society. Before he travelled to Irkutsk by rail and then on to China, he had been Deputy Commissioner in Burma, Administrator of Mashonaland in what is now Zimbabwe and was a special correspondent for *The Times* in the Far East. In his book *The "Overland" to China* (1900) he deplores much of what he sees around him, yet has to acknowledge the achievement.

Leo Deutsch (1855-1941)

Known originally as Lev Grigor'evich Deich, Leo Deutsch was a "political" sent to Siberia in 1884, not to return until the new century. He wrote of his time there in *Sixteen Years in Siberia: some experiences of a Russian revolutionist*, published in 1905.

Harry de Windt (1856-1933)

Harry de Windt was born in Paris and brought up in France and England. In 1876-8 he served as private secretary to his brother-in-law "the white Rajah of Sarawak".

He made several journeys through Russia and Siberia between 1887 and the Revolution. His first, which he describes in *From Peking to Calais by Land* (1889), was made before the days of the railway. It is surprising that he ever went back. In the introduction he says "I fear the general reader will find little to interest him in this record of our monotonous pilgrimage through Europe and Asia". This assumption did not deter him from making a 656-page book of it and going back for more. "The voyage," he continues, "though somewhat original, is sadly devoid of interest. Urga and Irkoutsk are, no doubt, well worth seeing, but a passing glimpse of these unique cities far from repays the discomfort, not to say hardship, which must be undergone on the caravan route ... I only trust this book may deter others from following my example."

Travelling with Harry de Windt must have been like going on an outing with Eeyore, and his writings are perhaps the most humorous. However, on further inspection, he found Siberia more to his liking, although he always avoided real enthusiasm.

His exploring led him to many places. He rode to India from Russia via Persia in 1889, inspected prisons in Western Siberia in 1890 and in Eastern Siberia in 1894. He attempted to travel from New York to Paris by land in 1896, but after a disaster was rescued by a whaler in the Bering Straits. He explored the Klondike, travelled in the Sahara and Morocco.

His books include *A Ride to India* (1890), *Siberia as It Is* (1892), *Through Gold Fields of Alaska* (1895), *Paris to New York by Land* (1903) and *Russia as I Know It* (1916).

Bassett Digby (1888-1962)

Born in London, Bassett Digby first worked in the London office of the *Chicago Daily News,* and a year later moved to Albany, New York to the Knickerbocker Press, where *he* probably met his travelling companion, R. L. Wright. He spent 1910 "travelling and studying in Siberia". He did a year on the staff of the *Philadelphia Public Ledger* before returning to Siberia to make ethnological studies and to collect flora and fauna. In 1914 he explored the north-east coast of Lake Baikal and discovered in north-eastern Siberia the skull and horn of an extinct woolly rhinoceros and the first tusks of a baby mammoth. Then, disguised as a Siberian peasant, he visited lamaseries along the Mongolian borders. He became war correspondent for the *Chicago Daily News* in Egypt, Scandinavia, the Balkans, Poland and Russia and after the war contributed to many journals.

His writings include *Through Siberia: An Empire in the Making* (with R. L. Wright, 1913), *The Mammoth and Mammoth-Hunting in*

North-East Siberia (1926) and *Tigers, Gold and Witch Doctors* (1928). Digby and Wright travelled jocularly together as far as Tomsk, which they wrote about in a chapter of their book headed "Tomsk: a city of orgies and education". From there, Digby went by sledge to the Salairskiy Kryazh Mountains and Wright went on to Irkutsk. They travelled by train and steamer, acquired a dog called Jack, went through Manchuria and reached the Pacific. They would have been great fun as travelling companions–if one could have kept up with them.

Peter Fleming (1907-1971)
Peter Fleming travelled widely, generally as Special Correspondent of *The Times*. His books describing these travels include *Brazilian Adventure* (1934), *One's Company* (a journey to China on the Trans-Siberian Railway in 1933), *A Forgotten Journey* (1952), a diary of a journey through Russia, Manchuria and northern China in 1934, *News from Tartary,* describing his overland journey from China to India in 1935, *The Siege at Peking* (1959) and *Bayonets to Lhasa* (1961).

Noble Frankland (1922-)
Educated at Oxford, Noble Frankland served in the RAF from 1941-45. He was Air Historian to the British Air Ministry from 1948-51 and Official Military Historian in the Cabinet Office 1951-58. From 1960-82 he was Director of the Imperial War Museum in London. *Crown of Tragedy,* the biography of Nicholas II, was published in 1960. He has also written several books and many articles on military and aviation history.

Sir John Foster Fraser (1868-1936)
In the autumn of 1901 the travel writer John Foster Fraser journeyed across Siberia and through Manchuria by train, boat and sledge. His book, *The Real Siberia,* published in 1902, reprinted 24 times in the next decade. He declared himself as being on a "mission of curiosity, with the average Britisher's prejudice against things Russian, and with my eyes open to see things I might criticise or even condemn". Some of what he saw he did condemn. But he saw too that "the popular idea about Siberia is altogether wrong".

Son of an Edinburgh clergyman, Fraser claimed to have been educated "by being turned loose in the library for some years" and by going through the training of a provincial journalist. His travelling began when, in the winter of 1895-6, he roamed the Mediterranean on cargo boats. In 1896 he cycled with two others around the world–19,237 miles in 774 days. Later he travelled in and wrote about Canada, the Balkan States, the famine regions of Russia (1906), Australia, South America, Russia during the Great War, and the Sahara.

His books include *Round the World on a Wheel*, *The Land of the Veiled Women* and *The Amazing Argentine*.

Bob Geldof (1953-)

Most of us know Bob Geldof because of either the Boomtown Rats or Band Aid, his crusade for Africa. He is also a Trans-Siberian traveller, having made the latter part of the journey in 1978 because it had "two great advantages apart from the obvious romance and mystery of so epic a trip; it would take me to places where nobody knew me and because it was a holiday, an expedition organized by an international travel company, my only responsibility would be to relax ..."

Guide to the Great Siberian Railway

Edited by Dmitriev-Mámonov and A. F. Zdziárski (a railway engineer) and translated by Miss L. Kúkol-Yasnopólsky, this book was published by the Ministry of Ways and Communications in 1900.

Many of the writers included in this book draw heavily on this guide–some even quoting straight from it without any acknowledgement! The *Guide* gives a very detailed description of the geography and history of Siberia (with many photographs) and has detailed chapters on the construction of the line up to 1897, the organization behind its construction, the technical conditions, the cost and the importance of the Great Railway "in connexion with civilisation and trade".

It contains much of the same sort of boring quantitative information which fell from the memory and lips of any good Intourist guide: "the town [Petropavlosk] contains 2,972 houses including 200 of stone ... on the average, a peasant household owns 6.1 horses, 4.1 head of cattle and 10 sheep ... the annual town revenue amounts to 60,000 roubles ... from 250,000 to 400,000 head of cattle driven from different parts of the Steppe region are slaughtered annually ..."

Esther Hautzig (1931-)

In June 1941 Esther Hautzig's family were arrested by the Russian soldiers then occupying their town of Vilna in north-eastern Poland because they were "capitalists and enemies of the people". They were sent "to another part of our great and mighty country"... to Siberia. In March 1946 they boarded the cattle trains that were to take them back to Poland. Esther Hautzig related her experiences in Siberia in her book *The Endless Steppe* (1968).

Lt Gen. Sir Brian Horrocks (1895-1985)

Commissioned in 1914, Horrocks served in France and Belgium and, in 1919, in Russia. He retired from the Army in 1949, after long and distinguished service. He became well known to millions of viewers through his television series. His autobiography, *A Full Life*, was published in 1960.

While a prisoner of war in Germany in the First World War he shared a room for many months with one other British officer and fifty Russian officers. "So," as he says, "I had perforce to learn Russian." When the War Office called in 1918 for volunteers who knew the language to go to Russia to help the White armies against the Bolsheviks, Horrocks volunteered. In April 1919 he landed in Vladivostok. He eventually left European Russia in October 1920, eighteen months after he had entered the country from the opposite side.

George Kennan (1845-1924)

Towards the latter part of his life George Kennan described himself as a writer and lecturer, but his first occupation was in a telegraph office. Born in Norwalk, Ohio, he went to Siberia in 1865 as an "explorer and telegraph engineer". It was from this period that his book *Tent Life in Siberia* dates. From 1866 to 1868 he was Superintendent of Construction of the middle section of the Russo-American Telegraphic Company in Siberia.

By 1877 he was Night Manager for Associated Press in Washington, DC, but left to investigate the Russian exile system in Siberia in 1885-6. It was his book and articles which gave the world its picture of Siberia as a land of exiles and convicts. Many novels about Siberian exile followed. In 1898 he reported the Spanish-American

War as special correspondent in Cuba. He continued to travel, being expelled from Russia in 1901, reporting on the eruption of Mount Pelee and the destruction of St Pierre as in 1902, and special correspondent in the Far East from 1904 to 1906.

His books included *Siberia and the Exile System* (1890), *Campaigning in Cuba* (1899), *The Tragedy of Pelee* (1902), *A Russian Comedy of Errors* (1915). *Misrepresentations in Railway Affairs* (1916), *A Biography* (1922) and many articles.

Annette M. B. Meakin (c.1890)

Annette Meakin was educated in England and Germany, studying music and classics. She was a traveller and writer, a life from which she diverted to qualify as a chemist's assistant in 1916 "to release a man for the front". Her books include *In Russian Turkestan* (1903), *Russia: Travels and Studies* (1906), *What America is Doing* (1911) and a biography of Hannah More (1911).

On a visit to Russia in 1896, Annette Meakin became "seized with a desire not merely to make the journey on the Trans-Siberian Railway, but to be the first Englishwoman to travel by that route to Japan". Friends in England smiled at the idea, but when she "unfolded the plan" to her mother and asked her to go too: "This she readily agreed to do, being quite as fond of travelling as myself."

They left London for Paris on 18 March 1900, there brushing up their French for the journey and studying "excellent maps and models illustrative of our proposed route which occupied several rooms in the Siberian section of the Exhibiton".

"Everyone knows," says Miss Meakin, "that the less luggage you have with you, the better and we were delighted to have reduced our luggage to a valise and hold-all, and a tea basket." But when they reached the Russian frontier on 21 May, bitter winds were blowing and snow lay on the sides of the streets.

They set out for Moscow with Miss Meakin suffering from a severe chill but undeterred and went slowly along the route of the "ribbons of iron", stopping off on their way in Omsk, Tomsk and Krasnoyarsk and diverting for a river trip on the Yenisey. The story of this journey is told in *A Ribbon of Iron* (1901).

Elsie Reid Mitchell (fl.1880)

See Helen Callista Wilson

Chris Moss (1966-)

Is a journalist and travel writer who has worked for *Time Out* and the *Daily Telegraph*. He is the author of *Patagonia: A Cultural History* (Signal 2008), a book that explores the mystique of South America's closest approximation to Siberia.

Murray's Handbooks for Travellers

In 1839 the *Handbook for Travellers in Denmark, Norway, Sweden and Russia* {being a guide to the principal routes in those countries with a minute description of Copenhagen, Stockholm, St Petersburg and Moscow) was 276 pages long. The second edition in 1848 added Finland and ran to well over 600 pages and, by 1871, the third edition had divided Scandinavia off from Russia.

In 1887 Murray issued the fourth edition of their *Handbook for Travellers in Russia, Poland and Finland* including the Crimea, Caucasus, Siberia and Central Asia. In 1893 they had to rush out a fifth edition because of "an unexpectedly rapid exhaustion of the Edition of 1887", due, they opined, to the fact that "Russia is being more and more frequented by travellers, British and American; for the continual extension of Railways within the Empire, the improvement of accommodation at Hotels, and generally the greater facilities offered to travellers, have given, as elsewhere, a strong stimulus to the tourist traffic".

Eric Newby (1919-2006)

In 1977 Eric Newby and his wife Wanda travelled on the Trans-Siberian Railway from Moscow to the Pacific with an official guide and a photographer. Through his resulting book, *The Big Red Train Ride* (1978), Eric Newby has provided a splendid stage-by-stage description of the journey for the armchair and the actual traveller alike. The enthusiasm of people to indulge themselves in this dream can be measured by the frequency with which the book is reprinted. Newby worked briefly in advertising before joining a Finnish four-masted bark in 1938 (an experience described in his first book, *The Last Grain Race).*

In 1942 he became a prisoner of war, escaping with the help of Wanda. For nine years he worked in the fashion business and then took off to become a traveller.

His books include *A Short Walk in the Hindu Kush* (1972). *Slowly Down the Ganges* (1966) and *A Traveller's Life* (1982).

The Rt Hon. Sir Henry Norman (1858-1939)

Educated privately in France and at Harvard and Leipzig, Henry Norman's first political activity was in starting a public agitation for the preservation of Niagara Falls, which resulted in its subsequent purchase by New York State. He was on the editorial staff of the *Pall Mall Gazette* and the *Daily Chronicle* until he retired from journalism in 1899, becoming a Liberal MP from 1900-23. He was interested in wireless and was appointed in 1920 to "draw up a complete wireless system for the Empire".

He travelled extensively. His writings about these travels include *The Preservation of Niagara Falls* (1882), *The Real Japan* (1892) and *All the Russias: Travels and Studies in Contemporary European Russia, Finland, Siberia, the Caucasus and Central Asia* (1902), based on 15 years' interest in Russian affairs, four journeys in the Russian Empire and residence in St Petersburg. His aim in writing was to encourage "the possibility of closer commercial and political relations between Russia and Great Britain".

Christopher Portway FRGS (1923-)

Christopher Portway was travel editor of a family magazine and writes on travel for many journals. His *The Great Railway Adventure* collects together a lifetime's experience of travelling around the world by train, including his journey through Siberia to the Pacific in 1973. He belongs to the old tradition of travellers who enjoys travel for no other purpose than its own sake.

His books include *Journey Along the Spine of the Andes, The Great Travelling Adventure* and *Czechmate*.

Morgan Phillips Price (1885-1973)

Morgan Phillips Price was the son of a Gloucestershire landowner. Educated at Harrow and Trinity College, Cambridge, he travelled in

Central Asia, Siberia, Persia and Turkey between 1908 and 1914. He became correspondent for the *Manchester Guardian* in Russia 1914-1918. In 1929 he became the Labour MP for Whitehaven for two years, and from 1935 until his retirement in 1959 was Labour MP for Gloucester.

He wrote *Siberia*, from which the extracts here are taken, *My Remembrances of the Russian Revolution* (1918), *Russia Through the Centuries* (1943), *Russia Red or White* (1947), *Through the Iron-Laced Curtain* (1949) and *Russia: Forty Years On* (1961).

He went to Siberia at the behest of friends who were engaged in the scientific exploration of the region. His own interest there was in social and economic matters and he looked at Siberia's potential for British investors. "Siberian railway stock," he says in his preface, "will prove, I think, to be a valuable investment." However, as he said, "speculation in land is not possible, as the land is wisely kept almost entirely in the hands of the Government."

Michael Myers Shoemaker (1853-1924)

Shoemaker described himself as an author who had "travelled the world over in the study of the people of the earth". Shoemaker's father was a railway engineer. When he was building the Kansas Pacific Railway, his sons spent their summer vacations in his private car, attached to the construction train, and "went slowly along the line as it was built ahead of them".

As a result of his travels he wrote *The Great Siberian Railway from St Petersburg to Pekin* (1903), *Sealed Provinces of the Tsar* (1895) *Islands of the Southern Sea* (1897), *Quaint Corners of Ancient Empires* (1899), *Wanderings in Ireland* (1908) and *Islam Lands: Nubia, the Sudan, Tunisia and Algeria* (1910).

James Young Simpson (1873-1934)

Simpson, who became professor of Natural Science at New College, Oxford, journeyed in Siberia during the summer of 1896 while the railway was still under construction. His book, *Sidelights on Siberia: Some Account of the Great Siberian Railroad, The Prisons and Exile System*, 1898, describes the terrain, the building of the "Great Siberian Iron Road" and his travels in Siberia.

His other writings include *The Self-Discovery of Russia* (1918) and numerous articles in literary and scientific magazines.

Doreen Stanford (1896-?)

Doreen Stanford's father was a mining engineer who liked to see the world. When her parents went to Siberia she was sent to school in England, but in 1916 her guardian aunts sent her off to join her parents. When the Revolution came and there was no way to leave except in truly atrocious conditions by train, the family set up an iron-monger's business in the main street of Krasnoyarsk. At last they too decided to leave and on 31 December 1919 set out eastwards with Doreen's fox terrier, Mimi.

In a month on the train they travelled 500 miles, a distance they could have covered on post horses. They then joined a Czech train carrying a battery of heavy artillery, travelling in an open wooden-seated compartment. Later they travelled in a train on which they inhabited two upper "shelves" of rough wood. At last their train "bumped and jolted" into a station three miles from Irkutsk, and a British officer took them and Mimi in his private coach. They reached Harbin on 5 March 1920 and then on to Vladivostok; it took a further two months to get a passage for home.

Doreen Stanford worked for the Land Owners' Association, becoming one of those many Englishwomen who put their outlandish backgrounds behind them. Her book *Sun and Snow: A Siberian adventure* (1963) describes those strange events.

Marcus Lorenzo Taft (?-?)

Marcus Taft travelled from China to Moscow in 1907 with his wife and daughter, who, he was assured by the compiler of Baedeker's *Russland,* were the first representatives of the fair sex, other than Russian, who ever visited Irkutsk. We know better, but it must have been pleasing for the Tafts. He wrote of their journey in *Strange Siberia: Along the Trans-Siberian Railway: A Journey from the Great Wall of China to the Skyscrapers of Manhattan.* They pressed on with their journey despite discouragement on all sides: "You had better not stop over at Harbin. It is very unsafe there. Even the servants in the hotels are all ex-convicts and criminals. They will rob you of your money and your passport," said a clerk in the Russian-Chinese Bank. "I would not advise stopping anywhere short of Moscow and Petersburg," warned a Scottish physician. "There is so little of interest in any Siberian town."

Paul Theroux (1941-)

One of the great railway books of this century is Theroux's *The Great Railway Bazaar* (1975). He set out in 1974 from Victoria Station in London with "the intention of boarding every train which chugged into view between London and Tokyo", and eventually returned home on the Trans-Siberian express.

By the time he boarded it at Khabarovsk, he was travel-weary and homesick. He wanted to be home for Christmas, but Russian bureaucracy foiled him.

Paul Theroux was born in Massachusetts, but lives in England. He is a writer, novelist and traveller. His later travel books include *The Old Patagonian Express* (1979), an account of his journey through North and South America, and *The Kingdom by the Sea* (1983), a tour around the coasts of Britain.

Bryn Thomas (1959-)

Born in Zimbabwe, Bryn Thomas read anthropology at Durham University and took to travel.

He made several trips on the Trans-Siberian railway and spent months reading about the railway in the British Library in order to create his *Trans-Siberian Handbook*, first published in 1988, and regularly updated since then. In 1991 he set up Trailblazers to publish route guides for adventurous travelers from Azerbaijan to New Zealand.

Samuel Turner (?-?)

Samuel Turner was a member of a leading English firm of food importers who saw it as "only natural that, having an eye to future trade relations, we should seek to increase our knowledge of Siberia and its potentialities". In 1903 he undertook the trip and was amazed by the Siberian butter trade which was, by 1904, exporting 681,857 cwt a year. He was convinced that the purpose of the railway was simply to open up the vast territory of Siberia for commerce and that the strategic purpose of the railway was minimal by comparison. He also turned his attention to climbing and exploring the Altai Mountains. His book *Siberia: A Record of Travel, Climbing and Exploration* (1904) combines commercial assessments with adventure.

Helen Callista Wilson (fl.1920-40)

A group of enthusiastic American radicals, seeing the new-born Communist Russia as a utopia where anything could happen, had a vision of skilled workers emigrating from capitalist America to proletarian Russia to colonize the great open spaces of Siberia. They called for funds and colonists, and by 1927 a community of roughly 400 American men, women and children were living in Siberia when Ms Wilson and Ms Elsie Mitchell went to join them as teacher and secretary. For two years they lived with the group in Kuzbass, south of Tomsk, watching the utopia crumbling, for they were "a group of individualists–as most radicals are–engaged in a socialist enterprise". But before they departed they had done well, installing a huge new turbine, making new records in coal production, furnishing local villages with electricity. The industrial romance took six years to build, blossom and die.

Ms Wilson and Ms Mitchell set off to wander, trekking south through the Altai Mountains accompanied by Ferghana, a fox terrier (surely related to Doreen Stanford's Mimi?). They then travelled north along the Irtysh River to Omsk and along the railway westward before setting off south again. After four months' traveling, they settled in Moscow where they wrote their book, *Vagabonding at Fifty* (1930).

Richardson Little Wright (1887-1961)

Richardson Wright was Sunday editor of the *Knickerbocker Press* in Albany, New York when his co-traveller Bassett Digby arrived on the staff from London. Wright became special correspondent of the *New York World*, *Chicago Daily News*, and the *London Daily Express* for their trip to Siberia and Manchuria in 1910. Unlike Digby he did not return to Siberia, but became literary critic of the *New York Times* (1911-14) and later Editor of *House and Garden*, until his retirement. His writings include *Through Siberia: An Empire in the Making* with Bassett

Digby (1913), *The Russians, an Interpretation* (1917) and many books on houses and gardens.

BIBLIOGRAPHY

Baedeker, Karl. *Russia with Teheran, Port Arthur and Peking* (Karl Baedeker, 1914)

Barber, Noel. *Trans-Siberian* (Harrap, 1942)

Baring, Maurice. *With Russians in Manchuria* (Methuen,1905); *A Year in Russia* (Methuen, 1907); *What I saw in Russia* (Methuen, 1927)

Bates, Lindon Jr. *The Russian Road to China* (Houghton Mifflin, 1910)

Blanch, Lesley. *Journey into the Mind's Eye: Fragments of an Autobiography* (Collins, 1968; Century, 1987)

Burr, Malcolm. *In Bolshevik Siberia* (H.F. and G. Witherby, 1931)

Clark, Rev. Francis. E. *A New Way around an Old World* (Harper and Bros, 1901)

Colquhoun, Archibald R. *The "Overland" to China* (Harper and Bros, 1900)

Deutsch, Leo. *Sixteen Years in Siberia: 1884-1900,* translated by Helen Chisholm (John Murray, 1903)

Dmitriv-Mămanov and A.F. 2dziarski. *Guide to the Great Siberian Railway* translated by L. Kŭkul Yasnopolsky (Moscow, Ministry of Ways and Communications, 1900)

de Windt, Harry. *The New Siberia* (Chapman & Hall, 1892); *Siberia as It Is* (Chapman & Hall, 1982); *From Paris to New York by Land* (George Newnes, 1904); *From Pekin to Calais by Land* (George Newnes, 1889); *Russia as I Know It* (J.B. Lippincott, 1907)

Digby, Bassett. *The Mammoth and Mammoth-Hunting in North-East Siberia,* (H.F. & G. Witherby, 1926); *Tigers, Gold and Witch Doctors* (Harcourt Brace & Co, 1928)

Digby, Bassett and Wright, R.L. *Through Siberia: An Empire in the Making* (Hurst & Blackett, 1913)

Fleming, Peter. *One's Company; A Journey to China* (Jonathan Cape, 1934)

Fraser, John Foster. *The Real Siberia* (Cassell & Co, 1902)

Geldof, Bob. *Is That It?* (Sidgwick & Jackson, 1986)

Greener, William Oliver. *See* Wirt Gerrare

Hautzig, Esther, *The Endless Steppe* (Hamish Hamilton 1968)

Horrocks, General Sir Brian. *A Full Life* (Collins, 1960)

Kennan, George. *Tent Life in Siberia* (G.P. Putnam, 1871); *Siberia and the Exile System* (Osgood &c McIlvaine, 1891)

Meakin, Annette M.B. *A Ribbon of Iron* (Constable, 1901)

Murray, John. *Handbook for Travellers, Russia* (John Murray, 1871); *Handbook for Travellers, Russia, Denmark and Norway* (John Murray, 1893)

Newby, Eric. *The Big Red Train Ride* (Weidenfeld & Nicolson, 1978)

Norman, Sir Henry. *All the Russias: Travels and Studies in Contemporary European Russia, Finland, Siberia, the Caucasus and Central Asia* (London 1902)

Portway, Christopher. *Great Railway Adventures* (Oxford Illustrated Press, 1983)

Price, M. Phillips. *Siberia* (Methuen, 1912)

Rado, Alexander. *A Guide Book to the Soviet Union* (Berlin 1929)

Russian Yearbook 1917 (Methuen, 1917)

Shoemaker, Michael Myers. *The Great Siberian Railway from St Petersburg to Pekin* (G.P.Putnam, 1903)

Simpson, James Young. *Sidelights on Siberia* (William Blackwood, 1898)

Stanford, Doreen. *Sun and Snow, a Siberian Adventure* (Longmans, 1963)

Taft, Marcus Lorenzo. *Strange Siberia: along the Trans-Siberian Railway: A Journey from the Great Wall of China to the Skyscrapers of Manhattan* (1909)

Theroux, Paul. *The Great Railway Bazaar* (Hamish Hamilton, 1975)

Thomas, Bryn, *Tran-Siberian Handbook*, (Trailblazer (7th edition), 2007)

Tupper, Harmon. *To the Great Ocean: Siberia and the Trans-Siberian Railway* (Secker and Warburg, 1965)

Turner, Samuel. *Siberia: A record of Travel, Climbing and Exploration* (T. Fisher Unwin, 1905)

Wilson, Helen Callista, and Mitchell, Elsie Reed. *Vagabonding at Fifty* (Coward-McCann,1930)

Wright, R.L. and Digby, Bassett. *See* Digby.

ACKNOWLEDGEMENTS

The editor and publisher acknowledge with thanks the use of material in this book to the following: the heirs of Lesley Blanch for excerpts from her *Journey into the Mind's Eye*; the Orion Publishing Group for excerpts from Eric Newby's *The Big Red Train Ride*; Paul Theroux and Penguin Books for excerpts from *The Great Railway Bazaar*; the heirs of General Sir Brian Horrocks for excerpts from *A Full Life*; the heirs of Annette Meakin for excerpts from *A Ribbon of Iron*; Harmon Tupper for excerpts from *To the Great Ocean*; Bryn Thomas and Trailblazer for excerpts from *Trans-Siberian Handbook*; the heirs of Malcolm Burr and Century Hutchinson for excerpts from *In Bolshevik Siberia*; the heirs of Bassett Digby and R.L. Wright and Century Hutchinson for excerpts from *Through Siberia* and Bassett Digby's *Tigers, Gold and Witch Doctors*; the heirs of Maurice Baring for excerpts from *What I Saw in Russia*; Methuen for excerpts from the *Russian Year Book 1917*; the estate of Peter Fleming for excerpts from *One's Company*; Methuen for the excerpt from *Siberia* by Morgan Phillips Price; Haynes Publishing (parent company of Oxford Illustrated Press) for excerpts from Christopher Portway's *The Great Railway Adventure*; Bob Geldof and Penguin Books for the excerpt from *Is that it?*; Chambers Harrap Publishers Ltd for excerpts from Noel Barber's *Trans-Siberian*; Chris Moss for the article 'Trans-Siberian Excess'.

The editor and publisher have made every effort to track down all owners of copyright material, and regret the use of any material included for which we have failed to locate the owners.

INDEX